THE BOOK OF THE
HAVANA CIGAR

THE BOOK OF THE
HAVANA CIGAR

COMPILED BY
BRIAN INNES

ORBIS PUBLISHING · LONDON

Frontispiece: 'The Pure Havana Cigar'
a drawing by the French artist Honoré Daumier

Text written by Kit Coppard
Fact boxes written by Geoffrey Hindley

First published in Great Britain by
Orbis Publishing Limited, London 1983
© Orbis Publishing Limited 1983

Originated in Great Britain by
SX Composing Limited, Rayleigh, Essex (text) and
Adroit Photo Litho Limited, Birmingham
(illustrations)

Printed in Spain by Grijelmo S.A., Bilbao
ISBN: 0-85613-546-1

CONTENTS

FOREWORD

THE cigar has always been a symbol of power and divine inspiration. Its smoke rises, curling lazily and luxuriously, ephemerally blue in the still air; not like that of a cigarette, thin and white and bitter, or the black cloud that clings around a pipe. There are phantoms in the smoke of the cigar, dreams of past loves, promises of future conquests.

In the Americas, medicine men for thousands of years used the smoke of tobacco as a means of direct communication with the gods; warriors were inspired by having the smoke blown into their faces before a battle; kings and emperors sought enlightenment in the smoking of cigars.

The word *cigar* most likely comes from the Spanish *cigarrar*, to roll – certainly it is evidence of the virtual monopoly that the Spanish colonies exercised over the making of cigars for three centuries: it was not until the Peninsular War that French and English soldiers discovered them. And then began the extraordinary cigar mania that swept western Europe. In 1823 a mere 26 pounds weight of cigars was imported into England, but seven years later the figure was 253,882! William Thackeray was then but a young man at Cambridge, and it would be 17 years before the success of *Vanity Fair*, but later in his life he wrote:

> I vow and believe that the cigar has been one of
> the greatest creature comforts of my life – a kind
> companion, a great stimulant, a cementer of friendships.

Cigars flooded into Europe from all the tobacco-growing quarters of the globe – from Brazil and Sumatra, from Jamaica and the Canaries, from the Philippines and from Tampa in Florida – but despite all attempts on the part of tobacco growers and merchants the hand-rolled Havana cigar has never been rivalled. The care devoted to the tobacco plant in the *vegas* of Cuba, the time taken to bring the leaf to its proper maturity, and the fact that the cigar, to attain its correct quality, must always be manufactured by hand, have inevitably made it an article of luxury. Yet, though kings and princes are almost extinct, though democracy is proclaimed in the four quarters of the world, even in the midst of revolution the cigar has remained the visible symbol of the leader of men.

For my part, however (and I have been a lover of the Havana for 30 years, and may well be the only British subject who was allowed his cigars as a fully-deductible expense against Income Tax!), I share the sentiments of Thomas Hood:

> I do not seek for fame,
> A general with a scar;
> A private let me be,
> So I have my cigar. . . .
> Some sigh for this or that,
> My wishes don't go far;
> The world may wag at will,
> So I have my cigar.

In the pages that follow, you can read the true history of the Havana cigar: its first discovery by the Spanish conquistadors, its ever-growing popularity, the stages, step by careful step, of its manufacture; the many artefacts, rich in charming detail, that are associated with it; and the many literary and historic figures who have praised it. From Lord Byron to Groucho Marx, wits and literati have had their say, but few have caught the love of the cigar so well as that most obscure of versifiers, Arthur W. Gundry:

> As I puff this mild Havana, and its ashes slowly lengthen,
> I feel my courage gather and my resolution strengthen;
> I will smoke, and I will praise you, my cigar, and I will light you
> With tobacco-phobic pamphlets by the learned prigs who fight you! . . .
>
> So I sing of you, dear product of (I trust you are) Havana,
> And if there's any question as to how my verses scan, a
> Reason is my shyness in the Muses' aid invoking,
> As, like other ancient maidens, they perchance object to smoking.
>
> I have learnt with you the wisdom of contemplative quiescence,
> While the world is in a ferment of unmeaning effervescence,
> That its jar and rush and riot bring no good one-half so sterling
> As your fleecy clouds of fragrance that are now about me curling. . . .
>
> I will puff my mild Havana, and I quietly will query
> Whether, when the strife is over, and the combatants are weary,
> Their gains will be more brilliant than its faint expiring flashes,
> Or more solid than this panful of its dead and sober ashes.

BRIAN INNES
London, 1983

CHAPTER ONE

THE HISTORICAL PERSPECTIVE

IN mid-November 1492 Luis de Torres and Rodrigo de Jérez, having completed a 14-day reconnaissance of the interior of eastern Cuba, reported back to their commander, Christopher Columbus. Five weeks before, the expedition had made its first, historic landfall at San Salvador, which Columbus, in one of the larger miscalculations of nautical history, proclaimed to be Japan – the fabled 'Cipango, rich in gold' praised (though never visited) by Marco Polo two centuries earlier. Columbus, surveying the apparently endless coast of Cuba, concluded that it must be part of mainland Asia – no less than the mighty empire of Cathay, one of the chief goals of his mission.

This was to have been the big moment for Torres. A Jewish scholar from Murcia, fluent in Hebrew, Arabic, and Chaldean, he had been specially picked by Columbus to enquire of the local inhabitants the whereabouts of the Great Khan and to serve as interpreter in the expedition's dealings with the Chinese emperor.

Torres' linguistic talents, we may be certain, were wasted in Cuba, but he and Jérez brought back some interesting information about the country and its inhabitants. They reported, among other things, that the islanders 'drank smoke'. Columbus's journal does not describe in detail how his seamen received this news from the first Europeans to witness the pleasures of tobacco. More than likely the response was a mixture of awe and hilarity, but if so it was misconceived: tobacco was to prove a greater economic resource to the Spanish than all the gold they plundered in the Americas.

These original Cubans, we should not be surprised to learn, favoured the cigar – or, at least, a thick, crudely rolled cylinder of tobacco leaves wrapped in a palm leaf. Within a few years other Spanish adventurers in the New World reported other methods of smoking enjoyed by Amerindians elsewhere. Ponce de León, obsessed with his search for the legendary Fountain of Youth in the Bahamas, stopped long

Columbus discovered the Antilles – and the habit of 'drinking smoke' in 1492. Within a generation tobacco reached Europe and began its climb to popularity

enough in Florida to observe Indians using pipes, while other explorers reported the use of snuff and of tobacco for chewing.

Early travellers in the lands of the New World varied widely in their opinions of the Indians. Most, like Gonzalo Fernández de Oviedo, viceroy of Santo Domingo, considered them useful chiefly as slave labour; others, notably the Dominican missionary Fray Bartolomé de Las Casas, praised their apparent simplicity and innocence, and sowed the seeds of the later European ideal of the 'noble savage'. Almost all observers, however, were fascinated by the Indians' smoking habits. The fragrant herb, it turned out, had many different names given to it by its Indian devotees all over the New World. The proud, warlike Caribs of the Antilles called it *cohiba*; to the Indians of the eastern seaboard of North America it was *uppowoc*; in parts of Brazil it was known as *petum*; and the Aztecs of Mexico called it *piecetl*. Whence, then, the origin of the word 'tobacco'?

The ultimate in social smoking?
Certainly the last word in economy. Two Caribs ensure that
not a puff of smoke is lost

Oviedo says in his *Historia general y natural de las Indias Occidentales* (1535):

> The caciques [tribal chiefs] employed a tube, shaped like a Y, inserting
> the forked extremities in their nostrils and the tube itself in the lighted
> weed . . . Those who could not procure the right sort of wood took their
> smoke through a hollow reed; it is this the Indians call *tobago*, not the
> weed or its effects, as some have supposed.

From Sacred Ritual to Social Habit

Until quite recently many historians and travellers cast doubt on the idea that the
American Indians were the first peoples to smoke tobacco. It is true that ancient pipes
and other smoking implements have been found in many parts of the Old World from
Europe to China. The ancient Greek historian Herodotus, for instance, wrote in the
5th century BC that the Scythians of the Black Sea region enjoyed inhaling the smoke
of a herb burnt upon a communal fire – reckoning it 'superior, in their estimation, to
any Greek vapour-bath'. In the Middle East, too, the hookah, narghile, and other
water-pipes have a very ancient provenance. But none of these ancient smoking
practices in the Old World involved the use of tobacco. A variety of herbs was used; in
the Middle East one of the most widely favoured was *Cannabis sativa*, from which the
Arabs obtained *dakka* (hashish). Again, in Europe during medieval times smoking was
sometimes recommended as a cure for various 'windy griefs of the breast' – but the
remedies consisted of herbs such as coltsfoot or, more drastically, preparations
including dried cow's dung.

The fact is there are no reports from pre-Columbian times of any plant used for
smoking, snuffing, or chewing that can be identified with tobacco – for the excellent
reason (as we now know) that the tobacco plant is indigenous to the New World.

From the admittedly rather skimpy evidence available, it is clear that the Amer-indians had been smoking tobacco for at least a thousand years before Columbus set foot on San Salvador, and probably for much longer than that.

It will remain forever a mystery who were the first native Americans to use tobacco for smoking purposes. An even more intractable problem is why, assuming an ignorance of the properties of tobacco, anyone should want to burn leaves in this way. Tobacco acquires its full flavour and narcotic qualities only after the leaf has been cured and has fermented. Even in the event that the first users of tobacco found the leaf tasty as a form of salad, they would have experienced none of the pleasures enjoyed by the modern tobacco chewer. It seems likely that the first Indians to experience the pleasures of 'my lady nicotine' burnt tobacco leaves that had fermented after being stacked to form compost. It is even possible that such compost ignited spontaneously, and that its smoke proved pleasurable to those standing near it. This explanation is more plausible than it sounds, for several tribes reported by early European colonizers used tobacco only in this way.

Fire and smoke have had magico-religious significance, among peoples all over the world, for hundreds of thousands of years. In particular, smoke curling and

The popular image of the tobacco-smoking savage in an 18th-century engraving. The tobacco plant, however, is closely observed

A Brief History of Cuba

By 1515 Cuba was part of the Spanish empire, conquered by Diego Velázquez, one of Columbus's original lieutenants. It was on his orders that Cortez sailed from Cuba on the expedition that conquered Mexico. Cuba became the assembly point for Spain's American treasure fleets and a honeypot for English and French buccaneers.

The island's native Arawak inhabitants had quickly succumbed to the brutalities of the conquistadors. Their labour was replaced with African slaves whose periodic risings against the oppressions of their Cuban masters mirrored the master society's struggle against Spanish rule and restrictive trade policies.

It was only in 1614 that Madrid officially authorized the cultivation of tobacco. Nevertheless Cuba flourished. Spain's enemies envied her 'Pearl of the Antilles' and in 1762 Havana was briefly occupied by the British. But Spain held on to her pearl, even when, in the early 1800s, her other American possessions were winning their independence. The mid-century saw a failed liberation campaign mounted with US help, and then pro-slavery US southerners tried to take over, prompting Spain to half-hearted concessions, punctuated by episodes of brutal repression.

In 1868 Carlos Manuel de Céspedes raised the standard of revolt. There were times during the Ten Year War that followed when it seemed that the US would intervene on behalf of the rebels. But they eventually capitulated to Madrid, in return for promises of reform. These were not honoured and bitterness and discontent mounted, and the readers in the cigar factories chose patently subversive texts – notably the works of José Martí, poet and man of action.

Arrested when only 16 for revolutionary activities, Martí spent years in exile, mostly in New York, where he founded the Cuban revolutionary party. He died in May 1895, fighting in the Battle of Dos Rios, the opening conflict in Cuba's War of Independence. Liberal opinion in the US was enthusiastic for the rebel cause; business interests also wanted the States to be involved. The sinking of the US warship *Maine* in Havana harbour gave the pretext, early in 1898. In the war that followed, America took the Spanish Pacific possessions of Guam and the Philippines and Puerto Rico in the Caribbean. Cuba found herself liberated from Spain only to become an American protectorate.

A treaty gave the US its naval base at Guantanamo and rights to intervene in

The port of Havana in the 18th century

Cigar labels celebrate the early days of Spanish rule, when armed caballeros supervised the labours of black African slaves

Cuban affairs to suppress revolutionary movements. American business aimed at a monopoly of the cigar industry. World War I brought soaring world sugar prices and brief, heady prosperity to Cuba. But this 'dance of the millions' was followed by depression in the 1920s.

America finally abrogated her protectorate in the 1930s and eased tariffs in Cuba's favour. In 1934 a student and military junta headed by Fulgencio Batista overthrew the regime of President Machado. Batista became the strong man of Cuban politics, and in 1952 inaugurated a new era of brutal dictatorship with a military coup. The following year, the young lawyer Fidel Castro unsuccessfully raised the standard of revolt.

In 1956 Castro returned to Cuba, landing in the southwest Oriente Province. With 11 others, who included his brother Raúl and Ernest 'Che' Guevara, he established himself in the Sierra Maestra, Cuba's loftiest mountain range. Their guerrilla campaign finally drove Batista into exile in January 1959.

Castro's coup, the orientation of Cuba towards the Soviet Bloc, and the cutting of economic ties with the US, master-minded by Guevara, alienated western opinion. The sugar and cigar industries were nationalized and agricultural collectivization announced. The great marques of the old companies were done away with. A number, notably Henry Clay, Corona, Cabañas and Murias, had anticipated government closure by withdrawing from Cuba to the US, the Canary Islands and elsewhere.

Within months, the government was disturbed by declining cigar sales, following news of Castro's plans and rumours that the old companies had sabotaged the great plantations of the Vuelta Abajo and taken away their finest plants and workers. The regime spared the tobacco industry its collectivization plans; the old ways continued and the Havana cigar is as fine now as ever.

American cigar smokers, however, had to endure the embargo of all Cuban imports to the States. In 1961 the US severed diplomatic relations and then supported the disastrous Bay of Pigs invasion by anti-Castro Cuban exiles. However, even this *débâcle* was overshadowed the following year by the Cuban Missile Crisis when the Soviet Union under Nikita Khrushchev attempted to establish missile bases on the island. President John F. Kennedy demanded the withdrawal of the missiles and eventually the Soviet Union complied. Yet Cuba remains a Communist outpost in the American hemisphere. In the 1970s she sent troops to support risings in Angola and Ethiopia. It is a piquant irony that this bogeyman of the capitalist world still supplies it with that ultimate emblem of luxury – the Havana cigar.

writhing above a sacred fire has customarily been associated with spirits or prayers ascending heavenwards. Magic among primitive peoples is almost invariably the exclusive province of the shaman, witch-doctor, or equivalent priestly member of the tribe. It is hardly surprising, then, that when the narcotic properties of tobacco were discovered the use of the leaf was reserved for ritualistic occasions. By rapid and continuous inhalation of tobacco smoke a priest might be helped into a trance-like state in which he became sensitive to messages from tribal gods.

The earliest extant document of a smoker is a 5th-century bas-relief from southern Mexico showing a Mayan priest with a crude, straight pipe (or possibly a cigar); in one of the most important Mayan religious ceremonies the priest would blow tobacco smoke in the direction of the sun and then to the four points of the compass. Later codices (picture-writings) of the Maya – whose civilization was fully as splendid as that of dynastic Egypt – contain many figures of cigar smokers. By the time of the Discovery, the Aztecs of Mexico had ceremonial pipes made from silver, tortoiseshell, and a variety of other semi-precious materials, and commonly mixed their tobacco leaf with liquid amber and with certain hallucinogenic drugs.

As the Europeans intensified their exploration and colonisation of the New World, it became apparent that tobacco had significant religious importance to virtually all Amerindian peoples who had access to the leaf. The depth of the cultural imprint of tobacco is evidenced by the number of peoples whose myths and legends linked the plant with their tribal origins. Among the Susquehanna Indians of Pennsylvania, for instance, it was believed that the tribe's fortunes were founded on

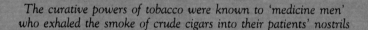

The curative powers of tobacco were known to 'medicine men'
who exhaled the smoke of crude cigars into their patients' nostrils

The Indian village of Secota on the Pamlico river in 1587. As well as maize and pumpkins, tobacco grows in tidy plantations

the gift, by a beautiful goddess, of maize, kidney beans, and tobacco; while among certain Mexican tribes tobacco was believed to be the incarnation of the wife of Tlaloc, the god of rain, to whom various fertility rites were dedicated.

For many Amerindian peoples, then, smoking originated as ceremonial, as an act of homage to the gods. Tobacco was a sacred herb whose cultivation was exclusively by the priestly class and whose use was restricted to rituals involving prayers for rain, for success in battle, or for other tribal needs. And, since the art of healing is traditionally bound up with magico-religious practices – as in the work of the medicine man, the sorcerer, the shaman – smoking was also associated with ceremonies designed to drive out evil spirits.

Yet while the sacred connotations of the plant were widespread, the European colonisers found that smoking had evolved, among many Amerindians, into a purely social habit as well. A possible link in the evolutionary chain from sacred to social use is the calumet pipe shared by Indian chiefs as a symbol of peace or as the seal to a contract. There can be no doubt that one of the reasons why tobacco developed into a social habit enjoyed by all lay in the plant's ability to prosper in a variety of habitats once it had been taken into cultivation. The transition from sacerdotal plot to family

The earliest European explorers of America found it difficult
to describe how tobacco leaves were rolled into cigar form

garden and thence to tribal plantation would have presented few technical problems. Tribal interchange, both friendly and piratical, helped to spread the plant from region to region; and there are numerous reports, from the 16th century onwards, of Amerindians using tobacco as barter currency in intertribal trade. All this implies a significant shift in social attitudes towards the plant – a shift exemplified, among other things, in the medicinal uses for which tobacco came to be used. Fresh leaves, for example, were used to dress open wounds, and tobacco smoke was commonly prescribed for respiratory complaints.

The widespread cultivation of tobacco hundreds of years before European exploration of the New World means that we shall never know the original home of the wild-growing plant. Tobacco is one of the Solanaceae, a plant family that includes not only henbane (another plant with narcotic properties) and deadly nightshade, but also a couple of other New World natives of universal significance – the 'Irish' potato and the tomato. There are more than 50 species of tobacco, but only two are of commercial significance today: *Nicotiana tabacum*, which is used in cigars, 'Virginia'-type cigarettes, and most pipe tobacco; and the somewhat smaller *N. rustica*, which yields a harsher-tasting tobacco and is cultivated today mainly in the Soviet Union and Asia. It seems likely that *N. tabacum* originated in Brazil, whence it spread naturally southward to the Tropic of Capricorn and northward to the Rio Grande. The stronger and more bitter *N. rustica*, possibly a native of Mexico, spread northward to the east and west of the Mississippi and thence into eastern Canada. (It was there, close to the site of the city of Montreal, that local Indians attempted vainly to instruct the French explorer Jacques Cartier in the art of smoking in 1534: 'We tried to imitate them, but the smoke burnt our mouths as if it had been pepper' – which is still the complaint of some on their first experience of *N. rustica*.)

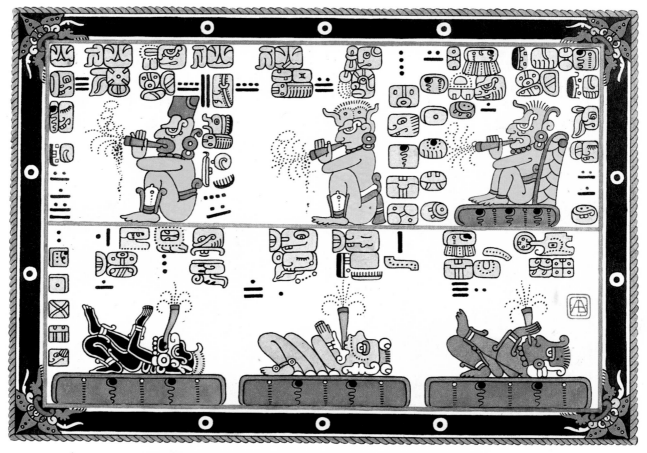

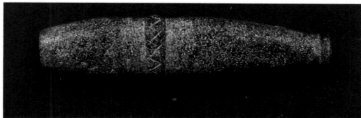

From the earliest times the Amerindian peoples attached a great ritual importance to tobacco: in one of the most sacred of Mayan religious ceremonies the priest would blow cigar smoke first in the direction of the sun and then to the four points of the compass. The pictorial codices of the Maya show many cigar smokers. Cigar holders, too, were widespread; the upper, in Mexican sandstone, is over 2000 years old; the lower comes from 16th-century California

The richly-decorated paper flaps that protect the cigars in their boxes frequently celebrate important aspects of the tobacco trade in Cuba. The quaint scene headed Vuelta Abajo (the area of Cuba where traditionally the finest tobacco is grown) shows the landing of Columbus in 1492, with a group of welcoming Indians and a flourishing tobacco plant; but in the background we find the port of Havana in 1865, with steamers, warehouses, and stately cigar factories. The label of La Cimiente (the fundamental) portrays two handsome Cubans in the traditional 18th-century costumes of the hidalgo; between them a tobacco plantation spreads before the distant skyline of Havana. Other, even older, representations evidence the long-established tobacco trade: the 17th-century Delft plate shows two Dutch merchants bargaining around a tub not unlike those still to be seen on plantations

The labels of the various cigar manufacturers, lithographically printed in many colours, embossed and gilded, developed into a specific art form. The graphic simplicity of La Imperiosa factory, with passers-by who include a lone cyclist, is set into a riotously rococo frame. The Partagás label celebrates the marriage of industry and art that characterized the many 'universal exhibitions' that were held in the second half of the 19th century. And the label of Antilla Cubana bears witness to the increasing industrialization of Cuba, with its steam engines and railway trains

Two of the labels illustrated here stir memories of William Shakespeare, although in very different ways. Romeo y Julieta was named deliberately for the star-crossed lovers – and it is said that when Pepín Rodríguez, the founder of the brand, failed in his attempt to buy the Capulets' house in Verona he nevertheless was accorded the concession of a cigar-stand in the entrance-hall, on condition that he gave a free cigar to every tourist visitor. On the other hand, the Por Larrañaga label, with its queen attended by her 'little Indian boy', may remind us of Titania in A Midsummer Night's Dream, although it also shows certain similarities with the el carro card of the Tarot pack. By contrast, the distinguished label of H. Upmann relies solely upon the richness of the many gold medals won at international fairs

Propietario: MANUEL LOPEZ

The richness and variety of cigar box labels is well-nigh inexhaustible.
Many, like that for La Gloria Cubana, get their inspiration from the
Spanish baroque style, combining Christian symbolism with figures
drawn from Greek mythology and the necessary stylized Indian. Others
take a more naturalistic view, like the charming 19th century
watercolour of Havana harbour (above left), or combine decoration
with instruction, as in the series of scenes (above) which show us various
aspects of Cuban rural life, from the tobacco plantation to the cockfight.

Cigars have figured in many forms of art, but probably most successfully in caricature. The spread of the luxuriant moustache in the 19th century, and the habit of greasing it thickly with pomade, provided cartoonists with an easy target

The daydreaming cigar-smoker is an appropriate image for the titlepage of this volume of waltzes by the popular Belgian composer Moens, published in Leipzig c. 1890: Erinnerung means 'fond memories'

Great care and dedication are given to the cultivation of the tobacco plant. Soon after the end of the rainy season the nursery-raised seedlings are planted out in the plantation fields, which have been hand-tilled and fertilized. After a month or so (top left) the plants begin to show the first signs of a growing maturity. Since it is the large leaves only that are required, the flowering head and the side shoots are pinched out (top right), and the plant may reach a height of nearly six feet, bearing eight to 12 of the large, almost rectangular leaves by the end of March (opposite). After harvesting, the leaves are strung together (above left) and hung from poles in the roof of the barn to dry. Then the dried leaves are tied into 'hands', buried for some time in pits, and transported to the factory where they are sprayed with water (above right) before being laid out to ferment further

Excess water is shaken from the 'hands' of tobacco leaves (top left) before they are laid out in heaps on the warehouse floor. Here they must be turned and moved frequently to control the temperature of the fermentation (top right). At the end of these various handling and fermentation processes the leaves are flexible and almost translucent, and the cured 'hands' are hung on racks (opposite) in controlled conditions of humidity and temperature until they are required for manufacture. Then they are inspected for flaws and blemishes (above left) and the central rib is stripped out to provide the half-leaves necessary for the making of cigars (above right)

NICOTIANA TABACUM. L.
Der gemeine Tobak.

Some tobacco is allowed to flower to provide seed for the next year. The
famous botanist Linnaeus once counted 40,320 seeds in a single pod, and
100,000 would fill an ordinary thimble

First European illustration of the tobacco plant, 1570: the caption describes it as 'the healthy and sacred tobacco of the Indies'

Tobacco Sails to Europe and Beyond

The early Europeans in the New World responded in a variety of ways to the mysteries and delights of tobacco. Many were impressed with the solace it evidently afforded Indian smokers and with its apparent capacity to increase stamina and endurance if food were short. Others were appalled by the very idea of imbibing smoke. Typical of the latter was the response of Girolamo Benzoni, a traveller from Milan, who in his *Storia del Nuovo Mondo* (1565) remarks that the people of the Antilles 'fill mouth, gullet, and the whole head with the powerful fumes until at last their monstrous lust is sated, when they fall about as beasts that have no reason, and lie senseless on the ground like dead men'. Although violent in his denunciation of 'this pestiferous herb', Benzoni allowed that it was widely credited with healing properties.

To the probably more susceptible sailors involved in the increasingly frequent New World voyages, the decision of whether to smoke or not to smoke was a question of pleasure, not principle. Nor surprisingly, many took to it avidly. Tradition has it that Rodrigo de Jérez, the companion of Torres in the Cuba reconnaissance, was the first European to acquire the habit. There can be little doubt that the first tobacco to reach Europe arrived in the pouches of sailors plying between America and the Iberian ports of Lisbon, Cadiz, Palos, and elsewhere, about the close of the 15th century.

As news of the real and imagined riches of the New World filtered north from the Iberian peninsula, adventurers in England, France, Holland, and elsewhere began to take an interest. The Spanish and Portuguese exerted a stranglehold on Central and South America, including the West Indies, so the northern Europeans confined their exploratory and colonizing operations mainly to North America. This geographical separation has profound implications in the history of smoking habits. In much of

Central America and throughout the West Indies and South America the dominant form of smoking was the cigar – or at least a rather crude version of what we now know as the cigar. By contrast, throughout eastern North America the pipe was used. So it turned out that for long the northern Europeans, and especially the English, who acquired the smoking habit invariably used the pipe, while the Iberians as invariably favoured the cigar. The cigar attained wide popularity north of the Pyrenees only in the 19th century, by which time the cigar industry of Seville was almost 300 years old.

Spanish and Portuguese sailors were also responsible for introducing tobacco to Africa and the Orient. The Portuguese, who pioneered the route to Asia via the Cape of Good Hope, took the leaf to India in the early 16th century, whence it spread via the Islamic connection to Iran and elsewhere in the Middle East. At about the same time Spain, in the person of Ferdinand Magellan (himself, ironically, a Portuguese), introduced tobacco to the Philippines, whence it spread to China, Indonesia, and most other lands in South-East Asia.

Tobacco Conquers Europe

Throughout the 16th century tobacco was regarded in most of northern Europe as an interesting botanical curiosity with somewhat vague though potent healing prop-

Jean Nicot, who introduced the tobacco plant to France

erties. The origin of this attitude among medical men is obscure, though it is known that a professor at Salamanca university recommended tobacco as a treatment for certain ailments as early as 1543.

The man who claimed to have introduced tobacco into France (in 1558) was one André Thevet, a failed Carmelite monk, who was one of the co-founders of the city of Rio de Janeiro; the veracity of his claim, however, is threatened by his reputation as a compulsive liar. What is certain is that Jean Nicot was the first Frenchman to make the plant at all widely known in Europe north of the Pyrenees. In 1559 Nicot, a humbly born citizen of Nîmes who had managed to get an appointment at the French Court, was despatched to Lisbon on an abortive mission to negotiate the marriage of the youthful Portuguese king and the daughter of Henry II of France. While in Portugal, Nicot became fascinated by that country's mercantile and colonial ventures, of which Lisbon was the centre. Nicot soon acquired samples of the tobacco plant and its seeds and sent them, with a wildly exaggerated report of their healing properties, to the Grand Prior of France. The latter, suitably impressed, passed on some samples to Catherine de Médicis (the now-deceased Henry's widow), who was notoriously obsessed with magic and the wilder flights of astronomy. Within a few years tobacco was being cultivated as a drug in French botanical gardens. Made into a medicinal snuff and known, among many other names, as *l'herbe de l'ambassadeur* (in reference to Nicot), its fame soon passed north and east across continental Europe.

Tobacco was introduced into England probably during the 1560s. One tradition, albeit a shaky one, gives priority to Sir John Hawkins, privateer and general ne'er-do-well, who is said to have found some leaf on a Portuguese slave ship he captured in 1565; the tradition has been embellished, though not made more plausible, by accounts of sailors having been seen smoking cigar-like objects in an Islington tavern about this time. The first certain date is 1585 when Ralph Lane, governor of Sir Walter Raleigh's Virginia colony, imported some plants and seeds. At all events Raleigh, whose fortunes were tied up in the Virginia tobacco plantations, did most to encourage the smoking habit in England.

Here, too, the early proponents of the weed became almost hysterically enthusiastic over its healing properties. No class of citizens praised it more effulgently than the apothecaries, who in the early days enjoyed more or less a monopoly of cultivating the plant in herbal gardens. With the growing prosperity of the Virginia Company, however, tobacco became the business of merchants; and as the role of smoking passed from panacea to pleasure, the apothecaries began to discern a truly appalling roster of evil consquences that must inevitably beset the habitual smoker. Such timely warnings fell on fertile ground in the shape of the royal ear. In his 'Counterblaste to Tobacco' (1604), perhaps history's longest and most powerfully sustained vilification of a member of the plant kingdom, James I allowed it to be known that smoking was

> a custom lothsome to the eye, hatefull to the nose, harmefull to the braine, daungerous to the Lungs, and in the black, stinking fume thereof, nearest resembling the horrible Stigian smoke of the pit that is bottomlesse.

More to the point, he raised the import duty on Virginia tobacco from 2*d*. to 6*s*. 10*d*. per pound – though he allowed leaf from Spanish and Portuguese sources to be imported at the old rate. The effect was to reduce the Virginia colony to the point of bankruptcy, and to create England's first (but not last) balance of payments crisis.

Neither regal execration nor crippling duties, however, could dampen the enthusiasm that Englishmen had by now acquired for the 'divine herb', as the poet Spenser had called it. By 1614, according to one contemporary observer, there were no less than 7000 shops in London where tobacco could be purchased. From being merely a pleasurable habit, smoking soon developed into a necessary accomplishment among members of the quality. To 'drink tobacco with a grace' was a hallmark of the gentleman. And for those to whom such an accomplishment did not come naturally, there were tutors who, for a price, would initiate them into the art and mystery of drinking smoke as elaborated in Ben Jonson's *Every Man Out of His Humour* (1605).

The English pipe-smoking habit soon crossed the Channel. As late as the first decade of the 17th century, smoking in northern Europe was still confined mainly to the seamen of Holland, France, and the Baltic states. From England its introduction to the European middle classes seems to have been pioneered by English students abroad, notably at the great Dutch university of Leiden.

Naturally, the enormously rapid spread of the smoking habit in England – even young children were encourage to puff at a pipe – brought a reaction from the arbiters of fashion. From the mid-1720s onward social trend-setters, who tended to ape French Court manners in most things, discarded the pipe in favour of the snuff box – snuffing having always been more popular in France than smoking. In many fashionable London lounges, smoking was forbidden, and Beau Nash outlawed the pipe from Bath at a stroke. Henceforward, it was confidently asserted, smoking would be the kind of solecism committed only by the most decadent rakes – and, of course, by the labouring classes, who could not be expected to know any better.

The Triumph of the Cigar

Ephemerality is of the essence of the dottier flights of fashion. Snuffing might, for a time, become the only permissible way for a gentleman to enjoy tobacco; but by the mid-18th century the pleasures and solace afforded by smoking – even of tobacco of the most execrable quality – were too firmly entrenched in the hearts of Europeans, from Cape St Vincent to Scandinavia, for the habit to be in danger of extinction. But in northern Europe the renaissance of smoking as a social accomplishment and an aesthetic experience marked a turning point: the cigar, rather than the pipe, was to become the fashionable and enduring vehicle of the profoundest smoking pleasure.

The Spanish and Portuguese, of course, had pioneered European use of the cigar; and maritime commerce between Iberian ports and the great trading centres of Genoa and Venice had effectively established cigars as the preferred method of smoking in the Latin and Balkan margins of Europe from the mid-16th century onwards. North of the Pyrenees, as we have seen, thousands of smokers had long enjoyed tobacco bought from Spain or Portugal; but most such tobacco came from Spanish or Portuguese colonies in America in which planters concentrated their efforts on producing leaf

*The earliest cigars were manufactured in small makeshift
factories, where female labour was always of great importance*

suited to the demands of pipe-smokers and, later, of snuffers. In Spain itself, not all
smokers could afford cigars. From the late 16th century many Spaniards puffed the
papelito, which was made from crushed tobacco wrapped in coarse paper; and by the
early 17th century this ancestor of the cigarette had acquired the unmistakable
hallmark of popularity: it had been formally denounced by the Spanish priesthood.

The earliest-known reference to cigars by an Englishman was written by a certain
John Cockburn. In 1731 he and several others were captured by Spanish coastguards
while sailing in the Gulf of Mexico. They were set ashore on the coast of Honduras,
where later they encountered some friars:

> These Gentlemen gave us some Seegars to smoke, which they supposed
> would be very acceptable. These are Leaves of Tobacco rolled up in such
> Manner, that they serve both for a Pipe and Tobacco itself. These the
> Ladies, as well as Gentlemen, are very fond of Smoking.

Almost certainly these 'seegars' had been locally produced, for by the close of the
16th century there were hundreds of makeshift 'factories' in Spanish America turning
out vast quantities of tobacco in crude rolls and other forms. But as the appetite for

cigars increased there developed a demand for higher quality in both tobacco and the end product. By the early 18th century cigar manufacture had become a flourishing industry in metropolitan Spain. The principal centre was the great southern capital of Seville. Cigars were first produced here in 1676, but production greatly expanded after the royal factories were opened in 1731; the quality of the product was safeguarded by the city's Casa de Contratación (Chamber of Commerce). The reputation of Spanish cigars soon passed beyond the frontiers of the Iberian peninsula. In 1779 Peter Wendler – a German painter in Italy who, on discovering his artistic talent to be minimal, turned to trade – was granted a five-year concession by the Papal government to manufacture *bastoni di tabacco* (tobacco sticks = cigars) in Rome. Within 10 years cigar factories were established in Germany and France. Northern Europe was gradually awakening to the delights of the cigar.

North America had already experienced these delights. The first Cuban cigars had reached New England in 1762, following the English campaign in Cuba, and within three years Connecticut tobacco – a disappointingly poor quality leaf grown from Cuban seeds – was available in New York. The first United States cigar factory opened in Connecticut in 1810, and although the quality of its products left much to be desired the American demand for cigars grew apace. The American word 'stogie', meaning an inexpensive cigar, was coined about this time: it derives from Conestoga, the centre for production of native leaf by Pennsylvania Dutch (Deutsch, i.e. German) immigrants in the early years of the 19th century.

An early 19th-century 'divan' in King Street, Covent Garden

*Cigars became increasingly popular in Europe during
the 19th century. A lithograph by Alexander ver Huell*

Even by the last years of the 18th century Americans and a few northern
Europeans had begun to realise what Spaniards and Portuguese had long known – that
cigars made from Cuban leaf were of a finer quality than any other. By 1810, as United
States customs returns indicate, Cuban cigars formed a significant fraction of some five
million imported cigars. Regular supplies of cigars, including those made from Cuban
leaf, began to be imported into England in 1814, after Wellington's successful
campaigns against Napoleon in the Peninsular Wars, when their Spanish comrades
introduced many English officers to the delights of the cigar. By 1820 a small quantity
of cigars from West Indian leaf was manufactured in Britain, and the following year an
act of Parliament set out regulations governing British production of 'seegars'. The
British cigar habit really took hold in the late 1820s: in 1826, according to the records,
a mere 26 pounds of cigars were imported into England; by 1830 the figure had soared
to more than 250,000 pounds – and this takes no account of large quantities of
'unofficial' (i.e. illegal) imports from Spain, Portugal, France, and Germany.

By the mid-1830s the 'cigar divan' had become fashionable in London. As its
name suggests, the divan's decor was modelled on whatever its proprietor conceived to
be the characteristics of a grand oriental lounge – a riot of tasselled cushions, sofas,
Persian carpets, and elaborate, tent-like drapes. Several of the grander divans offered
an authentically Turkish opulence; in others, the lack of taste and capital outlay

Special smoking compartments were established on trains.
'I say,' complains a passenger 'you know, here's somebody not smoking!'

resulted in an effect akin to an *Arabian Nights* pantomime cobbled together by a tatty provincial repertory company. About a dozen of the better divans attracted a ready clientele among the rising generation of fashionable cigar smokers, and they continued to enjoy a vogue until the great Pall Mall clubs began to set aside rooms especially for smokers during the late 1840s.

Although, by the mid-19th century, high-quality cigars had a devoted and steadily increasing following among the wealthy, Victorian society still frowned on the idea of smoking in mixed company. In most of the great country houses, those who wished to smoke had to repair to the billiards room; if there were no billiards room, the more desperate guests (and sometimes their host, too) might be found taking surreptitious puffs in the stables, or even in the kitchens after the servants had retired to bed. It was only during the last third of the century that it became the custom for the ladies to withdraw after dinner to allow the men to relax in the dining room over their cigars and the decanter of port. By then, however, cigar smoking had become a deeply entrenched habit among the aristocracy – indeed, in 1868 a law was enacted requiring the British railway companies to provide special smoking compartments in trains.

The triumph of the cigar among the wealthy and discerning was not, of course, confined to Britain. Most of northern Europe west of Russia fell a willing victim to the cigar habit. As we shall see, in many countries the taste for cigars was pioneered or encouraged by royal enthusiasts.

Havanas Lead the Way

All the major cigar-producing countries benefited from this revolution in smoking taste; lands as widely separated as Brazil, the Philippines, Jamaica, India, the Canaries, Indonesia, and North America all manufactured cigars of varying degrees of excellence. But although individual tastes in leaf varied then, as now, there was never much dispute among the cognoscenti that the profoundest and subtlest smoking pleasures were vouchsafed by the Havana cigars of Cuba.

The Spanish Court formally authorised cultivation of tobacco in Cuba in 1614, long after the indigenous Cubans, from whom the Europeans first learnt of the pleasures of smoking, had been wiped out by force of arms, disease, and the casual, senseless brutality of the conquistadors. Most of the Cuban leaf in the 17th century was shipped directly to Seville, where it was made into cigars of an increasingly varied range of sizes, shapes, and quality. Among the most popular cheap forms around the close of the 17th century was the *cigale* (locust), so named presumably because of its similarity in colour and shape to a large locust. Possibly our word 'cigar' (which has a much disputed etymology) derives from this term; though the Mayan word *sik'ar* (which pertains to smoking) and the Spanish *cigarrar* (to roll) are likelier sources.

All the comforts of a gentlemen's club, with carpets
and big brass ashtrays, aboard the Great Northern Railway

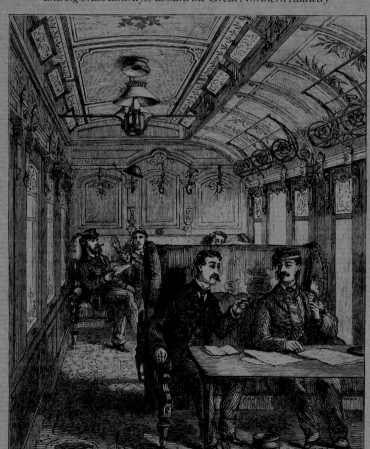

*By the 1890s 'smoking concerts' were all the rage. The opening
concert of the Royal Amateur Orchestral Society in 1893 was
graced by the presence of the Prince of Wales and his friends*

The Havana cigar today is the product of several hundred years of continuous
development. Cuban leaf has always enjoyed a head start over other cigar tobaccos on
account of the unique environment of soil and climate in which it is grown. But these
physical conditions, however irreplaceable, are merely the starting point in the
production of great tobacco. During the 17th and 18th centuries there gradually
emerged in Cuba an elite corps of tobacco specialists who, by patient experiments in
cultivation and breeding, came to understand how to improve and maintain the
quality of leaf. During the 18th century, too, a discovery was made that was profoundly to affect Cuba's economic and cultural future: neither the freshly harvested leaf nor
the partially or fully fermented tobacco travels so well as the manufactured and boxed
cigar. Production of the best Cuban cigars moved, about the beginning of the 19th
century, from Seville to Havana. It may confidently be asserted that the development
of the uniquely high quality of the world's greatest cigar dates from that movement of
manufacturing facilities from the Old World to the New.

Cuba, like its competitors, participated in the first great European boom in
cigar-smoking during the 1840s, and Havanas immediately and irrevocably entrenched themselves at the very top of the market. So great was the demand for them that
the production of Cuban leaf trebled during the course of that decade. The finest of all
Havanas during this period was the *regalia*, which was reserved for the exclusive use of
the Spanish Court. Exclusivity, indeed, was a much-sought-after privilege. In Spain it
extended also to the Cloth: unique, rather thick Havanas of special quality were
produced for the priesthood from tobacco selected and made up by monks. This is not

to say that cigars of the very highest quality were not available to other devotees wealthy enough to afford them. Names synonymous today with the finest Cuban leaf had already made their appearance in Havana's register of trademarks – Partagás as early as 1827, Por Larrañaga in 1834, and H. Upmann in 1844.

Throughout the second half of the 19th century and well into the 20th cigar consumption continued to expand throughout Europe and North America. Thereafter the ready-made cigarette was to take its place as the smoke of Everyman, though in recent years inexpensive cigars have begun to make a significant impact on the tobacco trade in Britain, following an already well established trend in continental Europe. Vice-President Thomas Marshall's celebrated aside in Congress – 'What this country needs is a really good five-cent cigar!' – was a wistful reminder, however, that cigars never were and never will be as cheap as cigarettes. For the connoisseur, moreover, the pleasure of the cigar is not to be measured in pounds, dollars, deutschmarks, or francs: which is just as well, for initiation into and the practice of the mysterious art of the Havana cigar can be as expensive (and as rewarding) as the development of the most subtly discerning taste in vintage claret.

What of today's Havana? The question is important not merely because, for the sentimentalist, things are never as good as they used to be but, more pressingly, because this ultimate expression of an aristocratic lifestyle is today the product of a communist republic. There can be little doubt that devotees of the Havana all over the non-communist world became alarmed when Fidel Castro's government assumed power in Cuba in January 1959. For a time it seemed possible that the new regime would insist on reducing the immense range of Havanas to a few standard types and sizes, and that the quality of the tobacco might be allowed to deteriorate to a common level of mediocrity.

That none of the despairing forecasts has turned out to be true is due to a variety of factors. One, certainly, is Cuba's need to export: although dwarfed by sugar as a foreign currency earner, Havanas nonetheless have always made a significant contribution to Cuba's balance of payments. Equally important, perhaps, were two other considerations: the pride of the cigar workers in their ancient craft; and the unsparing devotion of almost every Cuban – not least Fidel Castro himself – to the unique pleasures of Havanas in all their bewildering variety.

Today the cigar industry is part of a state monopoly, Cubatabaco – but one with a characteristically Cuban difference. For instance, about two-thirds of the very highest quality cigar leaf is grown by farmers with 160 acres or less who are permitted to own their land because of their consistent production record. Moreover, links with the pre-revolutionary past remain in the brand names of the finest cigars now coming out of Cuba: Bolívar, El Rey del Mundo, Hoyo de Monterrey, H. Upmann, Montecristo, Partagás, Por Larrañaga, Punch, Ramón Allones, Rafael Gonzalez, Romeo y Julieta. Retention of such titles would quickly have been discerned as little more than a crude marketing gimmick if today's Havanas remained true to the past only in name. In fact, connoisseurs the world over attest that the best Havanas today are at least as good as at any time in the past. For devotees of the divine herb, that means, as it has always meant, the supreme experience in smoking.

THE HALLOWED LEAF

NATURE has decreed that cigar tobacco attains its highest quality when grown in sub-tropical island environments within 25 degrees of the Equator. Havana leaf, of course, is the pre-eminent example of this; but its truth is confirmed by the best of the other cigar tobaccos, all of which are grown in or near the tropical zone. The quality of Cuban leaf was recognized by the early Spanish cultivators. Over the centuries Cuban seeds and plants, as well as Cuban farmers and cigar-makers, have been employed to establish cigar industries in many parts of the world. One of the more celebrated of such ventures occurred in 1886, when Vincente Ybor and a group of highly skilled Havana cigar-makers fled the oppressive Spanish regime in Cuba and settled in the infant city of Tampa, in Florida. Today Ybor City, Tampa's Latin Quarter, remains a centre of the American cigar industry. Yet in spite of a friendly climate and their technical know-how, these Cuban exiles never managed to produce leaf or finished cigars that could seriously aspire to the quality of choice Havanas. The same can be said of the excellent cigars produced by the firms who departed from Havana after the 1959 revolution. The reason in both cases is that the properties of any tobacco leaf are influenced profoundly by the purely local conditions of soil and climate in which it grows, and by a number of other local factors.

There is, indeed, a huge number of varieties of *Nicotiana tabacum* cultivated for production of cigar leaf; and each variety exhibits characteristics engendered by the specific conditions of soil and climate in which it grows. Evidently, Cuba offers uniquely favourable conditions that are impossible to duplicate elsewhere.

The Valley of the Vegas

'The most beautiful island I have ever seen' was how Columbus, wearied by weeks of featureless ocean horizons, summarised his brief sojourn in Cuba. The largest island in the Caribbean, Cuba lies like a great curved, rough-edged dagger between the coasts of Florida to the north, Yucatán (Mexico) to the south-west, and Haiti to the east. Tobacco is grown on large and small *vegas* (plantations) in four main regions: in Oriente province, near the towns of Bayamo and Nicaro; in the Remedios region of Las Villas province, between Sancti Spíritus and Santa Clara; in the Partido region south-west of Havana; and in the westernmost province of Pinar del Río. The quality of leaf varies considerably from region to region: that from Partido is valued chiefly for use as good-quality wrapper (the leaf forming the outer surface of the cigar), while Remedios leaf is excellent for blending purposes. For the true connoisseur, however, the supreme Havana may well be made entirely from leaf grown in Pinar del Río – and, specifically, in the area known as the Vuelta Abajo (Lower Valley). The most famous *vegas* in this area, which is about 100 miles long and about 20 wide, are located around the communes of San Juan y Martínez and San Luis, and elsewhere along the banks of the Cuyaguateje river, whose waters enrich the soil with alluvial deposits every year. On the eastern margin of the area is the Semi-Vuelta, where leaf of high excellence, though perhaps slightly less subtle in flavour, is grown.

Climate and soil, as we have already remarked, are key determinants in the production of fine tobacco. The luxuriance of the tobacco plants of the Vuelta Abajo seems to belie the fact that good harvests depend greatly on a relatively dry, though warm, winter growing season – Cuba receiving most of its annual rainfall from May to October. The sacred soil is famous for its almost rusty red colour. In fact, the rather thin top-soil is a fine, brown loam mixed with sand; but this overlies a reddish-brown,

A late 18th-century view, across to
the harbour and the distant city of Havana

*The artist's memory has failed him in this impression of an
18th century tobacco plantation: the leaves are far too small*

slightly gravelly subsoil, and it is the latter that becomes exposed when the *vegueros*
prepare the ground for cultivation. The quality of the leaf is intimately bound up with
the mixing of top- and subsoil and with the proportions of sand and gravel.

Cultivation

Nicotiana tabacum is one of those plant species, of which maize is a classic example,
that, having been domesticated by man, would probably not long survive in their
economically useful form if allowed to revert to the wild. The tobacco plant had more
or less assumed its modern appearance, in terms of size if not in luxuriance of growth,
in pre-Columbian times; for the Amerindian cultivators, though lacking formal
botanical know-how, were shrewd enough to deduce how to encourage growth of the
leaf at the expense of the rest of the plant. Since the 18th century, however, plant
breeders and tobacco technologists have succeeded, by dint of cross-breeding different
strains and varieties of *Nicotiana tabacum*, in developing plants that not only maximise
leaf production but also develop the desired physical and chemical properties that, in
the finished product, will result in cigars of high and consistent quality.

Domestication exacts its own penalties. A flourishing, wild-growing plant com-
munity has, almost by definition, acquired an ecological niche in which it is able to

compete successfully with other plants and in which it is free from, or capable of resisting, potentially destructive pests and diseases. The domesticated tobacco plant is a product of man; a tobacco plantation, like any other large area of soil devoted exclusively to the raising of a single plant species, is an inviting target for other plants, insect pests, and a host of bacterial, fungal, and viral diseases. Indeed, life on the *vegas* during the growing season is one of unremitting toil and care, requiring frequent inspection of each individual plant for tell-tale signs of pests or disease.

The growing season begins after the end of the rainy season, when nursery-raised seedlings are planted out. Considering the size of the mature tobacco plant, which may attain a height of six feet or more, the seeds are remarkably small. About 100,000 of them would fit comfortably into a thimble and would weigh less than half an ounce; Linnaeus, the great Swedish botanist, in an apparently morbid craving for exactitude, once counted 40,320 seeds in a single tobacco pod.

The seeds are raised in nursery beds under carefully controlled conditions. They germinate at a temperature of about 18°C (65°F), and within five or six weeks they attain a height of about 8 inches and are ready to be planted out. Each square yard of nursery bed produces enough seedlings for about 200 square yards of soil in the plantation. For over a month before planting out the soil will have been carefully tilled by hand, so that it is free of weeds, and then dressed with fertilizers, notably potash to enhance disease resistance and nitrates to encourage leaf growth.

The earliest signs of maturity in the plant become evident about a month after planting out, when the leaves begin to turn a lighter and more brilliant shade of green. In order to encourage the plant to concentrate growth and flavour-engendering nutriments in the leaves, the *veguero* pinches out the tip of the stem, so preventing development of the flower head. The same routine applies to the suckers (side shoots) developed by the plant in response to removal of the stem tip. Most plants will have yielded between eight and twelve of the oblong leaves, the largest up to 18 inches long, by the time harvesting has been completed toward the end of March.

The growing season is inevitably a worrying time for the *veguero* owing to the number and variety of the natural hazards that can ruin his crop; even the best-run *vegas* are operated on the assumption that about 15 per cent of the crop will be destroyed every year by pests and diseases. Dry weather is essential: the fields are never irrigated; morning dew and the occasional brief, light shower provide all the moisture the plants need. The commercial value of the harvest can be ruined in the space of three or four hours by a violent storm. Hailstorms are especially destructive; so, too, are the hurricanes that are notoriously prevalent in the Caribbean, although fortunately most of these occur during the summer. Fungicides and pesticides are regularly applied during the growing season, but they tend to diminish rather than eradicate diseases and pests. Among diseases the most dreaded is tobacco mosaic, whose visible signs – apparent only after the virus has taken hold – are a green and yellow mottling of the leaves. All plants, even healthy looking ones, in the area of those infected must be uprooted and destroyed as soon as the tell-tale signs appear. Among insect pests, the horn-worm is one of the most persistent. Some 3½ inches long, the green-and-white-striped horn-worm is the caterpillar of one of the larger hawk-moths, and is attracted to many plants of the Solanaceae family. Few *vegas* are free of the horn-worm during the growing season, and the most effective method of dealing with the pest remains the ancient but wearisome expedient of picking off the caterpillars by hand. If the *veguero* is not only vigilant but lucky, his harvested leaf will bear only a few small examples of the characteristic horn-worm holes; such superficial damage detracts neither from the quality nor the commericial value of the leaf.

On some cigars the wrapper appears to be stained with small, circular marks of a lighter brown than the rest of the leaf. This is caused when droplets of dew or rainwater form on the growing leaf. In bright, direct sunlight these droplets act as a lens or burning glass, resulting in the underlying leaf surface become bleached. While such marks, though marring the appearance of the wrapper, have little or no effect on its smoking qualities, they are rarely found on the choicest Havanas. The wrapper leaf for these – the very pick of the best areas in the Vuelta Abajo – is shade-grown, the plants being protected against direct sunlight for most of the growing season by means of muslin cloths stretched between poles. These muslin shades may cover many acres, and they must be erected at the beginning of each growing season and dismantled before the hurricanes begin at the end of summer. This method results in leaves of perfectly uniform colour – somewhat lighter in tone than the filler leaves – and with delicate, inconspicuous veins. But even with the best of intentions, some rain or dew may penetrate the muslin, and the presence of these marks is no indication that the leaf is not of the finest.

Harvesting of the leaves depends for its timing upon the requirements of the market. If light-coloured tobacco is required, leaves will be removed before they are fully mature; otherwise, harvesting waits until most of the leaves have acquired their characteristic rough, thick, yellowish-green, often rather spotty appearance. In either case, determining the exact moment to pick the leaves requires great experience and fine judgement on the part of the *veguero*. The flavour of the tobacco derives essentially from the sap in the interior of the leaf. In the young plant the sap is light green in colour; as the leaf approaches maturity the sap turns to a vivid emerald. The *veguero*'s decision to pick the leaf depends upon his capacity to discriminate between subtly different shades of sap colour.

Curing and Fermentation

The *vega* towards harvest time is a marvellous sight. Many of the plantations of the Vuelta are overlooked by the complex jumble of the Mogotes mountains – vast, steep-sided, green-clad mounds that rear dramatically from the floor of the valleys. The crowding of the plantations into the gaps between these bluffs means that the fields, though often large, rarely attain the monotonous rectangularity typical of single-crop farming elsewhere. The tall tobacco forms cool, delightful avenues of liquid golden-green, the topmost leaves vivid and almost translucent against the sun. The entrance gate to many of the larger *vegas* is guarded by a couple of tall, stately royal palms, whose slender trunks culminate in what appear to be giant feather dusters swaying gently in the breeze. More of these palms, either singly or in small groves, together with Cuban cedar and pine trees, are liberally scattered about the margins of

*Little has changed in the century since this and the following
photos were taken: Above: bales of tobacco wrapped in palm leaves*

the fields, offering a pleasant counterpoint to the studied regimentation of *Nicotiana*.

One man-made feature attracts the eye: rectangular, barn-like timber buildings, often with a thatch of palm leaves. Their apparently haphazard location – they occur every hundred yards or so, usually on the edge of fields but sometimes in the middle – is counterposed by the fact that their two longest sides invariably face east and west. These are the *casas de tabaco*, the curing barns, where the harvested leaf undergoes the first stage in the long journey toward the achievement of a choice Havana.

Immediately after picking the leaves are taken to the barn, where they are tied into bunches and hung on bamboo poles that are laid across beams in the roof. Almost all Havana cigar leaf is air-dried in this way. The curing process, which takes several weeks, substantially reduces the moisture content of the leaf: whereas before picking the leaf's water content accounts for about 25 per cent of its weight, by the end of the curing process the proportion has fallen to 10 per cent or less.

It is vital that the *rate* of curing is exactly right, otherwise the quality and flavour of the leaf will be impaired. If atmospheric humidity is too high, the leaves may be removed from the barn and exposed to the sun for short periods during the curing process. In the event of persistent rain, the air in the barn may be dried by the use of a charcoal fire. If humidity is too low the floor of the barn will be covered with

*The 'hands' of tobacco leaves laid out
on the floor of the tobacco warehouse to ferment*

water-soaked cloths. Fine adjustments to humidity are made by opening or closing any or all of several doors that are fitted high up in the smaller north- and south-facing walls. The temperature inside the barn must be controlled similarly, since heat is generated within the bundles of leaves as they begin the process of fermentation.

The fermentation of the tobacco leaf is caused by a complex of naturally-occurring bacteria and yeasts, and it is a remarkable fact that some of the finer subtleties of flavour in a particular leaf are attributable to particular species of bacteria. Indeed, the distinctive quality of Havana leaf is probably due as much to local bacterial flora as to the peculiarities of the Cuban soil – as true Roquefort cheese can be made only with the moulds that thrive in the caverns of Roquefort, or a fine wine should be made only in its own *domaine*.

When the leaf is taken from the curing barn it is very brittle. The bundles are laid carefully one upon another in a pit dug into the ground, and covered with the leaves of the royal palm, the trees of which are grown along the borders of the plantation. In a good year, when the growing season has been blessed with no more than two inches of rain spread evenly over the period, the leaf will be thick and juicy. Such leaf will be piled higher than leaf of lesser quality because the heat of fermentation will need to be intense; lighter leaf requires a less drastic initial fermentation.

*Inspecting and sorting the quality of the tobacco
leaf into the various grades of wrappers and fillers*

At all times the rate of fermentation – a function of the temperature in the
interior of the pile – must be carefully controlled, and it requires long experience and
the utmost skill to determine exactly when to halt the process. As fermentation
proceeds, the innermost bunches in the pile are brought to the outside and the
outermost ones buried within, so that all bunches undergo the same treatment. This
first fermentation lasts about two months, the pile attaining its maximum temperature
at about the halfway stage, and then gradually cooling.

When this first fermentation has ended, the leaf is pliable and in a condition to
be handled. Now comes one of the most important events in the journey from
plantation to factory: the *escogeda*, or selection, in which the leaves are sorted into
various categories. The two basic categories are *capas* (wrappers) and *tripas* (fillers);
but within each of these are several sub-categories pertaining to colour, length,
texture, and other physical properties. The selection, which takes place in villages
and communes all over the Vuelta Abajo, requires enormous skill and dexterity in the
escogedores, who work at great speed. Moreover, now that the first fermentation is
over, the true expert can get a pretty clear idea from the selection of the probable
quality of this year's 'vintage'. The *escogeda* is of great significance to the local people,
and the days of the *escogeda* are almost a rural festival in the Vuelta.

*The women of a cigar factory with their foreman. The wide
ethnic variety of the Cuban people is particularly noticeable*

The graded leaves are tied into bundles called 'hands', wound round at the butt
end with another leaf, and 320 hands are made up into a bale. Traditionally, the bale
should be wrapped in the bark of the royal palm, a material as essential to the ageing of
tobacco as the oak keg is to the maturing of fine wine. At the cigar factory warehouse,
bales of the same grade from different farms are broken open, blended together
according to the requirements of the individual manufacturer, and laid in large heaps
on the floor. At this stage, leaf intended for filler may have all or part of the central
stem removed.

The heaps are then sprayed with water to induce the onset of the next stage of
fermentation. This stage needs to be controlled with care: the fermenting heap of
tobacco is rather like a garden compost heap, and it must be turned frequently so that
the tobacco in the middle does not become overheated and damaged. To any but
those habituated to the experience, the odour of the leaf at this time provides an
overwhelming experience, somewhat like being trapped in a stable, since the vegetation gives off a considerable amount of ammonia.

When the heap is sufficiently and evenly fermented throughout the tobacco is
again racked until it has dried to a water content of about 12 per cent, and it is then
packed into bales, which are pressed and sewn up. These bales may be stored in the
warehouse for anything up to three years, during which time they go through a further
natural but less violent fermentation each year.

THE MAKING OF A HAVANA

E have seen that the journey of the Havana leaf, from seedling through harvesting, curing, selection, and various fermentations, may take up to 10 years. It is only at the end of this long journey, during which the leaf gradually acquires the requisite qualities of taste, strength, aroma, elasticity, and burning properties, that it is ready to be converted into cigars at the factories in Havana.

Yet even now the leaf must undergo further selection and refinement. The reputation of Havanas as the finest cigars in the world rests not only on the supreme quality of the leaf but also on the assurance – of vital moment to the true connoisseur – that each individual cigar bearing one of the dozen or so great brand names will possess, within astonishingly fine tolerances, the same taste, body, and aroma as its fellows in the same box. Indeed, even that degree of consistency is insufficient: cigars of a given brand must offer a more or less identical smoking experience from year to year. This question of consistency is difficult enough for cigar manufacturers catering for the popular market, where the average smoker is capable of distinguishing only between rather broad categories of strength and flavour. The true connoisseur of the Havana, however, is something else. He has spent many years cultivating and disciplining his senses of taste and smell to the point where he is capable of discriminating between the minutest inflexions of flavour. He has patiently worked his way through the truly vast variety of smoking experiences offered by the different brands and types of Havana, and has finally settled upon a favourite selection. He is simply not prepared to tolerate cigars whose taste is subject to sudden, random changes, however subtle.

One might reasonably suppose, given the matchlessly favourable environment of the Vuelta Abajo and the unremitting care and attention devoted to the leaf through all the stages of curing, cutting, and fermentation, that consistency in the quality and flavour of the leaf was assured. Not a bit of it; and the problem has little to do with plant diseases and pests and the unfavourable weather conditions with which the *veguero* have constantly to contend. No, the difficulties arise from the subtle effects on the leaf of the tobacco plant's astonishing sensitivity to even the smallest variations in the constitution of the soil. One might not, perhaps, be surprised to learn that leaf from one *vega* often tastes slightly different from that grown on another a few miles distant. The fact is, however, that leaf picked from plants in *adjacent rows* in the same field may vary in flavour. In each case the leaf may well be of the very highest quality; but it will not offer an identical smoking experience, because the variations will persist through the curing and fermentation processes.

It is one thing to be able to distinguish minuscule variations in flavour and strength between cigars while they are being smoked. It is quite another thing to possess the ability to examine the leaf and to determine how, by mixing certain quantities from different casks or consignments, absolute consistency of brand flavour can be secured. This is the daunting responsibility of teams of specialized selectors, who spend hours wandering, seemingly in a state of abstraction, among row upon row of suspended leaves examining them for the tiniest variations in colour, texture, elasticity, aroma, and other physical properties.

In the Fábrica

For the romantic or sentimentalist, the image of the cigar-maker was fixed for all time by Prosper Mérimée in *Carmen* (1845), with its picture of the girls in the cigar factories of Seville. The image was intensified, with intimations of a hectic sensuality, by the

El veguero (the planter), with his machete hanging at his hip, leans on bales of tobacco wrapped in leaves of the royal palm

The introduction of the reader, who would keep the cigarmakers'
minds engaged while their hands were active, was a potent educational
influence in the growing revolutionary fervour of Cuba

perfervid fantasies of other French observers, whose sensibilities were engaged less by
the quality of the product or the appalling squalor of the *fábricas* than by the golden
thighs of the girls engaged in rolling tobacco.

The historical reality of the Havana cigar factories is less voluptuous and more
interesting. Until recent years the cigar-makers were invariably men. As skilled
craftsmen they were regarded as the elite of the urban workers of Cuba, and from the
mid-19th century onwards they were to play a significant part in the rise and final
triumph of the Cuban independence movement. Ever since the days when the first
major factories were built in Havana, the workshops have been vast rooms in which
200 or more cigarmakers sit at row upon row of benches stretching from wall to wall.
At the front end of the room, facing the workers, is a raised platform.

Sometime during the 1860s a Havana newspaper owner suggested that the minds
of the cigar-makers might be improved if they were read to while they were at work.
One of the factory owners took up the idea, perhaps reasoning that the practice might
increase output while keeping his labour force in a state of happy docility. So it came
about that the now-famous readings of world literature began. At first the Bible was

The Great Marques

ABOUT the year 1600, Demetrio Pela, a native of the Canary Islands, settled in Cuba with an eye to the cultivation of tobacco. He sought the advice of an American Indian, Erioxil Panduca. Since these are the earliest names we have in the history of commercial planting in Cuba the partners have a claim to be the ancestors of the great marques of today.

By 1800 Cuban leaf had long provided the material for the finest Spanish-made cigars, though the home industry was still in its infancy. Then, in 1810, the Havana register of trademarks opened its books with the names of Bernardino Rencurrel and H. de Cabañas y Carbajol (a company already in business for more than a decade).

Thereafter, the register reads as a roll of honour. Within its first 40 years Partagás (1827), Por Larrañaga (1834), H. Upmann (1844) and La Corona (1845) were just four of the great names to be formally inscribed. In the 1850s came the company of Gustave Bock, the Dutchman who was the first non-Spanish European immigrant to establish a manufactory of cigars in Havana and also, as it happens, the presumed inventor of the cigar band.

In 1958, on the eve of the Castro Revolution, connoisseurs recognized some 20 grand marques. Among them were Partagás, Por Larrañaga, H. Upmann, Hoyo de Monterrey, Rafael Gonzalez, Romeo y Julieta, Ramón Allones, Punch, Bolívar, El Rey del Mundo, Montecristo, and Bock, La Corona, Cabañas y Carbajol, Villar y Villar, Murias, Henry Clay. The disruption caused by the revolution caused fears that traditional methods and the era of the great marques might be over. A number of the marques, chief among them the last six in the above list, withdrew from Cuba.

These houses still manufacture fine cigars, but they no longer have access to the finest leaf in the world from those magic acres of the Vuelto Abajo. The other great names became the property of the Cuban people. After a surprisingly brief period of revolutionary upheaval the old ways re-established themselves in the industry. Today, according to world experts, the great Havanas are of a quality unmatched by anything in the past.

Unfortunately, cigars marked 'Havana' are not always what they claim to be. In some cases, a fine product which includes some Cuban leaf in its composition pretends to the ultimate accolade, deserved only by cigars made of 100 per cent Havana tobacco in the island of Cuba itself. In other cases, the fraud is more unashamed. Either way, the green band, the official authorization of the Cuban government, is the only assurance of proper manufacture and brand authenticity.

To be sure, some things have changed. The factory which produces the Upmann marque is now known as the José Martí works, in honour of the poet revolutionary. There is sound justice in this since the cigar works have traditionally been in the fore of Cuba's revolutionary movements and the Castro regime has collectively honoured them for their historic role.

The symbols of the old houses continue just as the mystique of the Havana survives. The great cigar is a subject for deep connoisseurship. There are those who, given the year of the harvest from which the leaf for a given cigar was taken, can identify the maker or, given the maker, can identify the year.

Even before nationalization, not all the marques were independent. Six of them were associated in the group known as Tabacalera Americana, others were combined in the ownership of a single family. The great Menendez family of Havana were the proprietors of numerous brands, among them H. Upmann and Montecristo, the marque favoured by Orson Welles; the Palacios owned Hoyo de Monterrey and Punch. Jack Warner, the movie mogul, was smoking a Hoyo de Monterrey Panatela at the Palm Beach Casino in Cannes when he made his great gambling coup with a *banco* of one hundred million francs. The stub, said to be slightly chewed, was preserved in a silver box.

Each of the great marques boasts champions among the rich and famous and each has a fund of anecdotes to grace its proud history. Zino Davidoff, whose book details many such, records a dramatic personal experience of the almost miraculous qualities of the cigars of Villar y Villar in the magical climate of their homeland. Touring Cuba in 1936 in search of new sources of fine tobacco, he visited a small farm where the owner offered a Villar dating from the time of his grandfather as they discussed business.

The cigar in question was, in fact, 25 years old and Davidoff accepted politely though in some apprehension as to what he was letting himself in for. The cigar was excellent. The secret of its preservation proved to be 'an old thick wooden chest, slightly worm eaten . . . kept in a slightly humid earth cellar.'

*'The Tobacco Manufactory in different Branches' is the caption
to this engraving published in the* Universal Magazine *in 1750*

high on the list of material considered suitable; later, the readings were taken not only
from the work of Spanish writers such as Cervantes, Calderón, Unamuno, and others,
but also translations of Hugo, Zola, and Dickens. To a 19th-century factory owner,
the work of such writers was no doubt more than sufficiently inflammatory. But this
was not the end of it. Almost imperceptibly over the years, the nature of the reading
matter began to change: not always with the consent of the management, and often to
its extreme alarm, the workshop platform evolved into a source not only of cultural
nourishment but of political education. A culmination of this trend was the appearance on the platform of José Martí, one of Cuba's greatest poets and the first hero of its
independence movement.

Martí was to draw much of his revolutionary support from the tobacco workers,
both on the *vegas* and in the factories, and it was the cigar-makers who launched
Cuba's first clandestine newspapers. The political sophistication and fervour of the
cigar-makers has endured to the present day, and Fidel Castro officially proclaimed
them 'Heroes of Moncada' in recognition of their part in the 1959 revolution. The
director general for many years of Cubatabaco – who had indulged a fervent partiality
for Havanas since he was 12 years old – was one of Castro's comrades in the
mountains. And still the readings continue – stories and poetry, of course, but
leavened now with the writings of Che Guevara and other heroes and editorials from
Granma, the Party newspaper.

Hand-made Quality

Cigar-making, including the vital role of the *torcedor* (twister) who handles the supremely important wrapper leaf, is no longer the exclusive province of the Cuban male. Since the 1959 revolution it has been the policy of the Cuban government to open up opportunities for women to earn a living in skilled and semi-skilled manual work; and one of the areas that have witnessed a radical transformation of the labour force is the cigar industry. At first, of course, the takeover was very gradual and applied only to factories making cigars of lesser quality: the craft of constructing the *puro*, the great cigar, is not acquired quickly, and in any generation it is only a privileged few – men or women – who attain this summit of the cigar-maker's craft. But the extent of the transformation can be measured in the fact that today the José Martí factory, which makes H. Upmann and Montecristo cigars in the heart of old Havana, employs 520 women and only 190 men, and 220 of the women are engaged in making hand-rolled cigars. (Another facet of the mobilization of the labour force at all levels may be seen in the plantations during the growing season, when thousands of pre-university students – the doctors, engineers, artists of tomorrow – assist in the work of cultivating the tobacco plants under the watchful eyes of the *vegueros*.)

The great Havanas are all hand-made from start to finish – which partly accounts for their price. The hand-rolled cigar is pretty rare in this age of the machine; indeed, it has been rare for more than half a century. One of the first cigar-making machines was patented as long ago as 1883 by Oscar Hammerstein, who later found worthier and more lasting fame as one of the great Broadway impresarios. His machine was ingenious but essentially unworkable. But by the 1920s most American cigars were machine made, and the practice has now spread to the majority of cigar factories around the world.

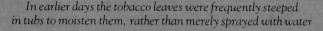

In earlier days the tobacco leaves were frequently steeped
in tubs to moisten them, rather than merely sprayed with water

*Stringing newly-harvested tobacco leaves
together to hang them in the rafters of the drying barn*

As early as 1925 one of the most famous Havana cigar companies imported an American machine and rashly exhibited its productive efficiency in the streets of the city. Immediate protests were forthcoming from the cigar-makers, strikes broke out, and more than one *torcedor* died in violent demonstrations that lasted for several days. The machine was put away, and was eventually shipped back to the United States.

It cannot be doubted that there was an element of Luddism in the attitude of the workers: the machine threatened the livelihood of hundreds of craftsmen whose expertise had taken many years to acquire and was, moreover, the living expression of a skill in which Cubans had led the world for 200 years. But there is more to the argument than that. The great cigars are hand-made not for the sake of luxury or exclusivity – though in the nature of things the cost of making them by hand renders them both luxurious and exclusive pleasures. No, the real issue is simply one of quality: so far, technology has failed to come up with a machine that makes cigars as good as those fashioned by the elite *torcedores* of Havana. There are two major areas of difficulty. In the first place, manufacture by a machine, however delicate it may be in operation, tends to produce small fractures in the surface of the filler leaves, and this leads to evaporation of the aromatic oils that contribute crucially to the cigar's flavour. Second, and perhaps even more undesirable, machines invariably select wrapper leaves that are thicker and coarser-textured than the smooth, delicate, membrane-like wrapper that turns a great Havana into an authentic masterpiece.

It might be supposed by those unfamiliar with the *torcedor*'s skill that production by hand must inevitably lead to at least some variation in size, shape, or density among individual cigars of a given type. The quickest way of disabusing anyone of such suspicions, of course, is to open a box of choice Havanas. But it may also be remarked that, over the years, the *torcedores* have shown themselves capable of reproducing exactly more than 950 individual sizes and shapes: they have had to, such are the personal, regional, and national tastes and foibles of Havana aficionados throughout the world.

The advent of female cigar-makers has had no effect on the uncompromisingly exacting standards of excellence that the production of the *puro* demands. For both men and women, training begins with a year's apprenticeship. Two years later, the more promising 'students' will have advanced to the point where they are permitted to call themselves *torcedores* – but they are still not ready to work on the *puro*. Only after the cigar-maker has passed through six ever-more-difficult grades of excellence is he or she accorded the final accolade of handling the wrapper of the greatest brands.

Constructing the Havana

A cigar consists of three basic components: filler, binder, and wrapper. The filler forms the interior of the cigar; it accounts for the greater portion of the cigar's mass, and it is the filler leaf that is subject to the art and science of the mixing process we mentioned above. Nevertheless, it is the wrapper, which constitutes no more than 8% of the mass, which contributes most of the flavour.

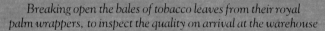

*Breaking open the bales of tobacco leaves from their royal
palm wrappers, to inspect the quality on arrival at the warehouse*

THE SMOKERS' ROOM

*George Cruikshank, who engraved this candid view of a cigar divan
in 1832, was not impressed with the dandies who frequented it*

DURING the 18th century, fashionable society in England and France took its tobacco in the form of snuff – pipes being mostly left to the lower orders. Service in the Peninsular War gave French and British troops the taste for the Spanish cigar but it was not until duty was reduced in 1829 that cigar smoking really caught on. Snuff taking was soon old-fashioned and almost from the start the House of Commons had a special smoking room set aside for the use of members. Elsewhere in the capital public smoking rooms, called 'divans' from the popular name for the Turkish court and its comfortable sofas, were soon doing a thriving trade. The London clubs followed suit and by the end of the century there was hardly a great country house in the land which had not converted one of its numerous drawing rooms for the use of smokers. They could be places of almost serious formality and were luxuriously appointed. 'The Lesson of the Master', a short story published in 1888 by Henry James, conjures up the setting.

The smoking-room at Summersoft was on the scale of the rest of the place: high, light, commodious and decorated with such refined old carvings and mouldings that it seemed rather a bower for ladies . . . than a parliament of gentlemen smoking strong cigars. The gentlemen mustered there in considerable force and in bright habiliments on the Sunday evening . . . in front of one of the cool fair fireplaces of white marble, the entablature of which was adorned with a delicate little Italian 'subject'.

There was another fireplace in the facing wall but in the mild days of spring and summer the focus of the room 'was provided by the table in the chimney corner, laden with bottles, decanters, and tall tumblers'. A ladies' room it may originally have been, but the conversion seems to have been adequate to its purpose and the 'parliament of gentlemen' could divert themselves by inspecting the fine old prints on the wall while refreshing themselves with Havanas . . . and tall tumblers.

'The Smoking Room at the Club': another cartoonist's view

Those 'bright habiliments' brought a touch of festiveness to the scene. When the ladies turned in for bed, the gentlemen wishing to smoke would adjourn to their dressing rooms and come down again to the smoking room, adorned in smoking jackets, usually of velvet in various colours, with wide and gorgeous lapels and often embellished still further with gold-braided frogging; they would then don their equally splendid smoking caps for the evening's business. These clothes also had a practical importance: worn for this evening ritual they, rather than the gentlemen's formal evening wear, absorbed the rich cigar smoke, while the caps protected the hair in the same way.

A typical domestic smoking room of the late 19th century

*Cigar makers in a
Havana factory, more than half a century ago*

The filler is enclosed within the binder. In all cigars, of whatever quality, the binder is responsible for the structural rigidity, and commonly is selected from the larger leaves, growing near the base of the plant, which tend to have a relatively high tensile strength. In many cigars, the binder is selected almost entirely for its physical properties and often has indifferent smoking qualities. In the choicest Havana, however, as much care is devoted to selection of the binder as to that of the filler and wrapper: like the other components, it invariably comes from the Vuelta Abajo, and makes its own characteristic and irreplaceable contribution to the flavour and aroma of the end product.

The shade-grown wrapper leaf forms the outer surface of the cigar. The best Havana wrapper is, quite simply, the highest expression of the tobacco grower's art: its quality has never been approached, far less equalled, anywhere else in the world. The visible indications of a great wrapper leaf include smoothness of texture, evenness of colour, and delicacy of structure; it must be very thin and without prominent veins. But more important than these visual indications are the wrapper's smoking qualities: its aroma, flavour, and strength must perfectly harmonise with, and subtly counter-point, those of the filler and binder.

We can understand, then, that it is not only in the careful blending of filler leaves but also in the almost unbelievably subtle task of achieving perfect complementarity in smoking qualities between filler, binder, and wrapper that the skill of the selectors attains its fullest expression.

This labelled flap from a box of Punch cigars, probably designed round
about the turn of the century, shows us that the traditional ways of making
cigars by hand, and the equipment used, have remained virtually
unchanged in the intervening years. The tobacco arrives at the factory in
its stencilled bales wrapped in the leaves of the royal palm (lower left); and
the cigars are rolled by hand at a small desk-like bench (upper left) where
the workers sit elbow to elbow. The finished cigars are tied into bundles,
each with its coloured ribbon (upper right), or packed into boxes made
from the wood of the Cuban cedar (lower right)

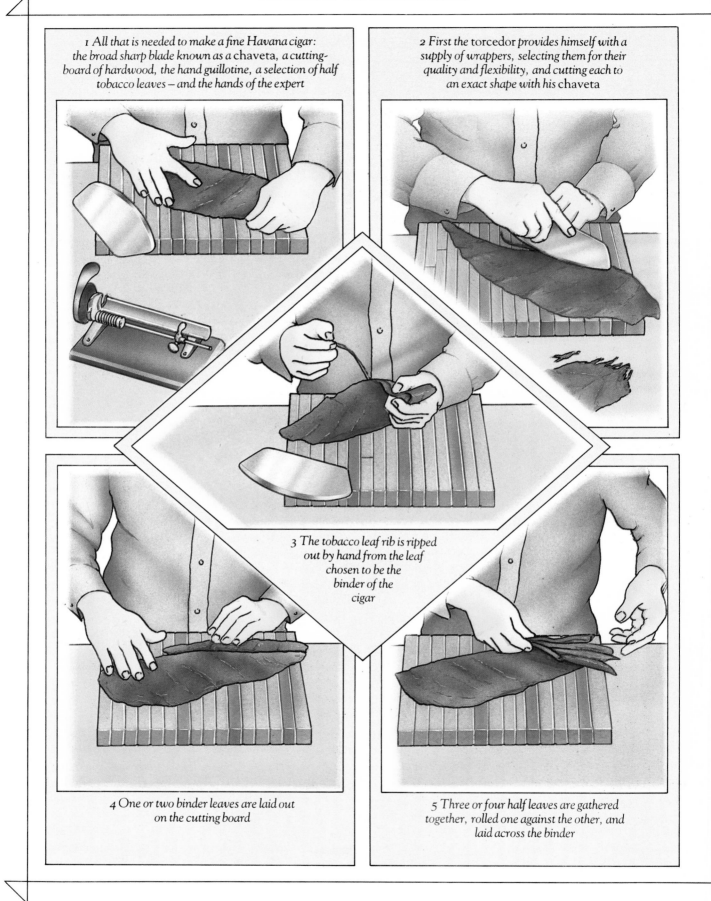

1 All that is needed to make a fine Havana cigar:
the broad sharp blade known as a chaveta, a cutting-
board of hardwood, the hand guillotine, a selection of half
tobacco leaves – and the hands of the expert

2 First the torcedor provides himself with a
supply of wrappers, selecting them for their
quality and flexibility, and cutting each to
an exact shape with his chaveta

3 The tobacco leaf rib is ripped
out by hand from the leaf
chosen to be the
binder of the
cigar

4 One or two binder leaves are laid out
on the cutting board

5 Three or four half leaves are gathered
together, rolled one against the other, and
laid across the binder

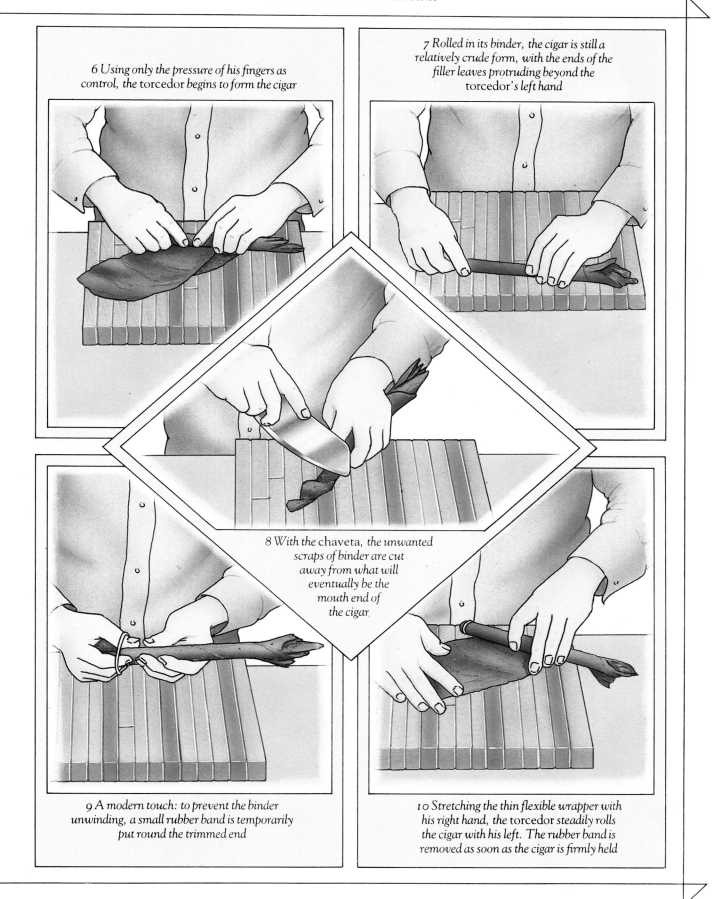

6 Using only the pressure of his fingers as control, the torcedor begins to form the cigar

7 Rolled in its binder, the cigar is still a relatively crude form, with the ends of the filler leaves protruding beyond the torcedor's left hand

8 With the chaveta, the unwanted scraps of binder are cut away from what will eventually be the mouth end of the cigar.

9 A modern touch: to prevent the binder unwinding, a small rubber band is temporarily put round the trimmed end

10 Stretching the thin flexible wrapper with his right hand, the torcedor steadily rolls the cigar with his left. The rubber band is removed as soon as the cigar is firmly held

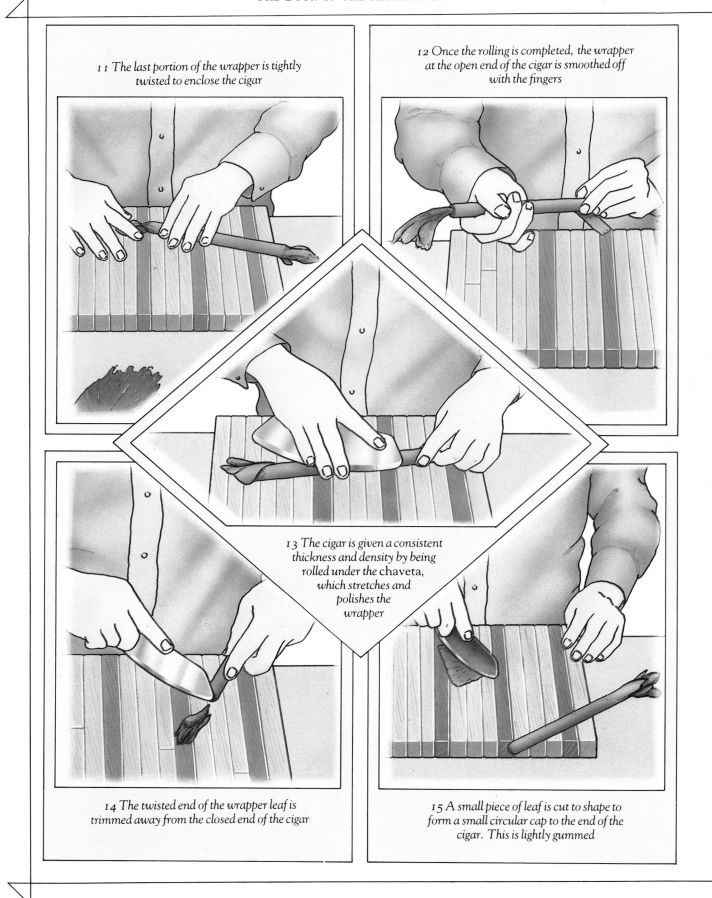

11 The last portion of the wrapper is tightly twisted to enclose the cigar

12 Once the rolling is completed, the wrapper at the open end of the cigar is smoothed off with the fingers

13 The cigar is given a consistent thickness and density by being rolled under the chaveta, which stretches and polishes the wrapper

14 The twisted end of the wrapper leaf is trimmed away from the closed end of the cigar

15 A small piece of leaf is cut to shape to form a small circular cap to the end of the cigar. This is lightly gummed

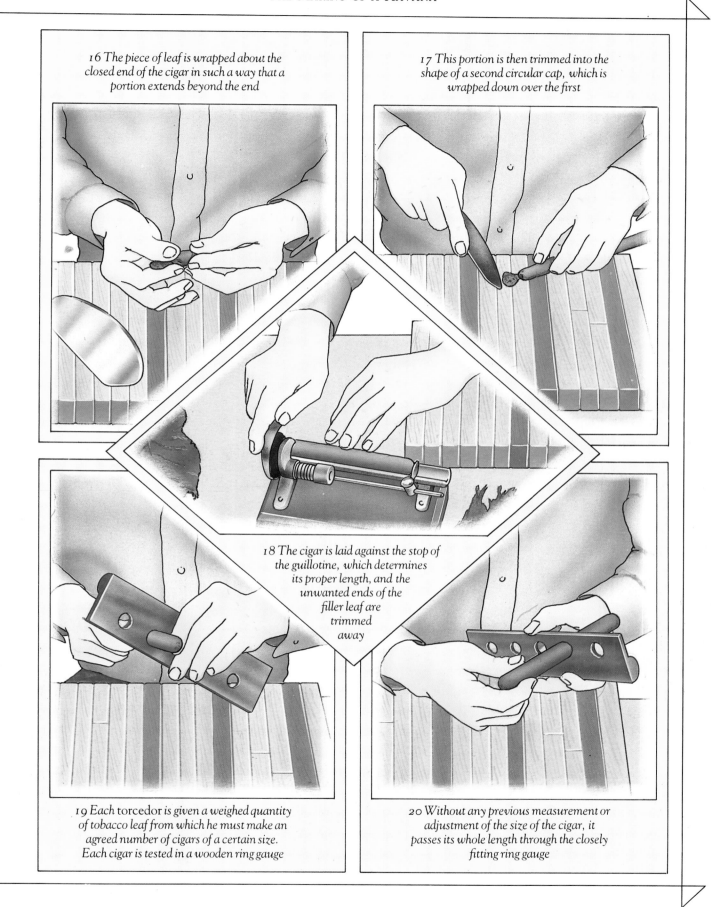

16 The piece of leaf is wrapped about the closed end of the cigar in such a way that a portion extends beyond the end

17 This portion is then trimmed into the shape of a second circular cap, which is wrapped down over the first

18 The cigar is laid against the stop of the guillotine, which determines its proper length, and the unwanted ends of the filler leaf are trimmed away

19 Each torcedor is given a weighed quantity of tobacco leaf from which he must make an agreed number of cigars of a certain size. Each cigar is tested in a wooden ring gauge

20 Without any previous measurement or adjustment of the size of the cigar, it passes its whole length through the closely fitting ring gauge

Quality control remains of the greatest importance, even under nationalization. Every batch must be sampled, a cigar being broken open to inspect the work and the condition of the filler leaf (opposite). The cigars must be weighed, to ensure that their content conforms to specification (top left) and samples of tobacco must be subjected to regular chemical analysis (top right). Then the cigars must be graded for colour and consistency of the wrapper leaf (above left), so that when they are finally batched for packing into boxes (above right) they present a carefully matched appearance

The last manual operation is the addition of the paper band with the name of the brand (opposite). The wooden tray is marked along the edge with a scale to check on the size of the cigar. Then the cigars must be stored, either as bundles of fifty (top) or in their cedarwood boxes (above). At all stages of their future life the temperature and humidity should be carefully controlled, for they are still living entities, and undergo regular further fermentation

Even the appearance of the name of Havana on a flap or label is no guarantee that the cigars are genuinely from Cuba: at least one of these labels (top and opposite) is from cigars manufactured in the USA. Since 1912 all genuine Havana cigars have been sealed with the Cuban Government Warranty (above) and no box or other pack that is not so sealed can be considered genuine. Boxes may be sometimes be found with the seal broken, but this should not be taken as a sign that an unscrupulous tobacconist has replaced the Havanas with imitations: the Customs authorities insist upon sampling every consignment

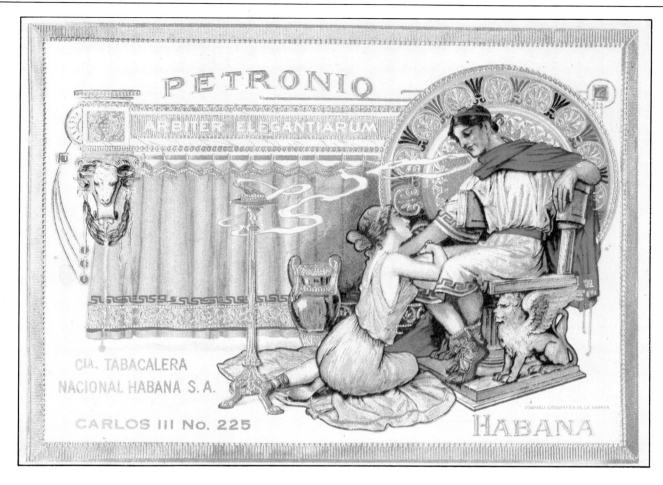

*Toward the end of the 19th century the popularity of the cigar, together
with its continuing significance as a symbol of power and prosperity, led to
an extraordinary proliferation of brands, and the designers of labels vied
with one another in the production of labels that suggested both the
attractions of Cuban tobacco and the discrimination and elegance of the
typical cigar smoker*

The art and skill of the printer were applied as much to the cigar bands themselves as to the labels. Special selections had their own distinctive bands, which might offer 'Fancy Tales of Smoke' or a 'Selección de Lujo' (de luxe selection), or feature the portrait of an European sovereign known to favour them. Some enthusiasts, such as the pianist Arthur Rubinstein (who at one time had his own tobacco plantation) would have their personal bands specially printed. The collecting of bands has developed into an international hobby

The first stage in production is concerned with the filler. Two to four half leaves, of various sizes depending upon the thickness and length of the cigar, are laid one on top of the other, very carefully rolled (not folded) within the binder leaf, and then trimmed to the required length. If we remember that by no means all cigars are parallel-sided, some being thicker in the middle, others tapering gradually along their entire length; and if we also remember that the density of the cigar must be exactly the same throughout – not merely for aesthetic reasons but to ensure that the cigar draws evenly from beginning to end – we can perceive that rolling and binding is a very demanding skill.

Next, the *torcedor* selects a wrapper half-leaf from a large number he keeps beside him on the work bench. While awaiting his attention, the wrappers are usually covered with a damp cloth, so that they remain supple. The *torcedor* lays the selected half-leaf on his cutting board. Then, using his *chaveta* – a broad, gently curving, and extremely sharp blade – he very carefully cuts out two wrappers. Each wrapper consists of a broad strip, cut lengthwise from the leaf.

The *torcedor* now takes a cylinder of filler in its binder and places it at an angle of about 45 degrees across the wrapper. Then he winds the wrapper around the binder, making sure that the overlap is the same all the way up the length of the cigar; at the same time he delicately rolls the wrapped portion of the cigar with the flat of the knife blade, thus 'polishing' and stretching the wrapper so that it fits smoothly and tightly over the binder. Then the protruding end of the wrapper is cut away, and two small 'caps' are cut from it and successively stuck down with a tiny blob of tasteless and colourless gum tragacanth, the whole being smoothly rounded off. The presence of these caps is a sure indication that the cigar is not machine-made. It is then guillotined at its other end (the foot) to the exact length required.

Each *torcedor* is provided with a measured daily supply of tobacco, from which he must make an exact number of cigars of equal size and weight. He checks the length of the made cigar against the scale on his guillotine, and its diameter in a wooden ring-gauge, so that every one of a batch of cigars as it comes from the hand of the *torcedor* is identical in size, and his daily quota is always exactly maintained.

After inspection the cigars are customarily bound together by a silk ribbon in groups of 50, known as a half-wheel. They now spend a period of a few weeks in a cedar cabinet. One might call this a resting period: the cigars are recovering, as it were, from the final effects of the third fermentation and are able to lose some of the dampness they acquired during the various stages of manufacture. After this, the cigars are sorted into various categories and sub-categories (we shall be dealing with this topic in the next chapter), and are then ready for packing.

The standard range of Havana boxes contain 10, 25, 50, and 100 cigars. But so personal is the relationship between the great Havana connoisseur and his cigar supplier that there are endless variations on these standard packs. One of the commonest variations is known as the Cabinet Selection. Whereas cigar boxes are customarily oblong in shape and are decorated with extraordinarily colourful labels (see final chapter), the Selection consists of a ribbon-tied half-wheel (50 cigars) in a plain, square box – a *boîte nature*.

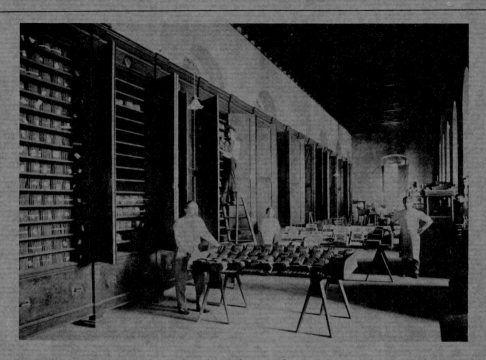

*The stock room of a
typical Havana factory, early this century*

While variety is the norm for box shapes, virtually all Havana boxes are made from Cuban cedar-wood, and large plantations of cedar, grown specifically for this purpose, are to be found all over Cuba. Like most other woods, Cuban cedar has the capacity to 'breathe'; but in terms of air circulation and humidity control, it is uniquely favourable to the preservation and final maturation of Havanas; and its natural smell is closest to that of tobacco. In some cigars, the filler is deliberately packed slightly more loosely than normal in the binder. When boxed these cigars are lightly compressed by the cedar-wood lid and by their neighbours on either side of them. As a result they not only acquire the correct density but assume, in section, that square shape with rounded corners favoured by many smokers.

We should also mention a well-established alternative to the cedar box. While most connoisseurs insist upon the superiority of fully mature cigars, an increasing number of smokers is claiming allegiance to the 'green' Havana – a cigar more or less in the fresh, slightly moist condition in which it leaves the factory. For such clients, Havanas are packed in air-tight jars, or singly in aluminium or glass tubes which effectively retard, though they cannot entirely eliminate, the maturation process.

Finally, a word about authenticity. Cuba exports cigar tobacco – though never the pick of the crop – all over the world, and many of the most popular cigar brands contain leaf shipped from the Havana warehouses. Some of the less scrupulous European manufacturers use this as a pretext for calling their cigars 'Havanas'. Do not be deceived by such impertinence. The only authentic Havanas are cigars made entirely from tobacco that has been grown, cured, fermented, rolled, and packed in Havana. Your guarantee of authenticity is the distinctive green Republic of Cuba warranty seal that appears on every box or jar of genuine Havanas.

CHAPTER FOUR

CHOOSING AND CARING FOR HAVANAS

W E have had a brief look at the history of the cigar, and at how tobacco is raised in the Vuelta and fashioned in the *fábricas* of Havana into cigars of surpassing excellence. It is time now for a quick excursion into the fascinating but elusive realms of cigarmanship: what one may look for in a fine cigar, some consideration of the enormous variety of Havanas available, and – a selection having been decided upon – how one can best keep a stock of cigars in good condition.

Evidence of the Senses

Taste is a very difficult topic; it partakes of so many subjective elements, and it operates at so many different levels. The loftier reaches of connoisseurship in cigars, as in great wines, seem to be attainable only by relatively few people, not only because of the time and money involved but also because of the concentration of aesthetic training and discipline they demand. More to our purposes here, such connoisseurship deals in subtleties and nuances of experience that seem scarcely amenable to verbal description or classification. A musicologist can describe in great detail the formal structure, and a critic can trenchantly define the artistic achievement, of a late Beethoven string quartet; but reading such analyses is not merely no substitute for listening to the music – it is an experience of a radically different order. The same kind of dilemma faces anyone endeavouring to communicate the nature of the finer subtleties or the total experience of smoking a choice Havana.

That being the case, perhaps the most useful office we can perform here is to cleave to fact, to provide a broad base of general information, suggestions, and hints from which the enthusiastic beginner may commence his exploration of what the poet Spenser called the 'soverane weed'.

First, it may be useful to define terms – the meanings of three basic expressions commonly used (and even more commonly misused) in describing the experience of

The manager's office in the factory of Real Allones at the turn of the century. Notice the combined humidor and safe

smoking a fine cigar. The terms are 'flavour', 'body' and 'aroma'; and it is no coincidence that these categories of quality are associated also with an activity closely akin to the aesthetic of the Havana – connoisseurship in vintage wine.

Flavour has to do with taste – with the nature of the specific response of the taste-buds to the presence of smoke drawn into the mouth. Human taste-buds can distinguish four basic tastes: sweetness, bitterness, saltiness, and acidity. In smoking good Havanas, the main subjective element of comparison is the relative degree of natural sweetness that distinguishes one cigar from another. Objectively, of course, all four elements are present, and it is our capacity (varying considerably from one person to another) to perceive the balance between such elements that gives rise to such terms as 'fruity', 'nutty', and so on, which attempt to summarise what is a highly complex permutation of taste-bud responses.

Flavour is also characterized as 'mild', 'medium', or 'full', and it is essential to realise that these expressions refer *not* to the strength of the tobacco but to its resources of flavour – very fruity, say, or mildly sweet. But to describe the flavour of a great Havana as 'fruity' or 'mild' is as adequate as describing our Beethoven quartet as 'tuneful': true in its way, but hardly scratching at the surface of the experience.

Body, in contrast, is an index of the tobacco's strength, and therefore of the broad physiological effect it has on the smoker. A tobacco's body is entirely distinct from its flavour. A full-bodied cigar of indifferent quality, for instance, may lacerate your palate even though it may be classified (correctly) as 'mild'. One is tempted to suppose that cigars and pipe tobaccos puffed by vision-seeking Amerindians in pre-Columbian times must have been aggressively full-bodied.

Finally, *aroma*, which concerns the scent of tobacco: it can be applied both to the delicate odour that rises from a newly opened box of Havanas and to the subtle fragrance of the smoke rising from the lighted end of a cigar. Even the most earnest student of the Havana has difficulty in assessing the aroma of the cigar he is smoking, for its effect is inextricably mingled with the effects of the cigar's flavour and body.

The combined effects, indeed, of flavour, body, and aroma – their individual nuances and their profound compatibility with each other – are what make the Havana such a remarkable smoking experience: the flavour, however mild, never losing its subtle delicacy; the body, however full, never harsh to the palate; the aroma, however penetrating, never offensive to one's companions.

There is a truly daunting range of Havanas available, providing an embarrassment of choices for every possible taste and occasion; a range, indeed, that it is well beyond the compass of this book to explore in any detail. But the problem of discovering one's favourites by the wholly delightful expedient of practical research may be simplified a little by classifying cigars according to two primary attributes – colour, and size and shape.

Colour

Perhaps the cigar tyro's most persistent misapprehension is that colour is an index of the tobacco's body – nor surprisingly, since a rich, dark-brown leaf seems to suggest greater strength than a light-coloured one. It is perfectly true that many cigars of dark leaf *are* full-bodied; but, strictly speaking, colour is an indication of flavour, the darker tobaccos almost invariably being fuller-flavoured than the lighter ones. Flavour, like body and aroma, derives partly from the growing leaf – that is, from the basic characteristics of the individual parent plant, from the part of the plant from which the leaf was taken, and whether the leaf was picked at the moment of optimum development or earlier or later – and also from the duration and intensity of the fermentations, especially the long third one. The reason why one can be confident that deep-coloured leaf is full-flavoured is that long fermentations, which increase the intensity of flavour, invariably produce a dark leaf.

In the complex blend of flavours contributed by filler, binder, and wrapper, that of the wrapper tends to be dominant. The experienced smoker of Havanas, of course, knows exactly what he is getting through long familiarity with particular brands: the flavour of his present consignment of, say, Bolívar, Hoyo de Monterrey, Montecristo, Romeo y Julieta, or whatever, duplicates, down to the finest inflexions, that of his previous consignment and will in turn be as exactly matched by next year's. To someone trying Havanas for the first time, one of the earliest lessons in what should develop into a liberal education is that of learning how the range of colour tones of Havana wrappers can be used to infer the flavours of the cigars as a whole. Cigars are classified, according to the colour of the wrappers, into the following broad groups.

Lightest of all is the *double claro*, or *claro-claro*, which has an almost blond wrapper, although the filler is commonly of a somewhat darker colour. The lightness

*'Why, what on earth is the matter with you? Given up smoking,
shaved off your beard, leaving the Club,' the heavily hirsute,
cigar-smoking friend asks. 'Got married, that's all' is the reply*

of colour is achieved by harvesting the leaf before it is fully mature and then drying it
rapidly with the heat from a wood fire lit outside the barn, the hot air being passed
through flues; a rarer and more costly double claro wrapper, known as *capa candela*, was
once dried, as its name suggests, by the heat of candles. The double claro wrapper also
undergoes a comparatively short and mild series of fermentations lasting a total period
of less than nine months. As one would expect, the double claro has the mildest
flavour of all the standard-range Havanas; it is also light in body as a rule, so that the
total smoking experience is one of great, though subtle, reticence.

Somewhat darker is the *claro*, in which the very light brown of the wrapper leaf
has an unmistakable tinge of green. For this reason, such cigars are commonly called
'fresh' – a misleading term, of course, since the claro wrapper (like every other type of
leaf) undergoes curing and fermentation. Like the double claro wrapper, the claro
comes from naturally pale leaf that was picked before it had fully ripened. It undergoes
about 48 days of natural drying in the barn. Again like the double claro its light colour
and intrinsically mild flavour are retained by means of a sequence of relatively short
fermentations totalling not more than 12 months.

The claro represents the most significant growth area in the world-wide cigar
market – the trend in every type of tobacco being toward mildness. The Havana claro
is justly celebrated for the delicacy of its aroma, and is responsible in large measure for
the significant increase in the number of women who now enjoy smoking cigars.

The next two groups, *colorado claro*, with light-brown wrapper, and *colorado*, which has a brown wrapper with a characteristic reddish tinge, are both highly aromatic, though slightly less so than the two previously mentioned groups. However, they offer a progressive intensification of flavour, though even the colorado, the fuller-flavoured of the two, is still strictly speaking a mild cigar.

Next come *colorado maduro* and the *maduro*. The first has a mid-brown wrapper and is of medium flavour and body. The maduro (the word means 'mature') has a dark-brown wrapper, and its filler leaf is often even darker. Although relatively low on aroma, the maduro has a rich, full flavour and is usually medium to full-bodied. It is, in short, the classic leaf for most experienced cigar lovers looking for the richest and most satisfying experience in Havanas.

Darkest of all, the *oscuro* has a virtually black wrapper and filler, very full flavour, and is often exceptionally full-bodied. It is grown in the open field, not under shade. For most modern European tastes the oscuro's flavour and body are too intrusive, and its aroma too negligible, to permit of the highest smoking pleasure, though it has plenty of devoted followers in Central and South America.

While these colour categories offer a general guide to leaf types and flavours, it is important to stress that it is *only* a guide. Such is the diversity of Havana leaf that there

A delightful advertisement for British Marcella cigars

is a considerable range of colours and flavours within each category. Remember, too, that although the flavour increases, and the aroma diminishes, with progressively darker tobaccos, colour is by no means an infallible guide to body, or strength. This is also a convenient moment to expose, once and for all, a notorious fallacy: namely, that the darker the leaf the higher the concentration of nicotine. The two factors are quite unrelated, and in some cases the darker tobaccos contain less nicotine than light ones. In any event, Havana leaf has a significantly lower concentration of nicotine than cigarette tobaccos.

Among Havanas imported into the United Kingdom, the standard colour range available is from claro to maduro, although the latter is only available to special order. You will find that the colour type is indicated on the side or bottom of every cedar box according to the following code: ccc (claro), cc (colorado claro), c (colorado), cm (colorado maduro), m (maduro); the absence of a code letter on some brands generally means that they are claro.

Size and Shape

If our remarks above about colour give only a very general picture of Havana types, what can one usefully say about sizes and forms? We mentioned in the previous chapter that models exist of more than 950 forms of cigar known to have been made in the Havana *fábricas*. The selection of sizes and shapes given below is generally accepted and can at least claim to be typical. But each of the Havana brands has its own version (and sometimes several versions) of a particular type which may differ somewhat in length, thickness, or shape from cigars of the same type made by the other great brands.

The classic cigar shape is the *corona* (do not confuse the term with the brand name: La Corona cigars are no longer made in Havana). It has straight, parallel sides, with a rounded and closed head (mouth end) and square, open foot (lighted end). The average length of the corona is $5\frac{1}{2}$ inches. Its diameter will be measured on a ring-gauge graduated in 64ths of an inch; at 42 gauge it is therefore about $\frac{2}{3}$ inch in diameter. There is a large number of variants on this classic shape that include the word 'corona' in the type name. The thing to remember about these is that they are variants only on length: they are all of much the same thickness as the classic corona. The smallest is the *half corona*, which is about $3\frac{1}{2}$ inches long; next come the *très petit corona* (about $4\frac{1}{4}$ inches) and the *petit corona* or *corona chica* (about 5 inches). Among the larger variants are the *corona grande* ($5\frac{5}{8}$ inches long) and the huge *double corona* (7 inches).

A cigar form that has made giant strides in popularity during the last 20 years or so is the parallel-sided *panatela*. This elegant cigar is slightly thinner than the corona (about $\frac{1}{2}$ an inch in diameter or 33 gauge) and 6 to 7 inches long. Like the corona, the panatela is rounded at the head and square-cut at the foot; in some Havana brands, however, it is delicately tapered toward the head. Most Havana panatelas are milder flavoured and have less body than coronas. The *small panatela* is $4\frac{1}{2}$ to 5 inches long and only 26 gauge, and it, too, has proved a popular answer to the increasing demand for rather mild-flavoured, light-bodied cigars of moderate size.

WHAT'S IN A NAME?

THERE are some twenty great houses in the dynasty of the Havana cigar, from Bolívar to Upmann, and each has a story to tell. Here are two of the stories behind those famous names.

DAVIDOFF Zino Davidoff's father was a cigar-merchant in Kiev before the Russian Revolution, and his shop was a regular meeting-place for revolutionaries. When the Tsarist police discovered this the family was forced to flee Russia, and the business was eventually re-established in Geneva.

Connections with the revolutionaries were maintained, however: one of Zino Davidoff's prized souvenirs is an unpaid bill for cigars, made out to Vladimir Ulyanov – later to be known as 'Lenin'.

In his twenties, Davidoff travelled first to Brazil, to learn the fundamentals of the tobacco trade, and then to Cuba: as he put it himself 'I discovered Cuba's perfume and her sensual warmth as an immature adolescent discovers an ardent, knowledgeable woman'.

On his return to Switzerland he began to deal in the finest quality cigars, and over the years he built up such a reputation for his expertise that he had customers in many countries other than Switzerland.

All went well until 1959, when Fidel Castro rose to power in Cuba. One of Castro's first moves was to nationalize sugar and tobacco production, and to abolish all cigar brand names. As Davidoff tells it: 'Several months later, two emissaries of the Cuban revolutionary government arrived at my shop. In essence they asked: "M. Davidoff, what are we to do? No one is buying our cigars. The sales keep getting lower."'

Davidoff has since withdrawn his claim that it was on his advice that Cubatabaco, the newly-formed national agency, allowed each of the individual cigar factories to retain its own name and image. Nevertheless, some

debt of gratitude was paid when, in 1969, Cubatabaco offered to set up a factory to make cigars specially to Davidoff's requirements, and bearing his own name. Within only a few years these simply elegant cigars, with the Davidoff name on an unassuming white band, have gained a reputation equal to any.

ROMEO Y JULIETA The fame of the Romeo y Julieta brand owes much to the activities of 'Pepin' Rodríguez Fernández. Born in Spain in 1866, he was taken to Cuba at the age of nine by his uncle, Don Antonio Fernández des Roces, who was a partner with the Marques de Pinar del Río in the Cabañas cigar factory. After an education in Cuba and the USA, Pepin began work in the Cabañas factory, eventually becoming a partner and then manager when the American Tobacco Company bought it.

In 1903, Pepin set up on his own; he bought the small and almost unknown factory that had been established in 1875 by Inocencio Álvarez and Manin García, with the brand name of Romeo y Julieta.

It was now that Pepin gave full rein to his energy and instinct for publicity, and within two years he had turned the obscure brand into one of the greatest in the world, with a factory that employed over 1400 cigar-makers alone. His racehorse, named 'Julieta', ran at Longchamp; and he sponsored the American flyer McCurdy, in a flimsy biplane of canvas and bamboo, on a circuit of Cuba. But his most famous attempt at publicity was the offer to buy the Capulets' house in Verona, where Romeo and Juliet had plighted their troth, and open it as a cigar-store. Foiled in this plan, he was nevertheless given permission to erect a small tasteful stand to display his wares, on the condition that every visitor to the house should be given a free specimen cigar.

'Have you tried Corona half-a-corona cigars?'
asks the Old Member.
'That's the half I throw away' is the disdainful reply

Of the same thickness as the corona (42 gauge) is another classic form, the *Lonsdale*, which measures between 6¼ and 6½ inches in length. It has straight parallel sides and is cut at the foot, but is closed at its rounded head.

With the exception of certain specially made panatelas, all the cigar types mentioned above are parallel-sided. But although this shape is now firmly entrenched as the most widely accepted, it is by no means the only cigar form available. During much of the 19th century and the early decades of the 20th, one of the most popular forms was the cigar that was fatter in the middle than at the ends. The classic type of this form is the *perfecto*, which varies between 4½ and 5 inches in length and tapers noticeably toward both the head and (sometimes to a lesser degree) the foot; the head is closed. A larger variant of this shape are the *ideales*, which may be as long as 6½ inches. The fattest example of the type is the pot-bellied *torpedo*, which is closed at both ends; it is now out of fashion, but a popular alternative is the 'pyramid' peculiar to the Montecristo brand.

These then are the basic types and sizes of the most popular Havanas. You will find that the great brands have their own particular dimensions that depart slightly in one way or another from the measurements given here; to confuse you further, you must realise that many brands do not always mention the type name (corona, panatela, and so on) on the box but use their own trade-name equivalents. There are also many intermediate sizes and forms, in addition to special sizes made by certain brands: one thinks, for instance, of the *demi-tasse* (about 3¾ inches long); or of the exceptionally long cigars, the *gigantes*, which may exceed 10 inches in length. There are also some very bizarre forms – none more so than the *culebra*. The word means 'snake', and the form is made up of three rather thin cigars plaited together, rather in the manner of entwined serpents; in this type the head is closed, the foot cut. They are not meant, however, to be smoked more than one at a time!

Occasion and Choice

The Havana smoker, it must now be apparent, has both an enviable and, perhaps, bewildering selection of cigars from which to choose. The permutations of colour, size, and shape of all the great brands amount to a total of several thousand cigars, each with its own distinctive character. This multiplicity of choice is offered not merely for the sake of variety. For the great cigar-maker, adequate coverage of his market requires that he attend to two quite distinct problems affecting the pattern of consumption. The first is the basic overall problem of offering a sufficient variety, in terms of flavour, body, and aroma, to appeal to as large a fraction as possible of the connoisseurs' market. The second problem, which is subsumed by the first but is also a vital consideration in its own right, is to provide cigars for the very various occasions that are appropriate for smoking during the course of the day.

This last statement may sound pretentious, as if protocol and an obsessive concern for the usages of polite society were more important than enjoyment of a satisfying smoke. That is not our intention: laying down the law as to which kind of cigar is permissible at a particular moment or occasion would be as foolish as it was impertinent. Nevertheless, there are a number of questions the experienced Havana smoker ponders, even if unconsciously, before selecting a particular cigar for a specific occasion.

The first thing that needs to be said is that the Havana is not merely a large version of a cigarette, to which the habitual smoker constantly resorts in order to satisfy a narcotic craving. Leaving aside all the essentially irrelevant implications of luxury, prestige, and conspicuous expenditure that cigar smoking carries for some people, a Havana is an enjoyable aesthetic experience or it is nothing. Such an experience can be fully appreciated only at leisure – when one has enough time and is sufficiently free of distractions to be able to give one's cigar the attention it deserves.

The bundle of three cigars known as culebras *(snakes). In Germany these are called* Krumme Hunde *or 'entwined dogs'*

*Two early 19th-century servants provide an opportunity
for social observation: 'What do you smoke, Thomas, Awanna?'*

During the morning and afternoon, many experienced smokers (except those
with jaded palates) prefer relatively mild cigars – claro or colorado claro – of panatela
size or even smaller. At the conclusion to a lunch it is sensible to match the strength of
one's cigar to the size and richness of the meal. A light lunch, or a series of rather bland
courses, may often be fittingly concluded by a mild-flavoured, light-bodied cigar; on
the other hand, nothing less than a colorado maduro is likely to offer much pleasure if
one's taste-buds have been exercised by a curry or other highly aromatic dishes. For
many businessmen and women, time is of the essence. Among such people there are
many discriminating Havana smokers who can devote only a few minutes during the
day to their preferred medium- or full-flavoured cigar. For such people a miniature
corona maduro is the perfect answer, providing a brief but intensely satisfying smoke.

The greatest moment of the seasoned cigar-smoker's day is at the conclusion of
dinner, formal or otherwise. This, as ever, is the time when cares of the day, and even
the more enduring exigencies of fate, can be put aside for a little while. It is the
occasion for one's most ambitious sortie into the manifold enchantments of the

'soverane weed'. For the true aficionado of the Havana, this may involve nothing smaller than a corona and, for the profoundest pleasure, a maduro or at least a colorado maduro. Dogma has no place in a book concerned with matters of taste, but one cardinal rule really ought to be observed with regard to your after-dinner cigar: linger for a little while over your coffee, brandy, or whatever before lighting your first cigar; a rest of 10 or 15 minutes will allow your palate sufficient time to prepare itself for this most fitting conclusion to the meal. The same should also apply if one decides to have a second cigar: pleasure deferred, etc. . . . . Incidentally, if one plans to smoke more than one cigar on such occasions, it is sensible to arrange matters so that each succeeding cigar is more full-bodied or fuller flavoured than its predecessor.

One small but important matter of fact should be mentioned here. A thick cigar, no matter of what flavour and body, is usually capable of disclosing its character more comprehensively and satisfyingly than a thinner cigar containing identical leaf. That is why many experienced smokers prefer even a half corona to a much longer, but thinner, panatela of identical flavour and body.

None of the foregoing observations will be news to the old Havana hand. Most connoisseurs derive their greatest pleasure from large, full-flavoured cigars, which

Not only cartoonists found the cigar a subject for pictorial study. This is 'The First Cigar' by the French artist Daumier

they believe offer not only a richer but a more complex experience than milder leaf. But there are plenty of highly discriminating smokers who, having thoughtfully researched most of the basic permutations, settle permanently for colorado or colorado claro of modest size. It remains for the newcomer to prosecute his own pleasurable enquiries with an open mind and not to be swayed by more seasoned smokers whose tastes are not his own.

Lighting Up

Examining, lighting up, and smoking a cigar are all matters requiring merely a little common sense – or, rather, they would be if they had not been invested by cigar snobs with a number of specious rituals that are at once crass and hilarious.

The cigar holder comes into its own, between the lips of this phlegmatic waiter in a German beer garden

A German manufacturer caused a scandal in 1966 by issuing a series of cigar bands that brought together Adenauer, Napoleon and Adolf Hitler

Preliminary examination of a cigar, however cursory, will show whether the wrapper is smooth, even, and without prominent veins, and whether the filler is firm and evenly distributed within the binder (if it is not, the burning and drawing properties of the cigar will be impaired). Examining the wrapper of a choice Havana, with its fine-grained texture and delicate sheen, is always a pleasure. Mature Havanas that have been well looked after sometimes bear traces of a white bloom; this is due to conditions in transit but is harmless, and is best removed with a very soft-haired brush.

It is at this juncture that the cigar snob will raise the cigar not to his mouth or nose but to his ear – a practice dismissed with apt contempt by knowledgeable smokers as 'listening to the band'. It is as productive of useful knowledge as listening to a lump of sugar. The band referred to is the circlet of paper around the wrapper, bearing the name of the maker within an often marvellously ornate and colourful design. The question of whether or not to remove the band before lighting up, or during the course of smoking the cigar, is another source of essentially bootless controversy. The band was invented originally (according to one tradition) to protect the fingers or, in the case of ladies, the gloves against stains and also to secure poorly rolled wrappers. Neither problem is relevant to the modern Havana. Removing or retaining the band is

Accessories for the cigar smoker – cutters, which could be
disguised as a miniature bottle of Bass or a Derringer pistol;
and a wide variety of decorative boxes designed to hold the
matches known at the time as 'Vestas'

now purely a question of whether one prefers the appearance of a cigar with or without it: your Havana will be near the end of its pleasure-giving life before the fire reaches the band. If you happen to prefer a naked cigar, take care to ensure that the band is not adhering to the delicate wrapper leaf. Then carefully slide the band over the cigar head. Never attempt to cut the band or you will almost certainly damage the wrapper. It is easier to slide the band off after the cigar has been burning for some time.

Coronas, panatelas, and many other popular types of Havana have a closed head that must be cut before the foot is lighted. One can do this with the teeth, with a knife, or with one of various types of cigar cutter. Unless one is anxious to project a tough-guy image, biting is not recommended because it usually results in a rather jagged-edged opening that is either too large or too small – and, in cases of extreme incompetence, a mouthful of tobacco shreds. We mention this method only because there is a surprisingly large number of smokers capable of making a perfect cut every time in this way. If you use a knife, make sure that the blade is smooth-edged and very sharp. The soundest method is to bring the cigar head to the blade and rotate it in the same direction (it may be right *or* left, remember) as that in which the wrapper was wound onto the binder. Try to complete the circle in one continuous movement, so that the aperture margin is smooth. It is particularly important that the cut should not be made so far down the body of the cigar that the cap or caps are completely removed, since this will result in the wrapper unwinding. For this reason it is possible, and sometimes desirable, to remove the top cap by gentle prising with a fingernail, after which no further cutting is necessary.

The simplest and in many ways the best way to make the cut is with a cigar cutter. The cigar snob regards the use of such mechanical aids as a solecism that betokens inferior blood; the cigar snob is an ass. Three types of cutter are available: a flat cutter, which slices the end off the head (as when one uses a knife); a cutter that makes a V-shaped furrow across the head; and a specialized form of scissors.

The size of the aperture you make is very important. Too large a hole permits too great a rush of smoke into the mouth; if the hole is too small, the suction you will need to exert will soon tend to concentrate the tar and other oils at the aperture, effectively blanketing the flavour of the cigar and burning the tongue. It may seem a trifle pernickety to insist on such fine tolerances. But the aperture is an important factor in gaining maximum enjoyment from your cigar, and you will soon become accustomed to making the correct cut almost automatically. If you are using the special cutter for the first time, remember that the V-shaped furrow has a deceptively large surface area; do not cut too deep. On no account use a match or some handy spike to pierce a hole in the head: the diameter will be much too small, and the 'tunnel' made in the interior of the cigar will soon begin to act rather like a sump, collecting tar from the filler and channelling it straight onto your tongue.

Before lighting up his cigar, the snob will warm it by running a lighted match, or even a candle, along its length two or three times. He does not know *why* he does this – merely that he conceives it to be ritual sanctified by time. The custom arose during the late 19th century because the wrappers of certain Spanish and other cigars of the period were stuck to the binder with a bitter-tasting gum. It was found possible to

THE CIGAR HOLDER

IN the last century, the cigar holder, far from being despised as it commonly is today, was used by many smokers. To judge from the examples that have survived this may have been as much for competitive display in the smoking room as for any other reason. Encouraged by the taste of their employers' wealthy clients, craftsmen allowed their fantasy to run riot. Holders (originally called 'cigar tubes') were fashioned from horn, wood, ivory or tortoiseshell with mouthpieces of amber, and were enriched with silver mounts and carvings. Some of the most delicate work was done in the ever-fashionable smoker's material, meerschaum.

A porous, white, clayey form of the mineral magnesium silicate, meerschaum is about as heavy as water, though some variants are lighter. In earlier times, fragments washed up on the shoreline were thought to look like petrified sea foam: hence the name, from the German *Meer* (sea) and *Schaum* (foam). Before it is fully dried out, the soft stone is relatively easy to work into the ornate, sometimes fantastical, forms famous in meerschaum pipes and cigar holders. In the 19th century the main centres of production were Vienna and certain German towns which imported the stone from Turkish Anatolia.

In the most elaborate examples, the function of the piece may be almost masked by the sculptural adornment. A pair of fiery Arab stallions curvetting upon the barrel of the cigar 'tube', animal heads, human heads, forms of every kind, which make these masterly little figurines well worth the attention of the collector. They were certainly treasured by their original owners, being sold and kept in specially moulded and hinged cases of papier-mâché covered with leather and lined with velvet, with the name of the cigar merchant proudly embossed in gold leaf within.

The finished meerschaum holder was given a wax polish but retained something of its porous quality, which explains the rich yellows and browns of many old examples. The mouthpiece of the holder, following the convention, was almost invariably made from amber – another material first known to man from examples washed up on sea coasts. In prehistoric times the Amber Route from the Baltic was one of the great lines of communication between the northern and southern peoples of the Eurasian land mass.

The final touch to the finest examples of the meerschaum cigar holder was generally provided by a band of sterling silver binding

A finely-carved cigar holder with a mouthpiece of amber

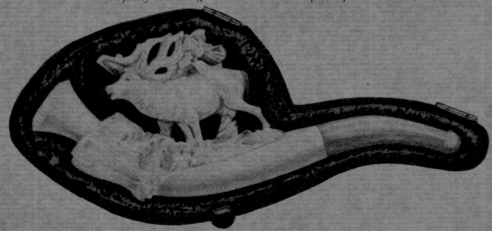

the join of the amber mouthpiece and the holder proper and engraved with some design or the initials of the owner, and the hallmarks.

It would seem that holders were generally used for the smaller sizes of cigars and, because variants of the tapering 'torpedo' shape were favoured in the last century, the collector will notice that the cup, hollowed at the end of the 'tube' to receive the cigar, is shaped accordingly. The result is that it is difficult to use one of these lovely objects today when the most common cigar shape is straight and cylindrical. The difficulty is that the 'square' end of the common modern cigar only engages the conical cup at one place and so is not securely gripped. From the collector's point of view this is perhaps as well since the holders are delicate pieces and break all too easily in use.

Each cigar holder, carved out of meerschaum and with a fitted mouthpiece, was sold in a handsome plush-lined hinged case

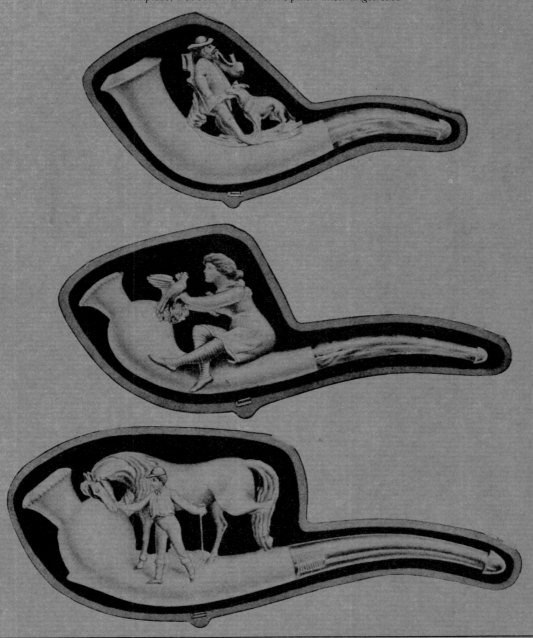

*The British importers of Upmann cigars have produced boxes
containing specially-large matches with cedarwood sticks*

alleviate the problem by heating gently any of the gum that was visible on the wrapper; this caused some of the bitter ingredients of the gum to evaporate. The gum ceased to be used at least 80 years ago; in any case, Havanas have never suffered from this failing. Do not warm your Havana: if you have stored it correctly it will be in perfect condition for smoking without baptism by candle.

It is important to use suitable materials for lighting your Havana. Avoid using a petrol lighter or sulphur or wax matches, all of which give off strong odours that will spoil the taste of your cigar, especially one of mild flavour. Gas lighters, wooden spills, and wood safety matches are all suitable. Whatever material you use, keep the flame about a quarter of an inch from the foot, and draw on the cigar while rotating it slowly. The rim of the foot should begin to glow first, then the fire will spread to the centre. To encourage development of a good live coal, draw on the cigar in quite gentle, short, even puffs. Once it is properly alight, the Havana most readily discloses its qualities if you are relaxed and, above all, refuse to be rushed: draw the smoke slowly into the mouth, and allow plenty of time between each puff to enjoy the matchless combination of flavour, body, and aroma. As the ash builds up, do not flick it off every minute or so, as one does with a cigarette, but allow it to fall into an ashtray when it is ready.

What to do if one allows one's cigar to go out? The cigar snob regards this as a gaffe of the highest order: no matter how little of the cigar has been consumed, he will evince disgust if you rekindle it. Ignore him: he is demonstrating an enslavement to bogus connoisseurship and a lamentable eagerness to waste good tobacco. The best way to relight your cigar is to take it out of your mouth and apply the flame first around the rim and then to the middle of the coal. As long as it is not carrying too much ash, the cigar will rekindle itself.

No discriminating cigar smoker inhales the smoke: the true joys of a Havana are to be discovered by allowing the taste-buds to respond to the extraordinary combination of sensations disclosed by the smoke when it is in the mouth. A good cigar offers one an extended interlude of surpassing pleasure: a Havana corona, for instance, when smoked at the best speed to appreciate its qualitites, will last as long as 50 minutes. By then about three-quarters of it will have been consumed and the live coal will be approaching the band. The remaining quarter will by now have lost most of its original flavour owing to the tars that have accumulated there as a result of your drawing on the cigar. You should now consign your cigar to the ashtray. There is no need to stub it out: the tar will soon extinguish the fire.

A couple of final points. Notwithstanding the extraordinary variety of people who take pleasure in the Havana, in a certain behavioural respect they can be divided neatly into two types: those who retain the cigar in the mouth for more or less the entire duration of the smoke; and those who hold it in the hand between puffs. There is little point in denouncing the first category as gluttons; the method happens to be some people's way, even if it is not yours. If you visit one of the Havana *fábricas* you will see plenty of *torcedores* with choice cigars clamped fixedly in the mouth as they fashion the masterpieces that you will later hold fastidiously in your hand; worse yet, they hold the cigars firmly between the teeth, not the lips. But do not fall into the error of supposing that they cannot appreciate to the full the nuances and inflexions of a great cigar. It must be said, however, that most experienced cigar smokers in Europe subscribe to the view that the most rewarding way to smoke a Havana is to take a puff about once every minute, then remove the cigar, retain the smoke in the mouth for

*A cigarstand in polished pewter, with a stylized figure
of a typical street urchin of the mid-19th century*

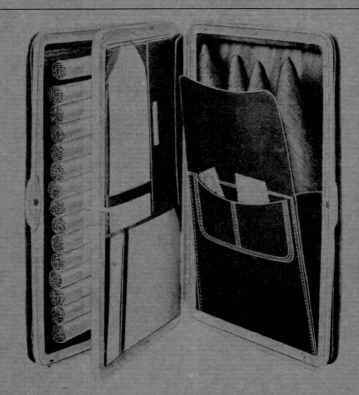

A handsome pocket case for cigarettes and cigars.
It is in leather, silk-lined, with a strong polished steel rim

about 10 or 15 seconds, expel it slowly, and allow the palate and tongue to rest for half a minute or so before the next puff. The argument is persuasive for at least one reason. If the cigar is stuck permanently in the mouth one's olfactory equipment is constantly stimulated by the smoke curling up from the live coal, and may eventually suffer a temporary loss of sensitivity in response.

Lastly, if you find that you cannot avoid wetting the head of your cigar, thereby loosening the wrapper, try using a cigar holder.

Laying in Stock

Anyone who has recently discovered the pleasures of the Havana and wishes to lay in some stock for the future, but is not quite certain which Havanas to buy, can at least be confident that, no matter what he chooses, he will be investing in the very pinnacle of the cigar-maker's craft. There are more than 20 great brand names from which he may make his selection: there are the long-established names – Bolívar, El Rey del Mundo, Hoyo de Monterrey and La Escepción (both from José Gener), Montecristo, Rafael Gonzalez, Gispert, Sancho Panza, Saint Luis Rey, Partagás, Por Larrañaga, Punch, Ramón Allones, La Gloria Cubana, Quintero, Romeo y Julieta, H. Upmann, José L. Piedra, Juan López – and two very recent brands, those of Davidoff and Dunhill. The former was named in 1969 after Zino Davidoff, the celebrated cigar merchant of Geneva; the latter is the latest to be introduced, and takes its name from the firm of Alfred Dunhill Ltd, whose London premises in Duke Street, St James's, are a temple to the faith of the dedicated cigar smoker.

Anyone wishing to lay in a stock, however small, should first become acquainted with the 'life' of a Havana. Many smokers of the ordinary, cheaper cigar naturally keep a box or two to offer to their friends and to satisfy their own immediate needs. If stored in a sensible way such cigars will keep in reasonable condition for several months. Laying in a stock of Havanas, however, is at once a more rewarding and a more taxing undertaking. The Havana is one of the very few cigars that continue to 'live', to mature, long after they have been packed in much the same way as a vintage claret continues to mature after it has been bottled.

Havanas undergo a fourth fermentation some five to eight months after their third one; and by this time, of course, those earmarked for the British market will have been in this country for several months. Some people like 'fresh' Havanas – those that have not yet begun the fourth fermentation – for immediate smoking; and many cigar merchants keep a proportion of their stock aside for this purpose. Most connoisseurs, however, prefer the mature leaf. In any event, once a Havana has begun its fourth fermentation it should not be smoked for another six months at least. This fermentation is known in the cigar trade as the 'sick period', and cigars in this condition are not normally put on sale.

How long should a choice Havana be allowed to age? This is rather like asking how long is a piece of string. All Havanas will offer you a richly satisfying smoke a

The elegant art nouveau interior of the Habana cigar shop in Berlin, 1898. The painted decoration represents cigar smoke

Boxes and Humidors

FROM an early point in the history of the Havana, makers began to offer their cigars packed in special boxes. For generations the preferred material has been the wood of the Cuban or 'cigar box' cedar, *Cedrela odorata*, strictly a member of the mahogany family but related to the true cedar and with a fragrance that recalls it. The wood is used for furniture and wall linings as well as cigar boxes and that fragrance is its secret, for it is held to repel insects that attack tobacco.

The earliest boxes made in Europe were generally of sycamore, and were embellished with transfer prints or pen and ink on paper drawings. Scottish merchants favoured tartan-ware boxes and these enjoyed a considerable vogue in Britain south of the border. But the cedar box came to replace its rivals and the simple prints and drawings gave way to colourful and elaborately designed labels. Traditionally printed in flamboyant hues and richly embossed with gilded patterns, they

are with us still. No doubt for collectors they can still yield their evocative and nostalgic moments – it has always been so. 'After lunch my father produced boxes of sparkling cigars – Valle, Clay, Upmann – which evoked for me visions of dancing girls.' Such was the memory of one middle-aged Frenchman earlier this century, as he looked back on life in Paris during the *belle époque*, known to the English-speaking world as the Naughty Nineties.

The makers' boxes themselves were handsome enough for some hosts to use when offering cigars to their friends, but in the smoking rooms of the grand houses more elaborate containers were employed. One such was a large, drum-shaped box. Closed, the top of the cylinder presented a handsome knob-like handle. When this was pulled up an interior of tin lining, designed to preserve a hermetic and nicely moist atmosphere within, could be glimpsed. More noticeable, however, were the six or more cigars which

English-made cigar cabinets of polished oak, from the 1901 'Illustrated Guide for Smokers' produced by Salmon & Gluckstein

A wooden drum packed with cigars and sealed with the Cuban guarantee

rose, splayed out around a central spindle and supported on metal tobacco leaves, to present a handsome flower of the best from Havana.

This forerunner of the modern humidor could still be used if the collector's instinct allowed. The cigar, like a good wine, is a living thing and needs attention. The simplest, and very effective device, is today provided by placing an open ended glass tube holding a moistened sponge in the place of one of the cigars in a box. Specially manufactured moisture pads are also made to lay in the bottom or top of the box. More elaborate

models, in Spain often made in the form of a pirate's chest, can hold up to 100 or even 500 cigars.

But the smoker needs also to carry his needs and the cigar case designed for the pocket has a long ancestry. Today, a simple rigid leather container is generally preferred. In the 19th century the case was of various materials, papier mâché being much favoured. Whatever the body of the case, it was often handsomely ornamented with marquetry work or with japanned lacquer or mother-of-pearl inlay.

*A trade advertisement, one of
many that appeared in the 1910 Tobacco Year Book*

month or so after completing the fourth fermentation – that is, more than a year, and in some cases more than 18 months, after they were boxed. But some, especially the darker, full-flavoured maduro, may not reach their peak for several more years. This applies especially to leaf from one of the great years: the Vuelta Abajo, like the great wine-growing regions of France, has its 'vintages'; and the dark leaf from one of these years – the leaf that later underwent the longest and most intense third fermentation – goes into cigars that will continue to improve for about 10 years and will remain in superb condition for another five.

The fourth fermentation is by no means the last. Each year, for a further four or five years, Havanas that have been properly stored undergo fermentation in mid- or late summer. To all except the initiated these fermentations are almost undetectable, and they become milder with each year that passes; in the early years, however, the process often results in tiny droplets of oil being exuded by the leaf and becoming deposited at one or both ends of the wrapper. These droplets, which dry to a light-coloured powdery consistency, may form a bloom on the cigar.

The complexities and decisions involved in ageing and maturation serve to emphasise the enormous importance of buying your stock from a knowledgeable cigar merchant. Only he can tell you which of your current order will be ready to smoke in a few months, which ought to be set aside for a couple of years, and so on. Such information is vital not only for enabling you to bring your Havanas to a state of perfection but also in allowing you to plan your operations in such a way that some fully mature cigars are always available. In short, laying in a stock of Havanas involves the same kind of logistic problems as planning a good and varied wine cellar.

Now all this careful planning and selection goes for nought unless you are able to provide your stock with the kind of environment in which these final years of in-box maturation can take place. Cigars have, in fact, been stored in a variety of unlikely places, none more improbable than that used in the early 19th century by the Rev. Charles Colton, a vicar of Kew, who discovered ideal storage conditions beneath the pulpit of his parish church. Wherever you choose to keep your cigars, the two key environmental factors are consistency of temperature and relative humidity. The temperature of the air in a house or flat often varies considerably from room to room – sometimes, indeed, from one part of a room to another part. Moreover, there is usually a considerable difference in temperature as between day and night. Relative humidity may also fluctuate considerably; and most central-heating systems tend to dry the air. Wide variations in temperature or humidity are inimical to the health of the maturing Havana.

The best answer is to set aside shelving space in a small room, or even a cupboard, devoted exclusively to this purpose. It should be maintained at a temperature of 60-65°F (16-18°C) and at a relative humidity of 55-60 per cent by night and day. Ideally, the shelves should consist of well-spaced slats, allowing the air to circulate around each box. If you are unable to provide these conditions in your home, the next best thing is to ask your cigar merchant to store them for you in one of his conditioning rooms. All the larger merchants of any repute have such rooms; indeed, any merchant without them has no business to be dealing in Havanas.

Cigars that are ready for smoking should be kept in a humidor. This is a box that provides suitable atmospheric conditions for your Havanas, though it tends to retard the maturation process. Humidors come in a vast range of styles, from plain to outrageously rococo, and in capacities ranging from 50 to 500 cigars and more; the larger models are fitted with shelves for storing each of the standard cigar sizes. The humidor's most important job, as its name suggests, is to ensure that the cigars do not become too dry. It will contain one or more humidifiers – a grille, usually made of aluminium, and containing some absorbent material. To make the humidifier work one merely has to soak this material in water, shake it thoroughly and dry it lightly with a towel. The slow evaporation of the moisture through the grille maintains humidity at the correct level within the box; under normal conditions a humidifier needs to be dampened about once a month.

The ideal conditions of a humidor are 55 per cent relative humidity, and a temperature of 65°F (18°C). If kept in such conditions, cigars will last seven to eight years before slowly drying out and becoming 'woody' to the taste, but the ordinary smoker cannot normally provide such ideal conditions in his home. However, the cedarwood box in which the cigars were packed makes an acceptable container, and in the temperate zones the average natural humidity is reasonably satisfactory; cigars can be stored with confidence in a drawer or cupboard, provided that they are well away from heat or cold, or from any source of strong smells. If they should become dry, they can frequently be restored by being kept (in their original closed box) in a cellar or similar dampish situation for a few days.

Although necessarily brief, this excursion into matters of taste, selection, and storing will have given the inexperienced Havana smoker an idea of the amount of time, thought, and discriminatory zeal the true connoisseur brings to his enjoyment of

*Cigar-smoking on the streets of Havana is as common as gum-
chewing on the streets of New York. The workers can only afford
the cheaper quality, but this lady's pleasure is undoubted*

the great hand-rolled cigar. The uninitiated will object that there are better things to do with one's time than acquire a taste for an expensive luxury. Such an argument is at once unanswerable and beside the point. It is true that the price of the great Havanas puts them beyond the reach of most smokers except on special occasions. There are, however, always some people who refuse to compromise in matters of taste, no matter what the price. Among cigar smokers such single-minded pursuit of excellence leads inexorably to the Havana, the nonpareil – which proves that sometimes it is even better to arrive than to travel hopefully.

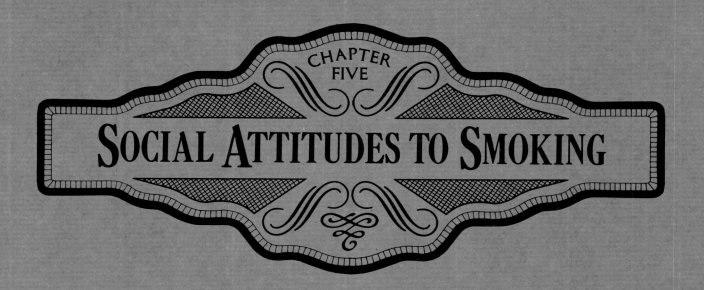

Chapter Five

Social Attitudes to Smoking

T HROUGHOUT its known history tobacco has engaged the emotions and ethical sensibilities of all who have, willingly or not, fallen under its spell. For some it has been a medium of revelation, opening the way to communion with the gods; for others it has seemed, no less magically, to offer a panacea for all bodily ills. For modern man tobacco – and pre-eminently the great cigar – has become associated primarily with the pleasures and consolations of the senses, to moralists an area equally productive of controversy as tobacco's older roles. In this final chapter we shall have a look at some of the attitudes and prejudices that have attended, and helped to shape, this evolution in man's use of the 'soverane weed'.

We have touched upon the enormous religious significance of tobacco among almost all the Amerindian peoples who came into contact with it. Perhaps nowhere was this significance, both spiritual and ceremonial, more dramatically elaborated than among the Aztecs of Mexico. According to contemporary accounts, one of their most ancient and hallowed traditions was the selection every year of a youth as an incarnation of one of their gods. For 12 months the youth lived a life of unexampled spendour, of ceremony, luxury, and sensuality – and at the end of his year he was ritually slaughtered in the temple of the sun. The tradition has unmistakable correspondences with myth-encrusted practices in ancient Greece and elsewhere, and has to do, at least in part, with the cycles of birth, maturity, death, and rebirth in the timeless calendar of the soil. Among the Aztecs the ceremonial sacrifice was unique in one respect: the youth's final act before immolation was to smoke a sacred, jewelled pipe of tobacco to honour the gods and to enjoin fertility on both soil and man.

Such practices, and indeed the entire connection of tobacco with 'primitive' religion, were shocking to the white explorers and colonizers, in whom missionary zeal contended with rapacity. They were impressed, however, by the Amerindian association of tobacco with the healing arts. And it was this aspect that engaged the attention

Are these two small figures from a Mayan codex fighting over
possession of a cigar, or enjoying the friendliest of smokes?

of Jean Nicot, who was primarily responsible for the early spread of interest in the
plant among men of learning in France, Germany, and Switzerland. His name, of
course, is forever linked with tobacco in the botanical name *Nicotiana*, which was
coined in France in 1570. Nicot never envisaged smoking as a use for the herb; a
French dictionary he compiled does not include this sense of the verb 'to smoke'.

It was Nicot's sensational, and often bizarre, claims for the curative properties of
the leaf that aroused the interest of apothecaries: open wounds, running sores, even
tumours were among a variety of serious complaints that a poultice of tobacco leaves
was claimed to heal. Nicot's advocacy was taken up and embellished by herbalists all
over Europe, and plots devoted to the cultivation of the plant became a familiar sight
in the gardens of the nobility, from Hungary to Spain, from Italy to Holland.

Smoking as a socially acceptable custom was pioneered in England – Raleigh,
with an eye to business, presenting his friends at Court with pipes and samples of
Nicotiana rustica. But in England, too, the curative properties of tobacco were
earnestly promoted by apothecaries and others after Sir Francis Drake reported that
the regular practice of chewing tobacco had kept his sailors free from scurvy and gastric
complaints. Sir William Vaughan, one of Queen Elizabeth's Court physicians, led the
way with his *Natural and Artificial Directions for Health* (1602). Some idea of the
scientific rigour of this work may be deduced from his recommendation that tobacco
should be smoked on cold, wet mornings of those months spelt with an 'r' – as
compensation, perhaps, for abjuring the pleasures of oysters. A certain Dr Butler, not
to be outdone in these realms of lunatic arcana, prescribed the smoking of 25 pipes of
tobacco for 'a violent defluxion of the teeth'. Francis Bacon was more cautious; he
discussed both the social and medical uses of tobacco in several of his works, and his
attitude was somewhat ambiguous. But he sternly warns pregnant women against
smoking, for 'it endaungereth the child to become lunatick'.

JAMES I ON SMOKING

*Frontispiece and title-page from a 17th-century pamphlet
which offered a variety of polemic against the smoking of tobacco*

TOBACCO, known in England by the 1560s, became a fashionable craze after Drake captured 'a great store of tobacco' from the Spaniards in 1586. The 'in' set of young gallants carried the habit to bizarre excesses. Supplied with equipment of gold and silver, they sought out 'professors of the art of whiffing', and smoked in public with foppish ostentation. In 1603 the priggish James VI of Scotland ascended to the English throne and made it his business 'as the proper physician of his politic body . . . to purge it of all diseases and evil-grounded abuses'. So runs the preamble to his *Counterblaste to Tobacco*, possibly the most famous anti-smoking tract ever penned.

He hated the habit the more because it had been made fashionable at court by Sir Walter Raleigh, whom he detested. Smoking, fumed James, 'was neither brought in by king, great emperor, nor learned doctor of physic . . . but sprang from a base and barbarous origin,

being begun by the Indians as a stinking and unsavoury suffumigation . . .' Why, demanded the king of his countrymen, did they imitate the beastly manners of these godless and slavish Indians? Was it merely for childish love of novelty?

Yet despite the royal thunderings some courtiers continued to smoke. Even worse, the colony of Virginia became increasingly devoted to the profits from its tobacco, imported into England duty free up to the year 1619. James tried to persuade the planters to find another profitable crop but when this failed aimed to extract the highest possible revenue by swingeing duties. Nothing, it seemed, could check the English devotion to tobacco. The royal campaign may even have added 'an element of pleasurable naughtiness' to smoking and so increased its allure. With James's death smoking lost its best advertiser – certainly the cult of excessive smoking began to decline after he was gone.

The earliest known illustration of a tobacco shop. The wooden
figure of a cigar-smoking Indian became a traditional shop sign

James I's violent antipathy to tobacco had the predictable effect of causing the
experts – or at least those with aspirations to courtly favours – to revise their opinions.
No *volte face* was more sudden or comprehensive than Vaughan's: in the fourth edition
of his *Directions* (1613) smoking was roundly condemned. James's personal physicians
were ardent interpreters of royal disgust with the weed, asserting among other things
that the use of tobacco must inevitably dry up the brain and cause the nails to fall from
one's fingers. Many writers took up the cudgels, and a host of satires and jeremiads at
the expense of tobacco poured from the presses. The title of a Dr Bushell's excursion
into literature – *Work for the Chimney Sweepers; or, A Warning to Tobacconists* – hints
at the tone and level of these effusions.

The violence of the controversy serves, if nothing else, to indicate the extent and
depth to which the smoking habit had taken hold in England by the early years of the
17th century. Every man of fashion, young as well as old, seemed to be under the spell
of what a contemporary poet called 'our holy herb nicotian'. When King James

Two pages and an illustration from Salmon & Gluckstein's 1901 'Illustrated Guide for Smokers'. The cigar case (top) is of 'finest calf leather, silk lined, with massive gilt chased frame and embroidered silk flap; with photoframe on right and secret recess for photo on the left'. The prices quoted for cigars (above) – even if these are British-made from a blend of Havana and Sumatra leaf – will bring a twinge of envy to every present-day cigar smoker

*Top: a painted cigar case representing the re-burial of Napoleon II in
1840. Upper left: an embroidered panel on a copper stand, with a watch
hook. Upper right: stand made from a reindeer horn. Above left: a
Staffordshire pottery stand with a head to hold matches. Above right: two
mid-19th-century wooden cigar containers, and a cigar holder made of the
silver-mounted legbone of a hare. Opposite: a cigar stand of Bavarian
porcelain, with a wooden cigar holder*

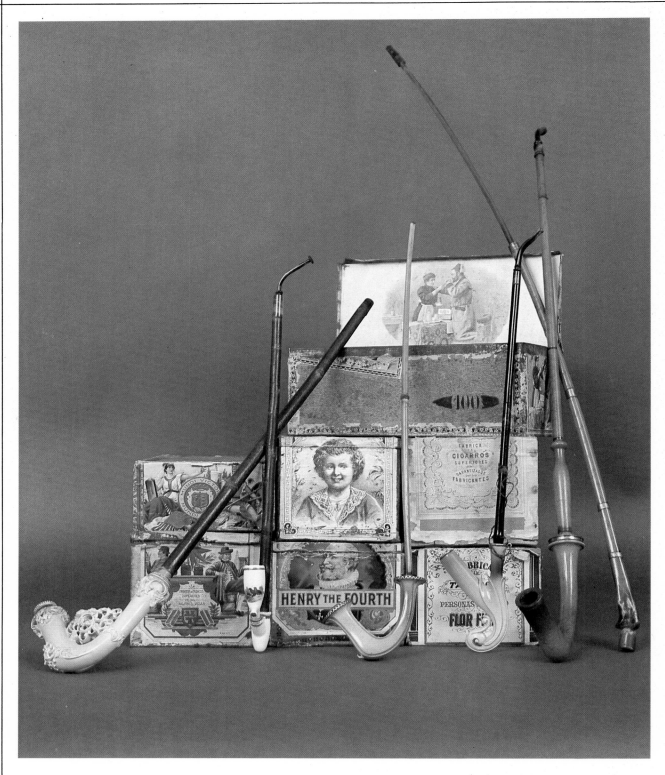

A collection of 19th-century cigar boxes and – a rather unusual sight – a number of long-stemmed cigar holders. Although these have the proportions of traditional meerschaum pipes, the size and shape of the holders shows that they are intended only for cigars

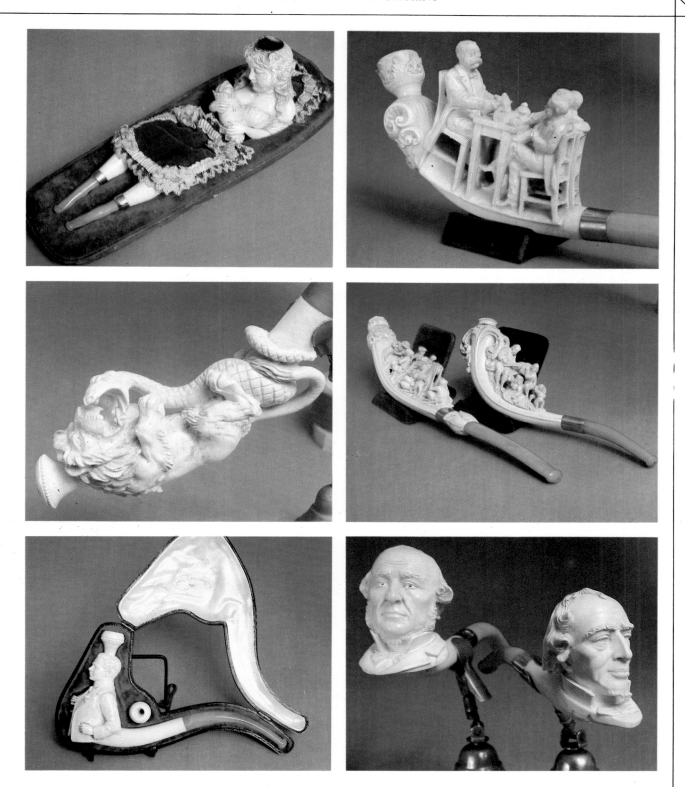

The intricacy and craftsmanship of these cigar holders jutifies their status
as collectors' pieces. From the coy girlish figure with its twin mouthpieces
modestly revealed beneath a tiny velvet coverlet, to the beautifully detailed
heads of Gladstone and Disraeli, every one is a masterpiece

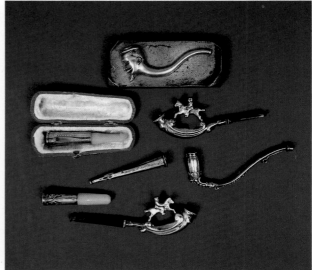

*Top left: a silver utensil described as a 'cigar snuffer', and a holder in
common pipeclay. Top right: four cigar holders in silver, together with a
rather battered silver case for a fifth, and two with amber mouthpieces.
Above: a baroquely erotic pair grace this meerschaum holder. Opposite:
two heads in meerschaum, with interchangeable mouthpieces*

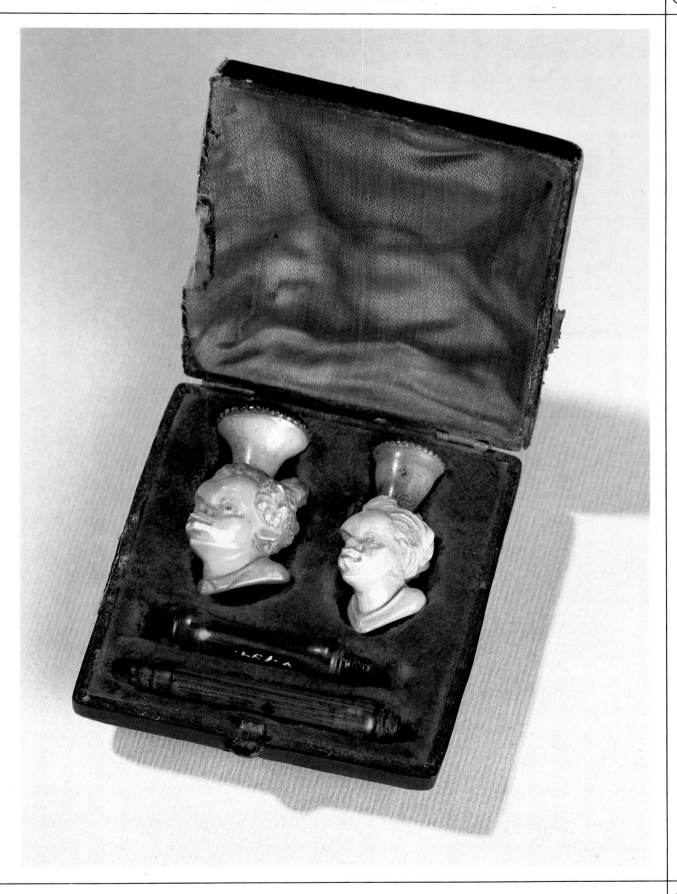

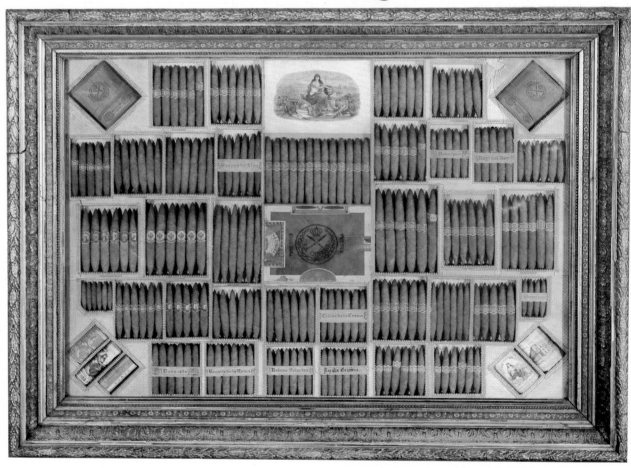

*Above: the cigar humidor of Alfred Dunhill's tobacco shop in St James's,
London. A wide selection of different brands is ranged in cabinets round
the walls, and the temperature and humidity are closely controlled through
vents in the ceiling. Dunhill have now introduced their own brand of cigar,
in a range of sizes. Opposite, above: a cigar chest in tortoise-shell, to hold
36 cigars. Opposite, below: a remarkable relic. Some 500 La Corona
cigars, in all their different sizes from demi-tasse to double-corona*

Graphic artists of all kinds have found the cigar a potent symbol. Above
left: a World War I poster from a Paris omnibus. Smokers are requested to
go to the rear of the vehicle and it is suggested that they should 'economise
on tobacco so that the soldiers should not go short'. The mid-19th-century
caricature (above right) portrays a typical Dutch dandy of the times, posed
before a billiard table with his cigar and Malacca cane. Opposite: a portrait
of the composer Jacques Offenbach, by the French artist Gustave Doré.
Overleaf: descriptions of the women cigar-makers of Seville evoked
lubricious images in the minds of many French writers, and inspired
Prosper Mérimée to conceive the heroine of his novel Carmen, the source
of the libretto for Bizet's opera. It is from this time that we derive the
misconception of cigars being rolled upon naked female thighs, but the
reality was closer to this portrayal of the Seville cigarette and cigar factory
by C. Meunier

*The 'contraband cigar' is smoked by an arriviste at Longchamp; the
'beginner's straw' (top left) by a young cadet; 'M. le Baron's pure
Havana' by his servant (top right); the 'planter's cigar' by a Cuban
peasant (above left); and the 'dude' by a young dandy (above right)*

*Some of the shapes and sizes of the Havana cigar. Top, left to right:
torpedo-shaped Montecristo No 2 (sometimes called a 'belicoso');
petit Lonsdale; 'Epicure' of Rey del Mundo; Romeo y Julieta 'Aguila';
corona; 'Romeo'. Above, downwards: demi-tasse; corona;
Montecristo No 5*

announced his intention of visiting Cambridge University in 1615, the Vice-Chancellor issued a hasty decree (rescinded immediately upon the king's departure from the town):

> Noe graduate, scholler, or student of this Universitie shall presume to take Tobacco in St Marie's Church uppon paine of final Expellinge the universitie.

The idea of using tobacco in church may seem curious or shocking to us today, but it was evidently less so in those times. The practice was not, of course, approved by all: Queen Elizabeth I had felt obliged to order beadles to search worshippers entering church and to confiscate any snuff boxes they found. In Italy, Spain, and Austria it became so common for priests to take snuff, and even to smoke, while celebrating Mass that in 1624 Pope Urban VIII issued a bull threatening excommunication to all who took tobacco into church. (Almost exactly 100 years later Pope Benedict XIII revoked the bull – one reason, according to cynics, being the well-attested fact that he was himself an ardent smoker.)

Excommunication was, of course, an appalling disgrace; but it could not have been as bad as some of the punishments meted out to tobacco devotees in eastern Europe and the Middle East, where the use of the leaf in any form was rigorously suppressed in the early 17th century. In Russia Tsar Michael, the first of the Romanovs, devised what he conceived to be a suitable scale of punishments. For his first offence a smoker was flogged, and for his second he was executed; a persistent snuff-taker had his nose amputated. In Turkey the penalty was also death, in spite of the fact that native poets had praised tobacco as 'one of the four cushions of the divan of delight'. In Persia the punishment sometimes took a rather colourful form, one merchant being burnt alive in his latest consignment of tobacco.

In the West, however, the habit of smoking, as a pleasure and as a solace, spread rapidly, especially throughout the contending armies during the Thirty Years' War (1618-48). Yet clearly the idea of smoking remained a controversial and emotive topic, for large numbers of books and pamphlets debating the morality of using tobacco and the medicinal properties of the leaf continued to be published in France, Holland, Germany, and Switzerland. None proved more popular than Johannes Neander's *Tobacologia* (1622), probably because none advanced so recklessly as this farrago of fantasy, old-wives'-tale, and historical distortion the virtues of tobacco as a panacea for every conceivable physical and mental complaint. That not everybody had been conned by Neander's feverish advocacy was demonstrated by a wise physician to whom the author sent a copy of the book. In one passage Neander had asserted that tobacco infallibly inoculated the smoker against syphilis. The physician dryly observed that more certain prophylaxis lay in staying out of brothels.

Nonetheless, the general proposition that tobacco possessed curative properties continued to be firmly held, sometimes as a matter of scientific conviction and sometimes as a matter of fervent hope. During the great plague of London in 1665 many physicians on their vain errands of mercy puffed furiously at their pipes not merely to keep the fearful stench of death from their nostrils but also in the belief that the fumes would guard them against infection. At this time, too, schoolchildren were required to smoke a pipe each morning to purge the classroom of any bubonic taint; and in churches, as many parish records testify, tobacco was mixed with incense to produce a sacerdotal fumigant.

Samuel Pepys, whose diary provides our most vivid record of life in London at this period, records that on 7 June 1665 he was walking down Drury Lane when he came upon several houses painted with the dreaded red crosses that betokened the presence of plague victims within. Feeling suddenly overwhelmed by nausea, Pepys bought some tobacco and, after lighting up, soon felt restored in mind and body. Pepys was one of the first writers to advocate the practice of chewing tobacco as a dentifrice. It is quite possible that he learnt the chewing habit from the unappealing General George Monck (a key figure in the restoration of the exiled Charles II), who, in common with many of the soldiers under his command, was addicted to the plug. Chewing was always more widespread in North America than in Europe; during the colonial period it was especially popular in the Connecticut valley, where the plug was known as 'fudgeon'. Although most people nowadays would agree with Amerigo Vespucci, who first reported what he described as 'this brutish habit' among islanders off the Venezuelan coast in 1499, chewing purely for pleasure has always had its advocates. Robert Southey was inspired to write an 'Elegy, on a Quid of Tobacco'.

Johannes Neander, the author of Tobacologia *(1622)*

The Tobacco Club instituted by Frederick William I of Prussia,
which held meetings in marquees erected in the palace gardens

Respectability and Fashion

Ever since its earliest days as a popular habit, smoking has posed a potential fire hazard in towns and cities, and from the mid-17th century onwards this danger began to exercise the minds of rulers all over Europe – especially those already disposed against tobacco on moral, medical, or aesthetic grounds. Infringements on the freedom of people to smoke when and where they liked were most rigorously enforced in the princedoms of Germany and in Switzerland. In 1652, for instance, the Electress of Bavaria decreed that 'tobacco-drinking' was to be strictly forbidden to 'the peasants and other common people'. As this and similar directives issued in most of the other electorates seemed to have little effect on the peoples' smoking habits, the lawgivers began to concentrate on prohibiting smoking in the streets and public buildings, and to ban the sale of tobacco except by apothecaries for medicinal purposes. Even these enactments were widely disregarded – as often by the constabulary as by anyone else – but they remained a source of annoyance, and often of violent anger, among smokers and those concerned with civil liberties, for many years; indeed, laws banning public smoking in Prussia were not repealed until 1848.

Surprisingly, in view of the attitudes of officialdom throughout the German-speaking lands, one of history's most fanatically enthusiastic smokers was Frederick

Women as Cigar Smokers

There's peace in a Larrañaga, there's
calm in a Henry Clay,
And a woman is only a woman, but a
good cigar is a smoke.

Kipling

ARCHBISHOP Las Casas, the cleric appointed by the Pope to preside over the spiritual well being of the conquistadors, recorded in the first edition of his *Memoirs* how two of the early adventurers returned from the interior of Peru with astonishing reports of men and women smoking flaming torches in their mouths. But later editions dropped the reference to these women smokers: what had at first seemed a freakish barbarian custom was by this time established in European society and the conventions already required that polite women should not partake of the weed – at least in public.

In Northern Europe, where the pipe was standard, women, generally of the lower classes, seem to have smoked quite freely, if paintings and engravings are to be credited. Learned authorities claimed medical properties for tobacco, a Dutch writer of the early 1600s recommending its juice for women in pregnancy. Society women generally abstained, at least in public.

In one respect, of course, women have a legendary association with the cigar. Cigars were being manufactured in Seville from the 17th century and women workers seem to have been employed from an early time. Various writers have left dramatic accounts of them. Maurice Barrès published a book about the cigar women called *Of Blood, Voluptuousness and Death* and Pierre Louÿs wrote the following description of the factory girls at work. 'The prudes wear a blouse, but most of the girls work with breasts exposed, clad only in a simple cloth skirt tucked up around their thighs. Some of the bodies, it is true, were unattractive but all were interesting and many were most beautiful, with full bosom and clear, shining skin.'

According to another French visitor, some of them smoked at their work, 'the cigar carried resolutely in the mouth with all the aplomb of a cavalry officer'. One would like to credit the startling image summoned up by these gallant Frenchmen; one of their more prosaic compatriots, however, described a Seville cigar factory as 'a horrible place, the faces of the women workers pale, drawn and poisoned by vitiated air, while besides many of the tables swaddled infants lie sleeping in their cots.' Henry Swinburne, an Englishman, reported seeing more than 500 women working in a single room.

Whatever the smoking habits of the Spanish women who produced Europe's finest cigars in the days before Cuban supremacy, the more adventurous of their society sisters began to experiment with the habit with increasing enthusiasm during the 19th century, as the fashion for the cigar moved rapidly northwards.

Lady smokers usually indulged themselves behind closed doors – in the women's Turkish baths frequented by the faster set, or in the privacy of their boudoir. One mid-century illustration shows an elegant German woman lighting a cigar from a candle while her maid peers out between the drawn curtains at the street below, as if to ensure that no unexpected visitors are on their way. A French picture of the 1840s depicts another lady with a sophisticated 'torpedo' between thumb and forefinger while her male companion pulls on a highly artistic pipe.

George Sand, the most famous woman of

*Above left: 'The Skater's Valentine – warranted first class –
an expensive article'. Above right: a more discreet pair of
lady cigar smokers, relaxing in the boudoir*

her day, writer of genius and mistress of many, the composer Chopin among others, opined that: 'The cigar numbs sorrow and fills the solitary hours with a million gracious images.' No doubt she also relished it as a way of irritating the conventions of bourgeois society. One evening at an intimate party in the residence of the Russian ambassador, held by the ambassador's wife to honour Chopin, Madame Sand lit up after dinner, to the astonishment of a young Russian nobleman who was an ardent admirer of the composer. Noting his consternation she observed composedly: 'I suppose, Sir, that a lady would not be permitted such liberties in a salon at St Petersburg.' 'Madame,' he replied, 'I know of no other salon in Europe where I recollect having seen a lady smoking a cigar.'

Perhaps the young man's knowledge of western ways was a little limited. In Holland, if we are to believe the cartoonists, some bold spirits enjoyed flouting the conventions by walking the streets in the long full trousers and short skirts popularized for liberated women by the American publicist Amelia Bloomer, their cigars alight at a jaunty angle in their mouths. Towards the end of the century English and American fashion prints show women skating in the elegant costumes of the day in sparkling winter landscapes, a cigar delicately held in their gloved fingers, while their admiring beaux push along eagerly in their wake. For such pioneers of women's liberation, the cigar was something of a talisman. No doubt they would have paraphrased Kipling's famous jibe as: 'A woman is indeed a woman and knows a good smoke when she has one.'

William I of Prussia. In 1713 he instituted what came to be called the Tobacco Club, which would hold meetings at Berlin, Potsdam, and elsewhere either within the royal palaces or in vast marquees erected in the palace gardens. At first these gatherings were small, formal affairs, but within a year or two they had been enlarged to include not only Court officials and senior army officers but ambassadors, foreign travellers, men of learning, and anyone else who happened to catch the king's eye. Meals would be taken, and vast quantities of wine and beer would be consumed; but the main purpose of the club meetings was smoking and conversation, the latter very often about burning issues of state. On many occasions when both the tobacco and the talk were good, the king would stay up all night, smoking continuously. The Scottish historian Carlyle, who was greatly influenced by all things German, was much taken by the idea of the club, observing: 'The substitution of tobacco-smoke for Parliamentary eloquence is by some held to be a great improvement.' Carlyle must, however submit to the charge of bias: tobacco, he averred, was 'one of the divinest benefits that has ever come to the human race'.

Outside the German-speaking world royalty had long discarded the idea of attempting the hopeless task of trying to deprive people of the pleasures of smoking. And, following James I's example, they soon realised that courtly coffers could be swelled by taxing the weed. In France, indeed, tobacco manufacture was made a monopoly of the king. Louis XIV must have had mixed feelings about this, for he detested tobacco in any form. Yet snuffing and smoking were enthusiastically practised at Court by the very flower of French society, not least by the royal princesses. In *Don Juan* (1665) Molière, the great contemporary observer of fashion, foible, and prejudice, has one of his characters assert:

> Whatever Aristotle and the great philosophers say, there is nothing like tobacco; it is the passion of all proper people, and he who lives without it lives for nothing. Not only does it refresh and cleanse the brain, it guides the soul in the paths of virtue, and teaches one to be a man of honour.

During the 18th century the controversy regarding the virtues of snuffing as opposed to smoking reached its zenith. For some it was an issue purely of fashion, of acceptable form. For others it was more a question of hygiene. Samuel Johnson, welcoming the ostracism of the pipe among men of mode, remarked testily: 'Smoking has gone out. To be sure, it is a shocking thing, blowing smoke out of our mouths into other people's mouths, eyes, and noses, and having the same thing done to us.' Yet if we grant some weight to his prejudice, we should also ponder Johann Cohausen's unappealing portrait of the snuffers' absurdly exaggerated affectations in his *Lust of the Longing Nose* (1720):

> Do but notice what grimaces snuff-takers make, how their whole features are convulsed, how they dip into their snuff-boxes in measured rhythm, cock up their noses, compose their mouths, eyes, and all their features to a pompous dignity . . .

Havanas Rule

The introduction of the cigar to northern Europe, and in particular the discovery in both Europe and North America of the delights of the Havana, effectively put a stop to the sterile debates about the best way to use tobacco. Those for whom to be fashionable was all-important could smoke whatever the arbiters of fashion decreed: for those to whom taste in this context concerned only the quality of the smoking experience, the cigar soon established primacy among the users of tobacco. As early as the second decade of the 19th century Lord Byron in 'The Island' (a poem partly inspired by the mutiny on the *Bounty* in 1789) proclaimed the predilection of that new breed, the connoisseurs of tobacco:

> Sublime tobacco! which from east to west
> Cheers the tar's labour or the Turkman's rest;
> Which on the Moslem's ottoman divides
> His hours, and rivals opium and his brides;
> Magnificent in Stamboul, but less grand,
> Though not less loved, in Wapping or the Strand;
> Divine in hookas, glorious in a pipe,
> When tipp'd with amber, mellow, rich, and ripe;
> Like other charmers, wooing the caress,
> More dazzlingly when daring in full dress;
> Yet thy true lovers more admire by far
> Thy naked beauties – Give me a cigar!

It cannot be denied that, notwithstanding this persuasive testimonial, the cigar was most effectually launched upon the path to prosperity by the company it kept. It

The 'Cigar Mania' of the early 19th century, in a cartoon

Bismarck, the Iron Chancellor, as famous for his cigar as Churchill

rapidly and most helpfully found patronage among kings, princes, and internationally admired men of affairs in every field, and its symbolic association with prestige and power as well as with aesthetic discernment has continued to this day.

In the mid-19th century the example was set by Napoleon III of France. Unlike his uncle Napoleon Bonaparte, who abominated smoking in any form but was a slave to snuff, Napoleon III was something of a connoisseur of cigars. His name in smoking history is secure as the recipient of a gift of probably the most expensive cigars ever made: a consignment of 20,000 Havanas stamped with his monogram, and tipped at the head with gold. The cigars are reputed to have cost £30,000 – which in those days was a kingly sum.

For Bismarck, the Iron Chancellor, the Havana became as potent a symbol in the public mind as it was later to be for Winston Churchill. There was a well-publicised occasion after the Battle of Königgrätz (Sadowa, in Czechoslovakia) in 1866 when Bismarck, inspecting the scene of carnage, came across a terribly wounded soldier begging for refreshment. Having nothing to offer him except his very last Havana, Bismarck lit it and placed it between the soldier's lips. Later, recalling the grateful smile of the soldier, Bismarck insisted 'I have never enjoyed a cigar so much as that one I never smoked'. He frequently praised the Havana as an invaluable aid to diplomacy – even interrupting the peace negotiations at the conclusion of the

Franco-Prussian War in 1871 to deliver a homily on the role of the cigar in helping to bring about the achievement of a just settlement.

Mention of war recalls to mind that Havanas were used, if only symbolically, in the cause of espionage during the 1914-18 conflict. Two German naval officers, having landed secretly in England, made a tour of the larger British ports in order to gather information on allied naval movements and dispositions. To anyone who asked, they were a pair of respectable cigar merchants, and their reports (to a base in Holland) were disguised as orders for shipments of Havanas. Each cigar size corresponded to a particular class of warship; thus, an order for 600 double coronas indicated that six battleships had been spotted at the port to which the imaginary consignment was to be dispatched. One hundred corona grandes represented a battle cruiser; 100 coronas represented a cruiser; and so on, down to 100 half coronas, which represented a submarine. The spies' ingenuity, however, was exceeded by their carelessness: they were soon discovered by British counter-intelligence and were later executed.

Among English royal patrons, the Havana is forever linked with King Edward VII. For much of his early life Edward's enjoyment of cigars must have represented a triumph of perseverence and cunning over formidable odds. Queen Victoria detested smoking of any kind and imposed a total ban on tobacco at Buckingham Palace, Osborne, and anywhere else she set foot. She never managed to suppress Edward's appetite for, or consumption of, Havanas – which seems to have been quite as shocking to her as his more notorious cravings for gambling and girls. Victoria was not alone in deprecating her son's smoking habits. On the occasion of his visit to America in 1860, one of the anti-tobacco societies in New York published *An Appeal to Lord Renfrew, Prince of Wales, on the Pernicious Effects of His Cigar and Pipe*. Neither this nor parental repression had any effect. It is said that on the very day of his accession when presiding over his first levee, he drew out a double corona with the words: 'Gentlemen, you may smoke'.

Among 20th-century men of power Winston Churchill was, of course, the archetypal cigar smoker. He worked quite exceptionally hard at reinforcing and burnishing this reputation: he is said to have smoked no fewer than a quarter of a million cigars in his life. His preference was for double coronas or Lonsdales of maduro leaf, and in later years his favourite Havanas had a band bearing his likeness.

Today the most notable, or rather the most noticeable, smokers of cigars are the plutocrats, the great oil magnates and show-business tycoons. Among the latter there are few more conspicuous consumers than the television mogul Lew Grade, who is reputed to spend more than £150 a week on Havanas. Among entertainers, the late Groucho Marx deserves mentioning not merely for the size of his cigars but, more strikingly (in view of his known passion for them), the fact that in the great Marx Brothers movies they are never lighted. But undoubtedly the greatest exploiter of the cigar in the world of entertainment is the American comedian George Burns. For him in his vaudeville days the cigar was not merely a trademark or prop: it was central to the punctuation, the very syntax, of his performance.

The world of arts and letters offers the full spectrum of social attitudes to smoking in all its forms. For opponents of tobacco the habit was summarized cryptically and for

A GARLAND OF PRAISE

'HOW happy they are, all those men,' wrote an Edwardian hostess, 'when we leave the dinner-table and they can settle down to the real pleasure of the evening, a good cigar! But why should we leave them? Why not break through the convention and stay behind to enjoy the aroma of those delicious leaves from Havana, and the talk they inspire?'

Many great writers have hymned the praises of tobacco and Lord Byron proclaimed his allegiance to the cigar in an ode, but it is those 'delicious leaves' that have inspired the

contemporary, Somerset Maugham, went still further. 'A good Havana is one of the best pleasures that I know. When I was young and very poor . . . I promised myself that if ever I had some money I would savour a cigar each day after lunch and after dinner. This is the only resolution of my youth that I have kept, and the only realized ambition that has not brought disillusion.'

During the 1790s, when France was in the grip of the Revolutionary Terror, the Duc de la Rochefoucauld-Liancourt prudently opted to go into exile in the United States, but not

 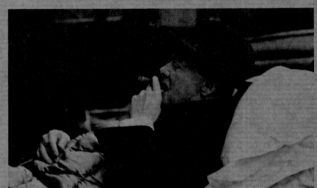

*Three 20th-century cigar smokers: the writer Evelyn Waugh (left),
Winston Churchill (right) and the Duke of Windsor (opposite)*

greatest loyalty. According to Franz Liszt, 'a good Cuban cigar closes the door to the vulgarities of the world.' As a pianist he dazzled the imagination of Europe in a series of concert tours which involved hours of travel on the continent's growing railway network. He never embarked on a journey without a large supply of Havanas, packed in an immense, three-layered box. At the end of his days he retired, as the Abbé Liszt, to a monastery, but not before he had secured a special papal dispensation to smoke his cigars at will.

'The most futile and disastrous day seems well spent when it is reviewed through the blue, fragrant smoke of a Havana cigar', wrote Evelyn Waugh, and his great English

without an ample supply of cigars. In 'a little eulogy for past services rendered' he gratefully acknowledged that the cigar had proved 'a great resource' on the long sea journey. 'Are you troubled by something? The cigar will dissolve it. Are you subject to aches and pains? The cigar will remedy them. . . . Do you ever feel faint from hunger? A cigar satisfies the yearning. If you have a pleasant remembrance or consoling thought, the cigar will reinforce it.' According to many, the cigar also clears the head. Marshal Foch, French commander during World War I, admitted to smoking a cigar on the eve of an offensive to sharpen his judgement for the decisions ahead.

The cigar has even been credited with political influence. It was the Indiana-born lawyer, Thomas R. Marshall, US Vice-President to President Wilson from 1913 to 1921, who made his mark on political science with the immortal observation: 'What this country needs is a really good five-cent cigar.' The Vice-President was no doubt unaware that Lenin was a cigar smoker, who left his tobacconist's bills unpaid when he returned to Russia from exile in Switzerland.

James I of England believed that men were bewitched by tobacco and it does seem that the Havana cigar, at least, can subvert the purest ideological loyalties. On his return from space, the American astronaut Colonel John Glenn was given the princely reward of his own weight in Havana cigars, despite the US embargo on Cuban imports. After the Castro revolution, the oil magnate Gulbenkian assured himself a continuing supply of cigars by arranging payments through a Soviet bank. 'Were the devil himself to take possession of the Vuelta,' observed the great capitalist, 'I would still smoke Havanas.'

Nor did the Communist revolutionary's takeover of the Vuelta affect the smoking loyalty of Sir Winston Churchill. He became a devotee of the Havana as a young man in the 1890s and smoked cigars till his death at the ripe old age of 91 in 1965. During the dark days of the Second World War, the Churchillian cigar was, for the British, almost as potent an emblem of victory as the war leader's famous 'V' sign. During the Blitz on London, one of the Luftwaffe's raids destroyed the famous London shop of Alfred H. Dunhill whose storage rooms held the prime-ministerial supply. Called to the scene in the small hours of the morning, the manager made a careful inspection of the damage and then hurried to the phone to report: 'Your cigars are safe, sir.'

No doubt Churchill found, as had Marshal Foch, that the cigar sharpened his judgement in the conduct of the war. For another famous Englishman, far across the Atlantic, the Havana proved a solace in exile. After his abdication as King Edward VIII in 1936, the Duke of Windsor left his native shores never to return. At the outbreak of war, the home government appointed him governor of the Bahamas, although he had demanded more active war service. He fretted under the petty round of official functions, but these at least afforded him the opportunity to inspect the factory and plantations of the great house of Por Larrañaga while on a ceremonial visit to Cuba.

Today, when smokers are under continual harrassment from the anti-smoking lobby, the final tribute to the Havana should, perhaps, be left to a doctor. Churchill belligerently claimed that his cigars helped keep him fit. One day, his wartime Field Marshal, Bernard Montgomery, told the great statesman: 'I do not drink. I do not smoke. I sleep a

great deal. That is why I am in 100% form.' 'And I,' retorted Churchill, 'drink a great deal. I sleep little, and I smoke cigar after cigar. That is why I am in 200% form.' And the testimony of our doctor bears him out.

The Scottish physician A. J. Cronin, world-famous for his novels of the doctor's life, provides heartening confirmation of the old Bulldog's splendid paradox. 'It can hardly be said,' wrote Dr Cronin, wearing his medical hat, 'that the Havana cigar is harmful – it contains only 0.064% of nicotine and, what is more important, no furfural, which is the really harmful element that may be found in some other tobaccos. So my advice is smoke your Havana cigar with a quiet mind and rejoice in the good it does you by inducing material relaxation and spiritual delight.'

*A powerful symbol, one that could be said to have inspired the
British nation throughout World War II: captured here by Strube*

ever by Horace Greeley, the 19th-century anti-slavery campaigner and founder of the
New York Tribune, who defined a cigar as 'a fire at one end and a fool at the other'.

This view would have been strongly endorsed by at least two of the giants of world
literature, Goethe and Tolstoy. Goethe's detestation of tobacco in any shape or form
is evident in many of his works; and his conviction that smoking ought to be abhorrent
to any man of taste and discernment must have led to frequent arguments with his
great friend and compatriot, Friedrich Schiller, who had an unassuageable appetite for
both pipe and snuff. Tolstoy's objections were essentially ethical ones. He insisted
that nicotine crippled one's moral sense; yet he succumbed to his craving for cigars at
intervals throughout his life.

Most people would agree that smoking, if any ethical problem at all, is one for the
individual rather than for society as a whole. William Makepeace Thackeray, who
sought tirelessly to expose the snobbism and vacuousness of polite society, would have
none of the 'silly social prejudice against smoking'. To the horror of those for whom
smoking in public was akin to debauchery, the hero of his 'Fitz-Boodle Papers' (1842)
observed: 'I for my part do not despair to see a Bishop lolling out of the Athenaeum
with a cheroot in his mouth . . .'

Of course, even among those capable of appreciating the delights of tobacco
there are people always ready to warn against the sins of excess. Mark Twain virtually
chain-smoked cigars (mostly stogies of indifferent quality, although he also developed
a taste for Havanas), his maxim being that eating and sleeping were the only activities
that should be allowed to interrupt a man's enjoyment of his cigar. Asked if he could

kick the smoking habit, he replied that of course he could – he had done so hundreds of times. The essayist Charles Lamb was also quick to defend himself on this score. When someone demanded to know how he had managed to become enslaved by the habit, Lamb replied: 'I toiled after it, Sir, as some men toil after virtue.' A voracious smoker, he eventually steeled himself to renounce his 'sweet enemy' – an event commemorated in his 'Farewell to Tobacco' (1805). The parting was shortlived, for he soon fell victim to the pleasures of snuff.

There is, of course, such a thing as going overboard in one's devotion to the weed. In his poem 'Betrothed', Rudyard Kipling, an ardent worshipper at the shrine of what he called 'the great god Nick o'Teen', unfolds the salutary tale of a man torn – but not for long – between his cigars and his possessive and too-fastidious fiancée:

> Open the old cigar-box; let me consider awhile.
> Here is a mild Manila, there is a wifely smile.
> Which is the better portion – bondage bought with a ring,
> Or a harem of dusky beauties, fifty tied in a string?
> Counsellors cunning and silent, comforters true and tried,
> And never a one of the fifty to sneer at a rival bride.
> Thought in the early morning, solace in time of woes,
> Peace in the hush of twilight, balm as my eyelids close.
> Open the old cigar box; let me consider anew.
> Old friends, and who is Maggie, that I should abandon you?
> Light me another Cuba; I'll hold to my first-sworn vows:
> If Maggie will have no rival, I'll have no Maggie for spouse!

We must conclude that, however admirable his devotion to the sacred herb – and Kipling himself was especially fond of Partagás and Por Larrañaga – the man had slid helplessly over the narrow boundary that divides love and obsession. He would, perhaps, have found a more fitting mate in George Sand, probably the most celebrated woman smoker in history, for whom 'the cigar numbs sorrow and fills the solitary hours with a million gracious images'. On second thoughts, perhaps not: the idea of an alliance between the French novelist and one of Kipling's heroes is enough to beggar the imagination. Somerset Maugham, however, obviously shared George Sand's views on the topic. In *The Summing Up* he wrote: 'A good Havana is one of the best pleasures I know . . . I like a mild cigar, of delicate aroma and medium length . . . After the last puff, when you put the stubby butt out and the last smoke curls away, who does not marvel at the work, the complicated enterprise, which has produced this half hour of pleasure?'

Ultimately, however subtle the inflexions, however rich and complex the experience of one's Havana, it is the solace, the soothing consolation offered by the sacred herb that counts for most, as expressed in Thomas Hood's artless quatrain:

> Some sigh for this or that:
> My wishes don't go far.
> The world may wag at will,
> So I have my cigar.

INDEX

Numbers in italics refer to illustrations

ACKNOWLEDGMENTS

The publishers would particularly like to thank the
Cuban Embassy in London, for kind cooperation and
helpful advice with many of the illustrations in this book.
They would also like to thank Nathan Chait, Elizabeth
Farrow and John Hall for permission to photograph illustrations from their respective collections of tobacco
ephemera.

Architectural Press, London.
Astleys Ltd., Jermyn Street, London.
BBC Hulton Picture Library, London.
Nathan Chait, The Pipe Shop, Hill Rise, Richmond,
    Surrey.
Cubatabaco, Havana, Cuba.
Deutsches Tabak-und Zigarrenmuseum, Bünde,
    Germany.

Alfred Dunhill Ltd., London.
Mary Evans Picture Library, London.
Elizabeth Farrow, The Dodo Shop,
    185 Westbourne Grove, London W11.
Fotomas Index, London.
Monty Frisco/Orbis
Mark Gerson/Orbis
John Hall, School of Graphic Design, Kingston
    Polytechnic, Kingston upon Thames, Surrey.
The Illustrated London News Picture Library,
    London.
Mansell Collection, London.
Musées Royaux des Beaux-Arts de Belgique.
New York Public Library.
Niemeyer Nederlands Tabacologisch Museum,
    Groningen.
Joseph Samuel and Son Ltd., Woking, Surrey.
John Topham Picture Library
Victoria and Albert Museum, London.

JOSEPH HOOKER'S
Rhododendrons of Sikkim-Himalaya

Kew Publishing
Royal Botanic Gardens, Kew

PUBLISHER'S NOTE

This facsimile edition of *The Rhododendrons of Sikkim-Himalaya* has been reproduced from an original held in the Library, Art & Archives of the Royal Botanic Gardens, Kew. The size of the original book is 36.5 × 50.5 cm, and the three parts were published by Reeve, Benham & Reeve, London in between 1849 and 1851. Each part has its own title page. The 30 plates and title vignette are coloured lithographs by Walter Hood Fitch after the author, and printed by Reeve, Benham & Reeve, Frederic Reeve, and Vincent Brooks.

This book has been produced to celebrate the life of Joseph Dalton Hooker, born in 1817. *The Rhododendrons of Sikkim-Himalaya* is not only a beautiful book in its own right but also a significant publication for a number of reasons. It is a landmark early publication by the young Joseph Hooker; it reveals some of the wondrous plants discovered by him during his important explorations in India (1848–51), with the plants themselves brought to life with stunning illustrations by renowned artist W. H. Fitch. Finally, the book introduced to the Victorian public new species of rhododendrons that were to become hugely popular and also to play a role in the evolution of British horticultural style and landscape design.

OPPOSITE
Chalk portrait of Joseph Hooker
by George Richmond, 1855.

Introduction

JOSEPH HOOKER IN INDIA

Virginia Mills, Joseph Hooker Correspondence Project,
Library, Art & Archives, Royal Botanic Gardens, Kew

Sir Joseph Dalton Hooker (1817-1911), is perhaps the greatest of the lauded Directors of the Royal Botanic Gardens, Kew. 2017 marks both the bicentenary of his birth and 170 years since he struck out from Kew for India, seeking botanical treasures in the Himalayas. The trip was to prove laborious, beset by natural and political perils, but Joseph Hooker's labours bore fruits, among them the sumptuous publication, *The Rhododendrons of Sikkim-Himalaya*, reproduced in this special edition.

The plant hunting trail would ultimately lead Hooker to elevated positions; not only Director of Kew but also President of the Royal Society. Thanks to a keen mind, thirst for knowledge, relentless hard work, networking and high standards Hooker would come to move in the circles of all the great thinkers of the day, as shown by his vast international correspondence held in the archives of the Royal Botanic Gardens, Kew. In his heyday he gained audiences with Prime Ministers, was sought as an advisor on major expeditions including that of Scott of the Antarctic, and orchestrated the transplantation of crop-species across continents. As a 'botanical emperor' Joseph Hooker became a widely known figure in Victorian society; certainly more celebrated than he is today. On the point of setting out for India in 1847, aged 30, these laurels were yet to be won. Hooker was recently engaged to be married but without secure income or promise of his much-desired career in botany, still largely a discipline for enthusiastic amateurs of means. He wrote to his fiancée Frances Henslow: 'foreign travelling … affords almost the only really good opening to a young man in…my line of life, & it is worth therefore sacrificing a few years to it'.

Travel to unexplored territories in the Himalayas was, for Hooker, an opportunity to make his name through new discoveries and observations of plants with botanical, horticultural and economic interest, also by surveying un-mapped areas and making observations of the wider natural world. His journals and notebooks contain observations on zoology, geology, meteorology, magnetism, ethnology and astronomy, but his chief aim was always botany and especially his own particular area of expertise; plant distribution and species variation. In this his interests intersected with his friend Charles Darwin.

'In travelling N. you come upon genus replacing genus, Natural Order replacing Natural Order.
In travelling E. or W. (i.e. N.W. or S.E. along the ridges) you find species replacing species, and this whether of animals or plants. Don't forget to send this to Darwin.' [*letter from Hooker to his father*]

The expedition to India and the Himalayas was being sponsored for the benefit of Kew and a horticultural return was expected. Hooker did not disappoint. Over four years in India, from 1848 to 1851, he and his local assistants collected over 5,000 different species of plants and Hooker also executed over 700 illustrations of plants. Of particular note amongst the haul were 25 previously undescribed species of the genus *Rhododendron.*

These chiefly came from Sikkim, a hitherto closed Himalayan kingdom on the border of British India. Joseph Hooker was to be the first European given permission to explore the region. The Rajah of Sikkim, Chomphoe Namgye was understandably wary of admitting foreign travellers who might survey his country, so the negotiations took considerable political manoeuvring.

Once access to this kingdom of secret plants was granted Hooker and his party — of porters escorts, Gurkha guards, translator, shooter and stuffer, and collecting assistants — was continually delayed, deliberately misdirected and denied vital provisions by the Rajah and his agents. The citizens of Sikkim had been instructed not to sell food to the expedition and they often had to scratch a living from the land, digging up edible roots; Hooker described himself as 'a starving wolf'.

At one point Hooker was briefly imprisoned by the Rajah for illegally crossing the border into Tibet. This was a major political incident and resulted in serious repercussions for the Rajah, who was threatened with invasion by British forces if he did not release his prisoners. Joseph Hooker himself shrugged off his period of incarceration. Despite recording being roughly handled in his diary he continued his explorations elsewhere with enthusiasm.

The rhododendrons were the horticultural jewels in the crown of Sikkim's flora. The genus is incredibly diverse with species prized by cultivators and gardeners, variously for their large clusters of flowers, evergreen foliage, and size; *Rhododendron falconeri*, one of 'Hooker's species', can grow to over 15m tall. They were not easily collected however. To gather seeds Hooker had to travel during monsoon season. He took to wearing woollen stockings and dusting himself in tobacco in an attempt to protect himself from leeches that were rife in the wet weather and often had to pick off a hundred a day. He was also afflicted by bites of mosquitoes and other insects.

The high terrain presented the risk of snow blindness which necessitated the wearing of tinted glasses and a veil. Altitude sickness was a real discomfort too but he was never the less able to ascend to over 18,000 feet, possibly attaining a greater height than ever previously recorded, to determine plant life that could survive at altitudes which had previously been imagined impossible.

Hooker would often return to his tent at the end of a day's collecting 'streaming with blood', 'mottled with bites' and suffering with incapacitating 'headaches that do not go off for hours'.

With no maps or roads progress was slow and hazardous: 'one often progresses spread-eagled against a cliff, for some distance and crosses narrow planks over profound abysses with no hold'. Hooker took surveying instruments with him to take measurements so he could make his own maps. Until he could trust his fellow travellers the actual map drawing was carried out only in secret in his tent. This furtive mapping, the British Government backing of the expedition and continuing payments made to Hooker from the Royal Navy have led to persistent speculation that Joseph Hooker was acting as spy as well as a naturalist in Sikkim. Though there is no record confirming this was an official role it is certainly true that the British military made use of Hooker's map when later annexing Sikkim.

The rhododendrons themselves were also a frustration; the mountains at 10,000 to 13,000 feet were covered with rhododendron scrub that had to be hacked away to make a path, they tore and bruised the traveller's shins mercilessly. *Rhododendron setosum*, a beautiful, purple-flowered dwarf species has such a powerful resinous scent that it causes headaches.

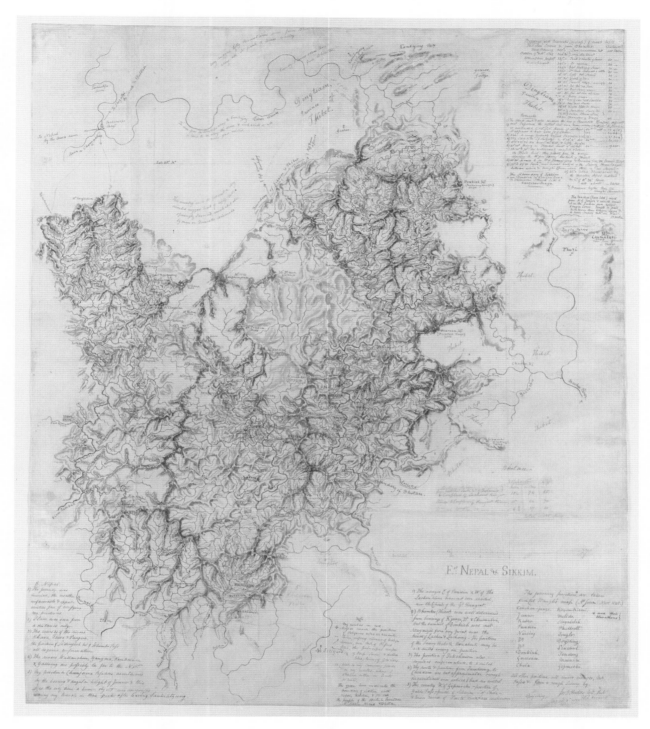

Map of the Sikkim and Himalaya region, produced using Hooker's rough surveys of the region,
with accompanying notes in his hand, c. 1850.

Hooker was an active collector himself and endured his share of the hardships in his pursuit of plants.
He was also assisted by knowledgeable local Lepcha collectors who were invaluable. They knew where to
find the choicest plants and could enlighten Hooker on the local vernacular plant names and ethnographic
purposes different species served. All of this information on habit and economic uses was duly recorded by
Hooker and sent back to Kew alongside plant specimens, drawings, seeds and ethnographic artefacts.

Among Hooker's more unorthodox collecting practices was training his dog to bring him roadside
shrubs, as he related to his younger sister in a whimsical, perhaps somewhat tongue in cheek, letter that
also claimed his canine companion was clever enough to assist with his correspondence.

Having caused such pains to secure, Hooker's plant collections faced myriad obstacles before reaching Kew. Specimens destined for the herbarium had to be dried and pressed and kept from rotting, no mean feat in the climate of India. This required drying paper; difficult and expensive to procure in India, a burden to carry and preserve on the march. As the expedition progressed further into the Himalayas Hooker sent porters with plant specimens gathered on their daily marches back to his base at the house of naturalist Brian Houghton Hodgson in Darjeeling. These were prepared by specially trained assistants before being sent on to Calcutta Botanic Garden and from there to Kew.

Seeds were sent in tin boxes in an effort to preserve their longevity, to protect them from damp and rot. Some were sent to be propagated at Kew, others would be sown at Calcutta and once the plants were strong enough to survive the rigours of a sea voyage shipment would be attempted by Wardian Case — glazed packing cases that resemble miniature greenhouses. Much material was lost at each stage and Hooker railed to his father when one of his finest collections of rhododendrons got ruined:

> 'I have to collect the troublesome things afresh…if your shins were as bruised as mine you would be as sick of the sight of these glories as I am'.

Despite the odds, the 1850 Kew Annual report recorded receipt of '21 baskets of Indian orchids and new species of rhododendron' just one of many shipments which were accompanied by drawings of the plants, detailing as far as possible their accurate colours (soon lost in pressed specimens), different stages of maturity and dissections of all their vital parts for identification and study. It was these materials and the efforts that went into procuring them that made the preparation of the *Rhododendrons of Sikkim Himalaya* back at Kew possible. The publication was completed whilst Hooker was still on Indian soil.

THE PUBLICATION OF *THE RHODODENDRONS OF SIKKIM-HIMALAYA* AND ITS RECEPTION

Cam Sharp Jones, Joseph Hooker Correspondence Project,
Library, Art & Archives, Royal Botanic Gardens, Kew

On the 6 August 1849, Joseph Hooker wrote to his father, William Jackson Hooker that 'all the Indian world is in love with you, it and me…' . The 'it' that Joseph Hooker was referring to was *The Rhododendrons of Sikkim-Himalaya*, the first volume having been published the previous spring in London.

Its publication in three volumes between 1849 and 1851 was an unparalleled commercial success for Hooker. The lavish illustrations produced by Walter Hood Fitch which accompanied the 33 rhododendron descriptions were, and still are, considered to be some of the finest examples of botanical illustration ever produced.

From the archives of Joseph Hooker and his father William, which remain at the Royal Botanic Gardens, Kew, it is possible to appreciate the process of drafting, illustrating and the eventual publication of this important work in greater detail.

When Hooker left England's shores in November 1847, his father, by that time the Director of the Royal Botanic Gardens, Kew, already had a plan that his son's travels in India would make a botanical mark. Writing to Dawson Turner on 27 March 1848, William Hooker remarked that the publication of Joseph's letters and other findings 'would keep Joseph in the mind of such persons as we would wish should not forget him.'

Indeed such a plan was quickly put into place with a short collection of published letters covering Joseph's journey from England to India. However by 1848, William's attention had been drawn to the new and beautiful species of rhododendrons that his son was writing home about. By February 1849, after Joseph had been in India just over a year, the idea of publishing a 'Rhododendrons' book had already been discussed by father and son. Joseph writes on 1 February 1849

'I have such heaps to tell & talk of that I scarce know how & where to begin. 1. Rhododendrons. Of these as of all my plants mss &c you are to make whatever you think proper. The [Flora Antarctica] nearly broke my back; & I do not contemplate any such great work...my present notion is to publish... large & expensive illustrations to a few Nat[ural] forms or genera. There are plenty of these without interfering with any you may select in the mean time. So pray go ahead with the Rhod[odendrons]. I hope to send drawings of 6 or 8 more species in spring. I will send you a small collection of these overland by March mail...'

From this and other references in letters between the pair, it is clear that William Hooker, who acted as the editor of all three volumes of *Rhododendrons of Sikkim-Himalaya*, was the guiding force behind its publication. By the time Joseph's reply reached his father back at Kew in March 1849, William had already started work on the publication. He had commissioned Walter Hood Fitch, the noted botanical artist and the Hookers' illustrator of choice, to transform Joseph's rough sketches of the rhododendrons in the wild, as well as the numerous specimens which were also arriving, into striking lithographs which were for the most part hand coloured by Fitch. To achieve the final result, Fitch would merge features from both the sketches and specimens to create 'complete' examples, then re-sketch the images onto stone ready for printing. Fitch was quite rightly proud of his skill at infusing 'life' into the dried and damaged specimens and incomplete sketches through his illustrations.

William Hooker arranged for *Rhododendrons of Sikkim-Himalaya* to be published by Reeves, Benham and Reeves, run by Lovell Reeve. Both of the Hookers had an established relationship with Reeve through the earlier publication of Joseph's *The Botany of the Antarctic Voyage* which had appeared in 1844, and also the ongoing publication of *Curtis's Botanical Magazine*, edited by William. By November 1848, discussions were occurring between Lovell Reeve and William Hooker about the possibility of a 'Rhododendron' book. Reeve established a subscription list for *Rhododendrons of Sikkim-Himalaya* which was subscribed to by many influential figures in the botanical world (see page 9). In a letter to his father dated 25 April 1849, Joseph remarks that 'If Reeves has 180 subscribers for the Rhod[odendron] book it will no doubt pay him well, as many persons in India will buy it I believe & it must be very beautiful', a comment which suggests there was increasing interest in the forthcoming publication.

In December 1848, the first plate of *Rhododendron dalhousiae* was complete and in a letter to his father-in-law Dawson Turner, William wrote 'both in execution and in subject, Rhod. Dalhousiae, it is the finest I think I have ever saw.'

The first volume of the work was published in April 1849 and received positive reviews both in terms of the skill of illustration and the speed at which such information was being transmitted from the subcontinent. By August 1849, the publication had made its way to India itself, and echoing his earlier sentiments, Joseph wrote to his mother, Lady Maria Hooker on 8 August; 'All the Indian world is in love with my Rhododendron book...really the feeling towards me thus displayed by perfect strangers is very gratifying.'

Rhododendrons of Sikkim-Himalaya was dedicated to the Princess Mary of Cambridge 'whose taste for the pleasures of a garden, the first and purest pleasures of our race, has made her feel peculiar interest in the Great National Establishment at Kew'. William had earlier debated whether to dedicate the book to Lady Dalhousie but changed his mind as he feared 'it would be thought overdoing the thing to dedicate the Books to her also'. This fear was grounded in the fact that *Rhododendron dalhousiae* had been named by Joseph for Lady Dalhousie following his acquaintance with her and her husband, the Governor General of India, Lord Dalhousie when travelling out to India in 1847.

In a similar manner, out of the eleven plates in the first volume, five rhododendrons which Joseph scientifically described for the first time, were named for colleagues and friends in India and England. Lady Dalhousie, Nathaniel Wallich, the wife of Dr Archibald Campbell — the Superintendent of Darjeeling and Agent for Sikkim, Dr John Forbes Royle and Dr Hugh Falconer were all honoured with a species named after them. In the second and third volumes of the work , Lord Auckland, Thomas Thomson, Brian Houghton Hodgson, Major Edward Madden, Michael Edgeworth (Commissioner of Multan) and Dr Robert Wight also received a similar honour. This practice of naming not only reflected Joseph's desire to thank those who had helped him on his travels and in his work, but also reinforced and maintained a relationship with his growing circle of correspondents and patrons. The ability to name a species after a noted figure also allowed Hooker to repay such support in a gentlemanly-like manner that would not be tarnished by the exchange of money.

Relationships were additionally established and reinforced by the gifting of the publication to colleagues and institutions. Hooker often wrote to his father asking for copies of *Rhododendrons of Sikkim-Himalaya* to be sent to him in India so that he could present them to specific people. An example of this is found in Joseph's letter to his father on 28 September 1849: 'Please tell Reeve to send me 2 or 3 copies of Rhod[odendron] book putting them down to my account. I will send one to the Rajah of Nepaul...'

Following the successful publication of the first volume, work continued on the remaining two parts. Joseph would write the descriptions whilst in India and then send them home to be edited by his father and illustrated by Fitch.

Both Parts two and three were published in 1851 and completed the masterpiece that William had been determined to produce. *The Rhododendrons of Sikkim-Himalaya* not only put the region of Sikkim and its botanical treasures on the map, but also announced Joseph Hooker as an influential force within the botanical world. The work was Joseph's most commercially successful publication and also his most accessible one for those interested in the flora of the world. No subsequent publication by Hooker would be as colourful or well-illustrated as *The Rhododendrons of Sikkim-Himalaya*. Although his later work would have a great impact on botanical science, it is perhaps the *Rhododendrons of Sikkim-Himalaya* that has had a lasting impact on the horticultural environment in Britain, for not only did subscribers to the publication acquire the book, but they also gained access to rhododendron seeds and plants, supplied by William and Joseph through Kew.

Mounds of rhododendron flowering under the native tree canopy in Kew's Rhododendron Dell, 19th century.

Sir Joseph Dalton Hooker's Impact on British Gardening

Ed Ikin, Head of Wakehurst Landscape and Horticulture

Joseph Hooker's explorations and introductions didn't just enrich British gardening, they inspired a whole new approach to horticulture. For years, garden style had swung between two poles, the mannered and pastoral. The former, embodied in bedding-driven styles such as the gardenesque, was viewed either as high art or artifice by critics, the latter, the 'English landscape style' bucolic or bland. One had to be 'swept away' to accommodate the other.

The arrival of compelling new rhododendrons such as Hooker's iconic *Rhododendron falconeri* and *R. hodgsonii* heralded a new horticultural language: *wild gardening*, later coined and codified by William Robinson. These extraordinary new garden arrivals, fully capable of arborescence, with shimmering, textured bark, intriguing indumentums and barely comprehensible, buxom trusses of flowers could only thrive in precise conditions redolent of their homelands. Shelter, dappled shade, humus-rich soils and minimal root competition were basic requirements to reap the ornamental rewards these new introductions offered, and such conditions already existed in Britain within the deciduous woodlands of Sussex, the south west of England, western Ireland and western Scotland.

And so it began, a new style of garden making. Niches and glades were carved out of native oak woodland and into it added breath-taking tracts of ornamental Himalayan wonder, a multi-coloured understorey, immediately exotic yet paradoxically harmonious: ecologically and aesthetically co-existent. Our native oak (*Quercus robur*) provided the perfect light and humidity levels whilst never competing with the new arrivals, their roots occupying space far deeper than their guests. Not only was this the birth of woodland gardening, a movement that gifted us some of our greatest gardens such as Knightshayes, Leonardslee, Caerhays, Mount Usher and Benmore, but also the initiation of a deeper trend; the notion that plants could thrive if their wild ecology was matched to garden conditions.

Hooker embraced the wild ecology of the plants he introduced, embedded for months within the wilds of Sikkim, Nepal and Tibet, challenged by the climate and hostile hosts, both human and animal, but exhilarated by the extraordinary mountainous landscape. Through Hooker's journals, the wild environment of his rhododendrons was evoked through compelling but precise language, providing a guide to those British garden makers seeking to establish their precious new arrivals. This evocation of landscape and a rich seam of new plants from Hooker and other Himalayan-exploring pioneers, enriched the woodland garden vocabulary further, adding sub-shrubs, herbaceous plants and bulbs. A direct line can be traced from the shift Hooker's plants inspired to William Robinson's notable words:

> ' "Wild Garden"…is applied essentially to the placing of perfectly hardy exotic plants under conditions where they will thrive without further care'.

Today, gardens such as Wakehurst, Kew's wild botanic garden in Sussex, are profoundly connected to Hooker's endeavour. Our 'temperate woodlands of the world' are composed of wild plants, selected and planted by Wakehurst's horticulturists and arborists with precise reference to the wild places they originate from. Our dramatic Himalayan Glade and Chile Bank create analogues of wild habitats that incorporate rather than isolate plants. Exploring Chile, Kyrgyzstan and the vast forest of America's west coasts is still a physical and mental challenge in the twenty-first century, despite satellite mapping, GPS and the latest in weatherproof equipment. Hooker's spirit, which drove him to explore perilous and uncharted landscapes whilst adroitly selecting garden-transforming plants, is with our modern-day plant hunters every time they step into these lands.

Tab. I.

J.D.H.del. Fitch.lith. Reeve, Benham & Reeve, imp.

RHODODENDRON DALHOUSIÆ, Hook. fil.

(in its native locality.)

THE

RHODODENDRONS

OF

SIKKIM-HIMALAYA;

BEING

AN ACCOUNT, BOTANICAL AND GEOGRAPHICAL, OF THE

RHODODENDRONS RECENTLY DISCOVERED IN THE MOUNTAINS OF EASTERN HIMALAYA,

FROM

DRAWINGS AND DESCRIPTIONS MADE ON THE SPOT,

DURING A GOVERNMENT BOTANICAL MISSION TO THAT COUNTRY;

BY

JOSEPH DALTON HOOKER, R.N., M.D., F.R.S., F.L.S.,

&c., &c., &c.

EDITED BY

SIR W. J. HOOKER, K.H., D.C.L., F.R.A.S., & L.S.,

Vice-President of the Linnæan Society, and Director of the Royal Gardens of Kew.

J. D. H. del. W. F. lith.

Reeve, Benham & Reeve imp.

KINCHIN-JUNGA (elev. 28,178 ft.) as seen from DARJEELING.

LONDON:

REEVE, BENHAM, AND REEVE, KING WILLIAM STREET, STRAND.

1849.

TO

HER ROYAL HIGHNESS,

THE PRINCESS MARY OF CAMBRIDGE,

WHOSE TASTE FOR THE PLEASURES OF A GARDEN,

THE FIRST AND PUREST PLEASURES OF OUR RACE, HAS MADE HER FEEL PECULIAR INTEREST IN

𝕿𝖍𝖊 𝕲𝖗𝖊𝖆𝖙 𝕹𝖆𝖙𝖎𝖔𝖓𝖆𝖑 𝕰𝖘𝖙𝖆𝖇𝖑𝖎𝖘𝖍𝖒𝖊𝖓𝖙 𝖆𝖙 𝕶𝖊𝖜,

AND WHO,

CONJOINTLY WITH HER ROYAL PARENTS,

HAS EVER BEEN FORWARD IN PROMOTING WHATEVER MIGHT TEND TO ITS USEFULNESS AND EMBELLISHMENT,

THE FOLLOWING FIGURES AND DESCRIPTIONS

OF A SERIES OF EMINENTLY BEAUTIFUL PLANTS, DESTINED SHORTLY TO ADD NEW LUSTRE TO ITS TREASURES,

ARE MOST HUMBLY DEDICATED,

BY HER ROYAL HIGHNESS' DUTIFUL AND OBEDIENT SERVANT,

THE EDITOR.

Royal Gardens, Kew,
March 15th, 1849.

LIST OF SUBSCRIBERS.

HIS ROYAL HIGHNESS PRINCE ALBERT.

HIS GRACE THE DUKE OF DEVONSHIRE.   HIS GRACE THE DUKE OF NORTHUMBERLAND.

THE RIGHT HONOURABLE THE EARL OF SHREWSBURY.   THE RIGHT HONOURABLE THE EARL OF DERBY.

GENERAL THE RIGHT HONOURABLE THE LORD GOUGH.

THE RIGHT HONOURABLE THE LORD BRAYBROOKE.   THE HONOURABLE LADY ROLLE.

THE RIGHT HONOURABLE THE EARL OF BURLINGTON.   HIS GRACE THE DUKE OF BUCCLEUCH.

HER GRACE THE DUCHESS OF ARGYLL.   THE HORTICULTURAL SOCIETY OF LONDON.

ROYAL LIBRARY, BERLIN.   ROYAL LIBRARY, LEIPSIC.

UNIVERSITY LIBRARY, EDINBURGH.   HULL SUBSCRIPTION LIBRARY.

W. T. Aiton, Esq., F.L.S., Kew.
J. Allcard, Esq., F.L.S., Stratford Green.
Dr. Walker Arnott, F.L.S., Kinross.
Messrs. James Backhouse & Son, York.
Professor Balfour, F.L.S., Edinburgh.
James Bateman, Esq., F.L.S., Congleton.
G. Bentham, Esq., F.L.S., Hereford.
Robert Bevan, Esq., Rangham.
Henry Birkbeck, Esq.
W. Borrer, Esq., F.R.S. (two copies)
Mr. E. Brande, Turnham Green.
John Brightwen, Esq., Great Yarmouth.
C. E. Broome, Esq., Elmhurst.
C. J. F. Bunbury, Esq., F.L.S., Mildhenhall.
Decimus Burton, Esq., Spring Gardens.
Dr. Bromfield, F.L.S., Ryde.
Archibald Campbell, Esq., Dover.
G. Charlwood, Esq., F.L.S., Covent Gard.
D. B. Chapman, Esq., F.L.S., Roehampton.
R. Clapham, Esq., Austwick Hall.
Rev. J. C. Clark, Chertsey.
Benj. Clarke, Esq., F.L.S., Barnes Green.
Dr. Cohen, F.L.S., Cleveland Row.
H. Collins, Esq., Berkeley Lodge.
W. Cubitt, Esq., Gray's Inn Road.
Sir T. Cullum, Bart., Hardwicke House.
Mr. J. Cunningham, Edinburgh.
Messrs. G. Cunningham & Son, Liverpool.
Miss M. N. Cunninghame.
Miss Richardson Currer, Eshton Hall.
S. Curtis, Esq., Victoria Park (two copies).
Mr. A. Dancer, Fulham.
Dr. Davis, F.L.S., Bath.
J. Dennison, Esq., Woolton Hill.
Mr. F. Dickson, Chester.
Messrs. Dicksons & Son, Edinburgh.
L. W. Dillwyn, Esq., F.R.S., Swansea.
Rear-Admiral Dixon, Belair.
G. Dorrien, Esq., Chichester.
Lady Farnaby, Wickham Court.
D. Ferguson, Esq., Belfast.
George Field, Esq., Clapham Common.
Joseph Fielden, Esq., St. Michaels.
G. F. Frere, Esq., F.R.S., Royston Hall.
W. Gardner, Esq.
Messrs. Garraway, Moyes, & Co., Bristol.
G. S. Gibson, Esq., F.L.S., Saffron Walden.
Capt. the Hon. Geo. Gough, F.L.S.
Mr. W. Gregory, Cirencester (two copies).
John Henry Gurney, Esq., Norwich.
Miss Gurney, Cromer (two copies).

Daniel Hanbury, Esq., Lombard Street.
Gavin Hardie, Esq., Blackheath.
Professor Harvey, M.R.I.A., Dublin.
S. H. Haslam, Esq., F.L.S., Kendal.
Messrs. Henderson & Co. Edgeware Road.
Charles Hennah, Esq., St. Austin.
Professor Henslow, F.L.S., Hitcham.
Rev. J. Heyworth, Hembury Hill.
Mrs. Hoare, Hampstead Heath.
Mrs. Hornby, Hornchurch.
M. Louis Van Houtte, Ghent.
R. Hudson, Esq., F.R.S., Clapham.
Robert Hutton, Esq., Putney Park.
Mr. James Ingram, Southampton.
Mr. E. Irons, Wynyatt Street.
Messrs. T. Jackson & Son, Kingston.
A. Johnstone, Esq., Halesworth.
Messrs. Knight & Perry, Chelsea.
Mrs. Lawrence, Ealing Park.
Charles Lawson, Esq., Edinburgh.
Messrs. J. & C. Lee, Hammersmith.
Professor Link, F.M.L.S., Berlin.
J. D. Llewelyn, Esq., F.R.S., Swansea.
Messrs. C. Loddiges & Sons, Hackney.
Messrs. Hugh Low & Co., Clapton.
John A. Lowell, Esq., Boston, U.S.
Messrs. Lucombe, Pince, & Co., Exeter.
J. Luscombe, Esq., Combe Royal.
Charles Lyell, Esq., F.L.S., Kinnordy.
Dr. I. T. Mackay, A.L.S., Dublin.
Mr. Marnock, F.L.S., Regent's Park.
Mr. W. Masters, Canterbury.
S. Maunder, Esq., Gibson Square.
Sir William F. Middleton, Bart.
Alexander Milne, Esq., Whitehall Place.
D. W. Mitchell, Esq., F.L.S., Sec. Zool. Soc.
Thomas Moore, Esq., Chelsea.
W. C. Morland, Esq., Hayes.
T. N. R. Morson, Esq., F.L.S.
Captain Munro, F.L.S., Druid's Stoke.
Andrew Murray, Esq., Cambridge.
Stewart Murray, Esq., Glasgow.
Dr. Neill, F.L.S., Edinburgh.
H. O. Nethercote, Esq., Moulton Grange.
Mrs. Nightingale, Embley Park.
H. S. Norman, Esq., Hull.
Thomas Nuttall, Esq., F.L.S., Rainhill.
Messrs. Osborne, Fulham.
R. Briscoe Owen, M.D., F.L.S., Beaumaris.
Messrs. W. B. Page & Son, Southampton.

Sir Francis Palgrave, Hampstead.
Mrs. Palmer, Bromley.
Algernon Peckover, Esq., F.L.S. Wisbeach.
Robert Pince, Esq., Exeter.
Mr. A. Pontey, Plymouth.
Miss E. Poyser, the Elms, Derby.
Mrs. Rawdon, Larkfield.
John Reeves, Esq., F.R.S., Clapham.
John Rogers, Esq., River Hill.
Mr. W. Rogers, Southampton.
Messrs. Rollisson & Sons, Tooting.
Messrs. H. Ronalds & Sons, Brentford.
Dr. Roupell, Esq., F.R.S., Welbeck Street.
T. B. Roupell, Esq., Madras.
Dr. Royle, F.R.S., Bulstrode Street.
Mr. Henry Shepherd, Liverpool.
Samuel Simpson, Esq., Lancaster.
G. Ure Skinner, Esq., Kings Langley.
Mr. Skirving, Liverpool.
Mr. John Smith, A.L.S., Kew Gardens.
R. H. Solly, Esq., F.L.S., Gt. Ormond St.
S. R. Solly, Esq., Surge Hill.
John Standish, Esq., Bagshot.
Rev. W. Stockdale, F.L.S., Ashby Hall.
Charles Stokes, Esq., F.L.S., Gray's Inn.
Hon. W. F. Strangway.
Rev. I. Swete, D.D., Cotham, Bristol.
Lieut. Col. Sykes, F.R.S., India House.
Henry Fox Talbot, Esq., F.L.S.
Dr. Thomas Thomson, F.L.S., Glasgow.
G. H. K. Thwaites, Esq., Bristol.
Miss Traill, Hayes.
Dawson Turner, Esq., F.L.S., Yarmouth.
C. H. Turner, Esq., Bruton Street.
Messrs. Veitch & Sons, Exeter (two copies).
I. H. Vivian, Esq., Eaton Square.
G. Wailes, Esq., Newcastle-on-Tyne.
Dr. Wallich, F.R.S., Gower Street.
Miss E. Walton, Barnsbury Square.
Dr. Waring, F.L.S. Marlings.
Mrs. Lee Warner, Walsingham Abbey.
Mr. Waterer, Woking.
Adam White, Esq., F.L.S.
J. C. Whiteman, Esq., Bryanstone Square.
Francis Whitla, Esq., Belfast.
J. Wild, Esq., Clapham Lodge.
John Williams, Esq., Birmingham.
J. H. Wilson, Esq., F.L.S., Oxford.
Jas. Yates, Esq., F.R.S. & L.S., Highgate.
Dr. J. Forbes Young, F.L.S., Kennington.

PREFACE.

DARJEELING, in the Sikkim portion of the Himalaya, the native country of the plants figured and described in the following pages, is situated in lat. 27° N., and long. the same as Calcutta, from which it is distant about 380 miles. Its elevation above the sea is 7,200 feet. The mean temperature of the year is about 55° of Fahrenheit, and that of each month, as detailed in a Calendar communicated by Dr. Campbell, the Hon. the E. I. C. Resident at Darjeeling, to the late Lord Auckland, and now lying before me, is as follows :—

January	.	.	.	41°	May	.	.	.	.	59°	September	.	.	.	61° 50′
February	.	.	.	43°	June	.	.	.	.	64°	October .	.	.	.	58° 50′
March .	.	.	.	53° 50′	July	.	.	.	.	65°	November	.	.	.	48°
April .	.	.	.	57°	August	.	.	.	.	65°	December	.	.	.	44°

"In five years," further observes Dr. Campbell, "there have been three heavy falls of snow : one in December, 1842 ; one in January, 1839 ; and one in February, 1841."

The mountain Sinchul, upon a spur of which, looking north, Darjeeling stands, attains an elevation of 9,000 feet, and to the west of it, next Nepal, rises another conspicuous mountain, Tonglo, reaching a height of 10,000 feet. Due north of Darjeeling, at a distance of only sixty miles, the horizon is bounded by the great snowy range (as seen, or rather attempted to be shown, in the vignette of the title-page), having for its principal feature the peak of KINCHIN-JUNGA, which has lately been ascertained to be 28,172 feet in elevation, the loftiest mountain yet known in the world. Dr. Hooker thus describes his first impressions of this scene :—" Much as I had heard and read of the magnificence and beauty of Himalayan scenery, my highest expectations have been surpassed ! I arrived at Darjeeling on a rainy misty day, which did not allow me to see ten yards in any direction, much less to descry the Snowy Range, distant sixty miles in a straight line. Early next morning I caught my first view, and I literally held my breath in awe and admiration. Six or seven successive ranges of forest-clad mountains, as high as that whereon I stood (8,000 feet), intervened between me and a dazzling white pile of snow-clad mountains, among which the giant peak of Kinchin-junga rose 20,000 feet *above* the lofty point from which I gazed ! Owing to the clearness of the atmosphere, the snow appeared, to my fancy, but a few miles off, and the loftiest mountain at only a day's journey. The heavenward outline was projected against a pale blue sky ; while little detached patches of mist clung here and there to the highest peaks, and were tinged golden yellow, or rosy red, by the rising sun, which touched these elevated points long ere it reached the lower position which I occupied.

" Such is the aspect of the Himalaya range at early morning. As the sun's rays dart into the many valleys which lie between the snowy mountains and Darjeeling, the stagnant air contained in the low recesses becomes quickly heated : heavy masses of vapour, dense, white, and keenly defined, arise from the hollows, meet over the crests of the hills, cling to the forests on their summits, enlarge, unite, and ascend rapidly to the rarefied regions above,—a phenomenon so suddenly developed, that the consequent withdrawal from the spectator's gaze of the stupendous scenery beyond, looks like the work of magic." Such is the region of the Indian Rhododendrons.

Perhaps, with the exception of the Rose, the Queen of Flowers, no plants have excited a more lively interest throughout Europe than the several species of the genus *Rhododendron*,[1] whether the fine evergreen foliage be considered, or the beauty and profusion of the blossoms; and it may probably be said with truth, that no kind of flowering shrub is so easily, and has been so extensively, cultivated, or has formed so vast an article of traffic, as that one oriental species to which the name seems more immediately to have been given, the *Rhododendron Ponticum*. Its poisonous qualities, too, have tended to bring it the more into notice; for, to eating the honey collected by the bees from that plant, (as well as from the *Azalea Pontica*,) in the neighbourhood of Trebizond, during the celebrated retreat of the Ten Thousand, were attributed the dreadful sufferings of the Greeks; so severe that their actions were said to resemble those of drunken persons or madmen. Major Madden has stated that cattle sometimes perish by feeding upon the foliage and flowers of *Rhododendron arboreum* in the mountains of Kamaoon. Dr. Hooker remarks, on a recent tour while exploring the mountain-passes leading into Thibet:—" Here are three Rhododendrons, two of them resinous and strongly odoriferous; and it is to the presence of these plants that the natives attribute the painful sensations experienced at great elevations."

The *R. Ponticum*, which inhabits the mountains of Asia Minor and extends as far west as Spain and Portugal, together with *R. ferrugineum* and *hirsutum* of the European Alps, *R. Dahuricum* of Siberia, *R. Chamæcistus* of the Austrian and Piedmontese mountains, *R. maximum* of the United States of America, and the arctic *R. Lapponicum*, were all the kinds known to Linnæus and to the botanical world so recently as 1764. The beautiful *R. chrysanthum* of Northern Siberia appeared in Linnæus' Supplement. Gmelin added the *R. Kamtschaticum* from Okotsk and Behring's Straits, and Pallas the charming *R. Caucasicum* from the Caucasian Alps.

Towards the very close of the 18th century, namely in 1796, *R. arboreum*, the first of a new form and aspect of the genus, and peculiar to the lofty mountains of India Proper, was discovered by Captain Hardwicke, in the Sewalic chain of the Himalaya, while he was on a tour to Sireenagur. The species has since been found to have a very extended range. It was published in 1805 by Sir James E. Smith, in the " Exotic Botany " of that author, and is characterized by its arborescent stem, very rich scarlet flowers, and leaves that are silvery on the underside. Sir James, on the authority no doubt of Captain Hardwicke, gives the height of the tree at twenty feet; but Major Madden, who found it on the mountains of Kamaoon, at elevations of from 3,500 to 10,000 feet, says he might safely have doubled that measurement. On Binaur, a *trunk* was found to be thirteen feet in girth, and another at Nynee Tal, sixteen feet; while a third, at Singabee Devee, was fourteen feet and a half in the circumference of the stem at five feet from the ground.

---

[1] So called, as is well known, from ῥόδον, a *rose*, and δένδρον, a *tree*: a name, however, which was given with equal justice to the Rose-bay, *Nerium Oleander*, the ῥοδοδάφνη of the modern Greeks.

It does not appear on record by whom the *Tree Rhododendron* was first introduced into Europe, probably by Dr. Wallich, about the year 1827. We know that to that distinguished botanist we owe the discovery, and the possession of most of them in our gardens, of other noble Indian species, such as *R. formosum*, *R. barbatum*, *R. nobile*, *R. campanulatum*, *R. cinnamomeum*, with their many varieties, the limits of which are not clearly defined; and the facility these kinds afford for hybridizing with *R. arboreum*, thereby rendering the produce more hardy, has occasioned the original type of this latter species to be almost lost to our gardens.

R. Nilagiricum (Bot. Mag. t. 4381) was introduced to our gardens by Messrs. Lucombe, Pince, and Co., of the Exeter Nursery, a species assuredly quite, and permanently, distinct from *R. arboreum*, though published and figured under that name in Dr. Wight's *Icones*. Dr. Wallich, about the same period, detected another distinct, but not less interesting, group of species, in Northern India, more allied to *R. ferrugineum* and *R. hirsutum*; namely *R. setosum*, *R. lepidotum*, and *R. Anthopogon*.

Drs. Horsfield, Blume, and Jack made known some species from the mountains of Java: they were *R. Javanicum* (a most lovely shrub, introduced to our gardens by Messrs. Veitch and Sons of Exeter, through their collector, Mr. W. Lobb, see Bot. Mag. t. 4336), *R. album*, *R. retusum*, *R. tubiflorum*, *R. Malayanum*, and *R. Celebicum*. Blume, we believe, first noticed a species as being epiphytal, in Java (" supra arbores "), his *R. (Vireya) album*. Mr. William Lobb informs me that several kinds are there epiphytal; and Mr. Low, who speaks of the fine Rhododendrons existing in Borneo, particularizes one which inhabits invariably the trunks of trees, and which he had the good fortune to send to England alive, though we fear it has not been preserved in our collections.

What may be the number of species, or what the kinds, detected by Mr. Griffith during his travels in Bootan, we do not learn from the volume of his Posthumous Papers recently published at Calcutta by Mr. M'Clelland; nor am I aware whether Dr. Wight has published the whole of them in the paper of that gentleman, in the Calcutta Journal of Natural History, vol. viii., on certain Rhododendrons of Mr. Griffith. In Dr. Wight's Icones he figures and describes only two, *R. grande* and *R. Griffithianum*; both very distinct from any found by Dr. Hooker in the adjacent territory of Sikkim. And in proof of the prevalence of the genus in Bootan, it may be observed that Mr. Griffith, in his Journal, when speaking of one single excursion (to Doonglala Peak, 12,478 feet of elevation), enumerates no less than eight distinct species; viz. :—

* *Floribus in racemis umbelliformibus.*

1. *R. arboreum ;* arboreum, foliis oblongo-obovatis subtus argenteis.
2. *R. ferrugineum ;* arboreum, foliis obovatis supra rugosis subtus ferrugineis.
3. *R. ——— ;* fruticosum, foliis oblongis subtus ferrugineo-lepidotis.
4. *R. ellipticum ;* fruticosum, foliis ellipticis.
5. *R. ——— ;* fruticosum, foliis ellipticis basi cordatis subtus glaucis reticulatis.
6. *R. ——— ;* fruticosum, foliis lanceolatis oblongis sub-obovatis subtus punctatis.
7. *R. undulatum ;* fruticosum, foliis elongato-lanceolatis undulatis subtus reticulatis.

** *Floribus solitariis.*

8. *R. microphyllum ;* fruticosum totum ferrugineo-lepidotum, foliis lanceolatis parvis.

In another place in Bootan (Pass of Rodoola, 12,000 feet), Mr. Griffith speaks of Rhododendrons as the only vegetation at the summit, and in the descent he traversed a "region of Rhododendrons."

It is not our intention, nor is it required by the nature of this little treatise, to enumerate all the Rhododendrons that are known in books: suffice it to say, that (exclusive of some Azaleas of Linnæus) thirty-two are distinguished by De Candolle in the seventh volume of his Prodromus, published in 1839; and enough has been here stated to show that the maximum of the species exists in Asia; for, commencing with Borneo and other Malayan islands in the tropics of the southern hemisphere, and proceeding north, we find them recorded in the mountain regions of all the intervening countries that have been botanically investigated, even to northern and extreme arctic Siberia. As we proceed westward into Europe, they gradually disappear, one only inhabiting Sweden and Norway (*R. Lapponicum*), and that seems not to extend to the western coasts.

In the vast continent of North America, the cool hilly grounds, with moisture, of the middle and southern states, yield only *R. maximum* (which, however, is found also in Canada), *R. macrophyllum*, Don, confined to the west side of the Rocky Mountains, *R. Catawbiense* and *R. punctatum*, which two have a very limited range. The anomalous *R. albiflorum*, with white flowers and deciduous leaves, is only seen in the Rocky Mountains, about lat. 52°. As might be expected, in the alpine and arctic regions the northern European kinds appear; for example, *R. Lapponicum* has been detected on the White Mountains, Massachusetts, on the summit of Mount Mary, Essex County, New York, at an elevation of 5,400 feet on the Rocky Mountains, in Labrador, and along the coasts of the Polar Sea; while in Behring's Straits, the *R. Kamschaticum* again appears. No species grows in Mexico or near the coasts of Oregon or California, and none in the isthmus of Panama. Throughout the whole of Africa [1] and Australia, the genus is unknown; and it will be observed that it only enters the southern hemisphere through the medium of the Indian Archipelago.

When it is borne in mind that, as above stated, Mr. Griffith, in an excursion to one mountain in Bootan, detected eight species,[2] and that the author of the present work, during a very limited sojourn in Sikkim, and with little means of prosecuting extensive researches, owing to the nature of the country and the hostile feeling entertained towards the English by the Rajah, yet collected and described eleven species, of which nine were new, it may, I think, be fairly conceded that if the maximum of Rhododendrons be in Asia, their head-quarters are on the lofty ranges of the Eastern Himalaya, where the mild and moist atmosphere is eminently suited to their habit.—ED.

---

[1] Boissier, indeed, in his *Voyage Botanique en Espagne*, says of the *R. Ponticum* :—" Hab. verosimiliter in Atlante,"—but I know not upon what authority.

[2] How far these species may accord with those of Sikkim, or whether any will do so, cannot be determined, until the Hon. the E. I. C. shall be pleased to unlock the treasures contributed by Mr. Griffith to the Herbarium stores in the possession of the Company; and there is now happily a prospect of this long-wished-for event taking place. The few Rhododendrons that have been edited by Dr. Wight we know to be very different and of peculiar interest.

THE

RHODODENDRONS

OF

SIKKIM-HIMALAYA.

IT has been well remarked by the illustrious Wallich, (the Father of Nepalese Botany,) that in Nepal the genus *Rhododendron* claims the highest rank amongst the plants of that rich kingdom. From the proximity of Sikkim to Nepal, a similarity in the botanical features of these countries might be expected; and also that the difference should rather exist in individual species than in the genera or higher groups. The outline of the two countries is very similar, their latitude the same, so is their geology, and the difference in climate is slight, and only evident in the increased humidity of the eastern region.

Rhododendrons are distributed in Sikkim as they are in Nepal, crowning those sub-Himalayan hills which attain 7,000 feet of elevation, and at a still greater altitude increasing in number of species and individuals: some species being replaced by others which have no greater, perhaps less, apparent adaptation for resisting vicissitudes of climate, and yet accompanying several of the more local kinds throughout the elevations they severally attain.

I. As is frequently the case with large genera, one or more species, distinguished by peculiarity of distribution, often present some anomalies in botanical or other characters, whether in the unusual habit, mode of growth, or singular outline, colour, or more important feature. So it is with the Sikkim *Rhododendrons*. *R. Dalhousiæ*, the only one found so low as at 7,000 feet, and thence upwards for 3,000 feet more, differs from all its congeners of Northern India in its epiphytal mode of growth,[1] its sweet-scented flowers, slender habit, whorled branches, and in the length of time during which it continues in bloom. It is much the largest-flowered species with which I am acquainted, and has more membranous leaves than any of the others. With all these striking anomalies, it does not, however, present one character of calyx, corolla, stamens, or pistil, entitling it to separation from the genus. In possessing a large foliaceous

[1] In Sikkim, *Vaccinium* offers a parallel case. The *V. serpens* (?), an epiphyte on very large trees, inhabits a much lower level and ranges through many more feet in elevation than any of its congeners. [In Borneo it will be remembered that Mr. Low discovered epiphytal Rhododendrons; and Mr. William Lobb, several in Java. ED.]

calyx, it is one of the most perfect plants of the whole, and in its characters of flower and fruit is far more closely allied to the typical or scarlet-flowered group, than is the section to which the following belongs.

II. *Rhododendron Falconeri*, a white-flowered species, is eminently characteristic of the genus in habit, place of growth, and locality, never occurring below 10,000 feet. On the other hand it is peculiar in its ten-lobed corolla, numerous stamens, and many-celled ovary, superb foliage and many-flowered capitula. This multiplication of parts and development of foliage and trunk give it a striking appearance; but there is an almost total absence of calyx, an organ sufficiently evident in other species. It is allied to a species discovered by the lamented Griffith in Bootan, the *R. grande*, Wight, published in the Calcutta Journ. Nat. Hist. vol. viii. p. 176, [and since in Dr. Wight's Icones, vol. iv. p. 6. t. 1202].[1]

III. A third white-flowered group contains but one Sikkim species, the *R. argenteum*, a very conspicuous tree at an elevation of between 8,000 and 9,000 feet. In beauty of foliage it nearly equals the last mentioned (*R. Falconeri*), and the flowers are larger than in any but *R. Dalhousiæ*, and of the same form as those of the scarlet group; the stamens are of the normal number, but the ovarium is many-celled. Though evidently distinct, this species combines the characters of most of the other groups. In size of flower and colour, as already observed, it resembles *R. Dalhousiæ*, as it does in its unusually membranous leaves;[2] in the colour of the flower, size of foliage, small calyx, and many-celled ovarium, *R. Falconeri;*—while the number of stamens, general habit, silvery under-surface of leaf, &c., connect it with *R. arboreum*.[3]

IV. A singular set includes the dwarfish kinds to which *R. cinnabarinum* and *R. Roylii* belong. The flowers are small, the corolla is subcoriaceous, narrowed at the base of the tube, and its colour is a peculiarly dirty brick-red, somewhat iridescent with blue in bud, and its lobes are rounded, subacute, not notched or wrinkled. The calyces are small, coriaceous, and squamous in both; in one the lobes are remarkably unequal. In the number of stamens, cells of the ovarium, &c., they agree with the usual characters of the genus.

V. Of the normal or typical group, indicated to be such by the number of species it contains, by the prevalence of scarlet flowers, uniformity of corolla and number of parts, there are two subdivisions: one has a fully developed calyx, in the other the calyx is very small and coriaceous. *R. lancifolium* and *R. barbatum* represent the former section, in both of which that organ is as conspicuous as in *R. Dalhousiæ*. *R. arboreum*, *R. Wallichii*, and *R. Campbelliæ*, belong to the latter section. The species of this group known to me are all trees, of contracted range and gay flowers.

VI. The little *R. elæagnoides* may be classed in another group: it is a very alpine plant, of which I possess only the foliage and fruit. Its scaliness (a character which seems most conspicuous in the smaller and more alpine species) allies it to *R. cinnabarinum*, but it is apparently single-flowered and calyculate.

The sub-Himalayan mountains are surely the *centrum* of this truly fine genus, distinguished by the number and variety of its species and groups, by the great size and eminent beauty of several, which form conspicuous features in the landscape over many degrees of longitude, through a great variety of elevations, and clothe a vast amount of surface.

---

[1] From this figure and description it will be seen, that although in many respects near *R. Falconeri*, especially in the dense many-flowered capitulum, smallish many-cleft corolla, numerous stamens and cells of the ovary, yet that it is quite distinct in the smaller cuspidate leaves, white and scaly beneath, and in the deeply ten-lobed corolla. ED.

[2] The term *membranous* is of course used comparatively here; in no species is the foliage truly so,—*less coriaceous* were the better, though more cumbrous, term.

[3] Dr. Hooker had here stated of *R. argenteum*, that *R. Griffithianum*, Wight, in Calcutta Journal of Natural History, vol. viii. p. 176, is probably a close ally of this; but that has since been published in Dr. Wight's Icones Plant. Indiæ Orientalis, vol. iv. p. 6. t. 1201, and proves to belong to, or rather to constitute, a very distant section, having very lax racemose flowers, a nearly entire, spreading, scutelliform calyx (quite unlike that of any other species), many (15 ?) stamens, and ten cells to the ovary. It is a native of Bootan. ED.

The Neelgherries, Ceylon, and the Malay Archipelago contain, each, some species which prove the affinity of their Floras to that of the Himalaya. The same is the case with the great mountains of Northern Asia, Central, Southern, and, especially, Eastern Europe, the Ural, and Pontus. The genus extends even to the Polar regions, diminishing in the size of the species and number as we recede from the Himalaya: in North America they appear again, though under a very different aspect from that they present on the subtropical mountains of Asia.

Wide though this distinction is, it is far from uniform, the Himalaya itself offering most remarkable anomalies. My friend Dr. Thomson (now engaged in a botanical mission to Thibet) informs me that the genus is not found in Cashmere; nor, during all the wanderings of that intrepid and indefatigable naturalist in the Trans-Sutledge Himalaya and Thibet, has he met with one representative of it. He detected, indeed, in the country south of the Chenaub, both the *R. arboreum* and *R. campanulatum*, and which is probably their western limit.

In North-west India, the genus *Rhododendron* is first seen on the Kunawur hills, and advancing east, follows the sub-Himalayan range for its whole length, the species increasing in number as far as Sikkim and Bootan; thence the genus is continued to the Mishmee hills, the eastern extremity of the range, crossing the Brahmaputra to that lofty range which divides the water-shed of the Irawaddi from that of the Brahmaputra.

Though scarcely found, throughout this long line of upwards of 1,200 miles, below 4,000 feet, the Rhododendrons still affect a warm and damp climate, where the winters are mild. The English naturalist, who is only familiar with the comparatively small hardy American and European species, would scarcely expect this. A certain degree of winter-cold and perpetual humidity is necessary; but the summer-heat is quite tropical where some of the genus prevail, and snow rarely falls and never rests on several of those peculiar to Sikkim.

R. arboreum, according to Captain Madden, inhabits various localities between 3,000 and 10,000 feet: this is in Kamaoon, where, of course, the genus would descend lowest; and the range is incomparably greater than that of any other species, at least of those found in Sikkim.[4] Dr. Griffith, after extended wanderings in Bootan, gives the limits of the genus in that country as between 4,292 and 12,478 feet, which is a lower level by 3,000 feet than they are known to descend to in Sikkim. In the extreme east of Assam, where the Himalaya itself diverges or sends lofty spurs to stem the Brahmaputra, on the Phien Pass to Ava, Rhododendrons ascend from 5,400 to 12,000 feet, to the upper limit of arboreous vegetation, and perhaps still higher.

During my limited excursions in Sikkim, I gathered eleven species (and I believe that more exist), a greater number than Griffith obtained in Bootan; so that I cannot but regard this longitude as the head-quarters of the genus in the Himalaya, and that chain as the especial region of the genus in the Old World. Here too I may remark (as is the case with the *Coniferæ* of Tasmania and *Cacteæ* of Mexico), the species are most limited in habitat, where, numerically, the genus is the largest, the *R. arboreum*, however, having a much wider range than any other species found in Sikkim.

[4] Dr. Hooker had here inserted "where *R. arboreum* is unknown," that is, in Sikkim. But one of his own excellent figures, sent home as representing a new species, is, I have no hesitation in saying, the true *R. arboreum*, coinciding entirely with the original figure of Sir James E. Smith (Exotic Botany, Tab. 6), and with original specimens given me by the same distinguished botanist and existing in my own Herbarium. Nor need we be surprised that Dr. Hooker should have fallen into this error, with few books and no authentic specimens to consult; especially when it is borne in mind that his eye had been accustomed to the plants that pass under that name in our gardens, but which have been so hybridized by cultivators, either to increase their beauty or with the intention of rendering the offspring more hardy, that an original plant or tree of *Rhododendron arboreum* is almost as rare in England as is the normal single-flowered state of the *Corchorus* (*Kerria*) *Japonica*. Let it be further observed that other distinguished Botanists have confounded distinct species with the *R. arboreum*: I allude especially to the plant so called by Dr. Wight of the Neelgherries (Icones Plant. Ind. Orient. tab. 1201), which is the *R. Nilagiricum* of Zenker (Plant. Nilag. cum Ic., and of Bot. Mag. tab. 4381). No one who compares native specimens of these two plants can have any hesitation in pronouncing them distinct. ED.

Westward again, as far, indeed, as the western termination of the Himalaya, the species descend lower than in Bootan: an anomalous fact, for which, in our ignorance of the contrasting features which may distinguish the Eastern from the Central Himalaya, I can only assign conjectural causes. Among these may be the proximity of the ocean to the Sikkim portion of the range, and the presence of heavy mountain-masses covered with winter, and even perpetual, snow, to the south and east of the upper extremity of the Brahmaputra, whereas the genus is found nearly 2,000 feet lower than in Sikkim. The descent of the snow line in Upper Assam to 14,000 or 15,000 feet, is no doubt due to the same causes, and this is a most remarkable fact. Uniformity of temperature, excessive humidity, and a broken surface, produce the same effect here as in the high southern and antarctic latitudes,—favouring the formation of snow and its permanence, and also extending the range of tropical forms upwards to a greater elevation, and the descent of temperate or arctic forms to a lower one; of which no stronger proof can be required than the descent of *Rosaceæ* and *Ericeæ*, and the great elevation which *Rafflesia*, *Balanophora*, and other eminently tropical genera, attain on the Himalaya.

Too much stress cannot be laid upon this fact, that the snow-line ascends with the latitude on the Himalaya, from 14,500 feet at its south-east extreme in Upper Assam, south of the Brahmaputra, lat. 27° N., to 20,000 feet at its north-west extreme in the regions near and beyond the Sutledge, in lat. 36° and 37° N. Had the level of perpetual snow remained uniform throughout these 600 miles of northing, then climate would have only annihilated the effect of distance from the equator. But if we allow that, *cæteris paribus*, a degree of latitude is the index of a change of 300 feet in the snow-line, we must also allow that the limit of perpetual snow is 8,000 feet lower in Upper Assam than its height on the Sutledge Himalaya would indicate, being 15,000 instead of 23,000 feet; and, *vice versâ*, that if 14,500 is that limit at Assam, as determined by latitude alone, in Kunawur we should have it at 11,000 instead of 20,000.

Only four species, *R. Dalhousiæ*, *R. Campbelliæ*, *R. argenteum*, and *R. arboreum* grow near Darjeeling. The second and fourth form scattered bushes at 7,500 and 8,000 feet: the *R. argenteum* is a small tree, at 8,000 and 9,000 feet, strangely associated with *Balanophora*, *Convallaria*, *Paris*, *Sphæropteris*, *Laurus*, and *Magnolia*.

It was on the ascent of Tonglo, a mountain on the Nepalese frontier, that I beheld the Rhododendrons in all their magnificence and luxuriance. At 7,000 feet, where the woods were still dense and subtropical, mingling with Ferns, *Pothos*, Peppers, and Figs, the ground was strewed with the large lily-like flowers of *R. Dalhousiæ*, dropping from the epiphytal plants on the enormous Oaks overhead, and mixed with the egg-like flowers of a new Magnoliaceous tree, which fall before expanding and diffuse a powerful aromatic odour, more strong, but far less sweet, than that of the *Rhododendron*. So conspicuous were these two blossoms, that my rude guides called out, " Here are lilies and eggs, Sir, growing out of the ground!"—No bad comparison. Passing the region of Tree-Ferns, Wallnut, and Chestnut, yet still in that of the Alder, Birch, large-leaved Oak (whose leaves are often eighteen inches long), we enter that of the broad-spathed *Arum* (which raises a crested head like that of the Cobra de capel), the *Kadsura*, *Stauntonia*, *Convallaria*, and many *Rosaceæ*. The paths here are much steeper, carried along narrow ridges or over broken masses of rock, which are scaled by the aid of interwoven roots of trees. On these rocks grow *Hymenophylla*, a few *Orchideæ*, *Begonia*, *Cyrtandraceæ*, *Aroideæ* of curious forms, the anomalous genus *Streptolirion* of Edgeworth, and various *Cryptogamiæ*, and the *Rhododendron arboreum* is first met with, its branches often loaded with pendulous mosses and lichens, especially *Usnea* and *Borrera*. Along the flat ridges, towards the top, the Yew appears with scattered trees of *Rhododendron argenteum*, succeeded by *R. Campbelliæ*. At the very summit, the majority of the wood consists of this last species, amongst which and next in abundance occurs the *R. barbatum*, with here and there, especially on the eastern slopes, *R. Falconeri*.

Mingled with these are *Pyri, Pruni*, Maples, Barberries, and Azaleas, *Olea, Ilex, Limonia, Hydrangea*, several *Caprifoliaceæ, Gaultheria,* and *Andromeda;* the Apple and the Rose are most abundant. *Stauntonia*, with its glorious racemes of purple flowers, creeps over all; so do *Kadsura* and *Ochna;* whilst a Currant, with erect racemes, grows epiphytally on *Rhododendron* and on *Pyrus*.

The habits of the species of *Rhododendron* differ considerably, and, confined as I was to one favourable spot by a deluge of rain, I had ample time to observe four of them. *R. Campbelliæ*, the only one in full flower early in May, is the most prevalent, the ropes of my tent spanning an area between three of them. Some were a mass of scarlet blossom, displaying a sylvan scene of the most gorgeous description. Mr. Nightingale's[1] Rhododendron groves, I thought, may surpass these in form and luxuriance of foliage, or in outline of individual specimens; but for splendour of colour those of the Himalaya can only be compared with the *Butea frondosa* of the plains. Many of their trunks spread from the centre thirty or forty feet every way, and together form a hemispherical mass, often forty yards across and from twenty to fifty feet in height! The stems and branches of these aged trees, gnarled and rugged, the bark dark-coloured and clothed with

[1] At Embley near Romsey, Hants, the seat of William Edward Nightingale, Esq., whose beautiful grounds boast of drives through what may really be called woods or groves of Rhododendrons, many of them self-sown.—The mention of these grounds (adorned with exotic Rhododendrons) by a naturalist luxuriating amidst the aboriginal species of the lofty mountains of Sikkim-Himalaya, makes me desirous to introduce here a brief notice of the plants in question. I could not trust my own memory for a correct statement of what it has been my privilege to see, but Miss Nightingale has obligingly communicated to me the following particulars :—

"Our Rhododendrons were chiefly planted about thirty years ago: the largest number are in an exceedingly wet 'bottom' of deep black peat full of drains, sheltered with sloping banks of Birch and Fir, with a good deal of Laurel, large Kalmias and Azaleas near the road. This part was originally a nursery-garden of about four acres: the shrubs have been cut continually to keep the road clear, and now make a bank seventeen or eighteen feet high. They are scattered over the high ground (a dry black sand) for about two miles, where they cover another bank of heathery soil and another bottom of the deep peat. There are not above a dozen of the *R. maximum* amongst them, and about three times as many of the *arboreum* and hybrid Scarlets which we find quite hardy, but which seem to flower best in the high and dry situations. The *Ponticum* and var. *roseum* seed themselves to a great extent, and the consequence is an immense variety in the shape, size, and colour of the flowers, hardly any two plants being quite alike.

"The largest single Rhododendron is one hundred and fifty feet round and twenty feet high: there are several of ninety-seven and ninety-eight feet round, but these have been cramped for room by their neighbours. The tallest I can find grows between a Birch and a Portugal Laurel, and is twenty-five feet high, its single upright stem measuring nineteen inches in circumference. It is quite an exception, for they fork generally immediately on emerging from the ground; and though there is one which measures five feet ten inches in the girth of its trunk an inch from the ground, yet as he leaves his good ways and divides immediately after, I am not sure you will grant him his diploma as a tree. The forks are from eighteen inches to two feet in circumference. The variegated kind, with long footstalks to the flowers, has perhaps the thickest stem with us. The outside branches of the large individuals root themselves all round and make impenetrable thickets. We plant out the seedlings, which come up very thickly wherever an open space gives them room, and they are now scattered over most of the wild ground about.

"I think this is pretty nearly all we have to tell, but we may add that the Kalmias and Yellow Azaleas are some of them ten feet high and wide in proportion."

It may be interesting to record some particulars of another favoured spot for Rhododendrons, namely, Penllergare, Glamorgan, the seat of Dillwyn Llewellyn, Esq., who writes in reply to my queries :—

"The soil and climate of this district suit that class of plants well, as is attested by the seedlings of the common *Rhododendron Ponticum*, which appear in thousands throughout our woods. The rough sketch I enclose is of this species: it measures in height fifteen feet ten inches, and completely covers a circumference of one hundred and ten feet. The plant grows by itself upon a lawn, without any trees to overshadow or interfere with it, and it forms a perfectly symmetrical and compact shrub, with dense foliage and short-jointed wood.

"We have also a specimen of *R. arboreum*, var. *roseum*, nine feet four inches in height, and in circumference forty-eight feet : it was planted fifteen years ago and has never received the slightest protection. Like the last, it stands alone on a lawn, and is of a beautifully compact form. It has 3,200 flower-buds now upon it. The single stem from which it rises measures one foot nine inches in girth.

"The American species also flourish here with great vigour. A specimen of *R. Catawbiense* measures nine feet six inches in height, and covers forty-one feet six inches of circumference: this, however, is much younger than either of the preceding. It is also growing under the shade of large oak-trees, for which reason it is somewhat drawn and not so fine and thick in its growth as it might otherwise have been."

It may be observed that Mr. Loudon, in his Arboretum Britannicum, has not described any specimens of *Rhododendron arboreum* of the size above given. The largest he has noticed are at Wimbledon House, thirty-three feet in the spread of its branches; at Cuffnells in Hampshire, thirty-nine feet ditto; Woburn Abbey, twenty-eight feet ditto; Shipley Hall, Derbyshire, fifty-six feet ditto, and sixteen feet the greatest height. ED.

spongy moss, often bend down and touch the ground: the foliage, moreover, is scanty, dark green, and far from graceful; so that notwithstanding the gorgeous colouring of the blossoms, the trees when out of flower, like the *Fuchsias* of Cape Horn, are the gloomy denizens of a most gloomy region. *R. Campbelliæ* and *R. barbatum* I observed to fringe a little swampy tarn on the summit of the mountain,—a peculiarly chilly-looking, small lake, bordered with *Sphagnum*, and half-choked with *Carices* and other sedges: the atmosphere was loaded with mist, and the place seems as if it would be aguish if it could, but was checked by the cold climate. *R. barbatum* had almost passed its flowering season: it is a less abundant and smaller tree than the last mentioned, but more beautiful in the brighter green and denser foliage, clean, papery, light-coloured bark, the whole forming a more picturesque mass.

Along the north-east and exposed ridges only, grew the *R. Falconeri*, in foliage incomparably the finest. It throws out one or two trunks, clean and smooth, thirty feet or so high, sparingly branched: the branches terminated by the immense leaves, deep green above, edged with yellow, and rusty red-brown below. The flowers are smaller, but more numerous in each head than in the two last mentioned (*R. Campbelliæ* and *R. barbatum*).

The temperature of the earth in which the above species grew, was, in the middle of May, at twenty-seven inches below the surface where the roots are chiefly developed, $49° 5'$ at all hours of the day: that of the air varied from $50°$ to $60°$.

In naming the new species before me of this eminently Himalayan genus, I have wished to record the services of some of those gentlemen who, besides Mr. Griffith (to whom a species had been already dedicated by Dr. Wight), have most deeply studied the vegetable productions of the country: they are Drs. Wallich, Royle, and Falconer. With their names that of Dr. Campbell, the Political Resident at Darjeeling, author of various excellent Essays on the Agriculture, Arts, Products, and People, &c., of Nepal and Sikkim, is no less appropriately associated; and in compliment to his amiable Lady I designate that Rhododendron which is most characteristic of Darjeeling vegetation; while to the Lady of the present Governor-General of India, I have, as a mark of grateful esteem and respect, dedicated the noblest species of the whole race. *J. D. H.*

Tab. II

J.D.H. del. Fitch, lith.

Reeve, Benham & Reeve, imp.

RHODODENDRON DALHOUSIÆ, Hook. fil.

RHODODENDRON DALHOUSIÆ, *Hook. fil.*

Lady Dalhousie's Rhododendron.

Tab. I., II.

Frutex gracilis, ramis remotis verticillatis vage patentibus, foliis obovato-ellipticis obtusis coriaceo-membranaceis subter pallidioribus sparse rufo-punctatis, basi in petiolum attenuatis, floribus (amplis albis) 3–7 capitato-umbellatis, lobis calycinis foliaceis oblongis obtusis, corolla campanulata basi profunde 5-foveolata, staminibus 10 filamentis inferne pilosis, ovario 5-loculari.

Hab. Parasitical on the trunks of large trees, especially Oaks and Magnolias. Sikkim-Himalaya: elevation 7,000–9,500 feet. *Fl.* April to July.

A straggling *shrub*, six to eight feet high, always seen growing, like the tropical *Orchideæ*, among moss and Ferns and *Aroideæ*, upon the trunks of large trees : the *stems* clothed with a reddish papery bark, the *branches* straggling, patent, whorled, the whorls distant; each branch bearing its leaves and flowers only at the extremity. *Leaves* few, patent or reflexed, petiolate, about four inches and a half to five in length, elliptical-obovate, between coriaceous and membranaceous, obtuse at the base, attenuated below into a more or less downy *footstalk*, about half an inch long, the margin plane (not revolute), the upper surface darkish-green, inclining to a yellow hue, even on the surface, beneath paler, dotted with very minute, scattered, rusty-coloured scales or points (scarcely sufficient to change the general tint), the mid-rib prominent, the rather close parallel *nerves* scarcely so. *Flowers* three to seven in a terminal, umbellate *head*, the spread of which is greater than that of the leaves. *Peduncles* nearly an inch long, stout, cylindrical, downy. *Bracteas* ligulate, membranaceous. *Calyx* large, deeply divided almost to the base into five ovato-elliptical, very obtuse, spreading, foliaceous lobes. *Corolla* very large, three inches and a half to four inches and a half long, and as broad at the mouth, campanulate, white, with an occasional tinge of rose, in size and colour and general shape almost resembling that of the white Bourbon Lily, *Lilium candidum*, very fragrant. At the contracted base of the tube are five deep foveolæ. *Lobes* of the *limb* nearly equal, very broad, rounded, waved, spreading. *Stamens* ten : *filaments* longer than the tube, curved upwards, downy below. *Anther* oblong-ovate, dark purple-brown. *Ovary* ovate, furfuraceous, five-celled, tapering into the thickened *style*, which is longer than the stamens. *Stigma* an orbicular, convex disk.

Certainly, whether we regard the size, the colour, or the fragrance of the blossoms of this plant, they are the noblest of the genus *Rhododendron*. The odour partakes of that of the Lemon. In age the flowers assume a delicate roseate tinge and sometimes become spotted with orange, which rather adds to, than detracts from, their beauty.

Tab. I. Represents a plant of *R. Dalhousiæ*, on a very reduced scale, in its native locality.

Tab. II. Flowering branch. 1. Stamen. 2. Anther. 3. Pistil :—*natural size.* 4. Section of ovary. 5. Pollen with boyau :—*magnified.*

Tab. III.

J.D.H. del. Fitch, lith.

Reeve, Benham & Reeve, imp

RHODODENDRON BARBATUM, Wall.

RHODODENDRON BARBATUM, *Wall.*

Bristly Rhododendron.

Tab. III.

Arboreum, foliis elliptico-lanceolatis acutis basi obtusis coriaceis marginibus subrecurvis utrinque glaberrimis subtus pallidioribus supra impresse venosis, petiolo tuberculoso longe ramulisque glanduloso-setosis, bracteis alabastrisque viscidis, floribus dense capitatis mediocribus sanguineis, lobis calycinis foliaceis viscidis ovato-ellipticis appressis, staminibus 10, filamentis glabris, ovarii glanduloso-hirsuti loculis 5–8.

RHODODENDRON barbatum. *Wall. Cat.* no. 757. *Don, Syst. Gard. and Bot.* vol. iii. p. 844. *De Cand. Prodr.* vol. vii. p. 721. *Hook. in Bot. Mag.* sub Tab. 4381; *in Gard. Chron.* 1848 (with a wood-cut).

HAB. Gossain Than, *Wallich.* Summit of Tonglo, in Sikkim-Himalaya, alt. 10,000 feet. *Fl.* April.

A *tree*, from forty to sixty feet high, branched from the base. Main *trunks* few, inclined, compressed, clothed with reddish, papyraceous *bark*, destitute of Lichens and Mosses. *Branches* numerous, floriferous at their apices. *Leaves*, in the very young state, sparingly hairy and ciliated; when fully developed, five to seven inches long, and from one and a half to two inches and more wide, elliptical-lanceolate, acute, rather broader above the middle, the margins reflexed and rough to the touch from the presence of minute harsh ciliæ, penninerved; the *nerves* sunk on the upper surface, and there dull but full green, paler and quite glabrous beneath and destitute of scales or down of every kind, but turning to an ochraceous tint when dry. *Petioles* short, (half an inch) thick, somewhat tubercled and beset with long, rigid, black *setæ* or hairs, glanduliferous at the point: these hairs or bristles often extend a little way up the mid-rib beneath. *Flowers* moderately sized, of a deep puce or blood-colour, collected into a compact, globose *head*, four to five inches in diameter. *Bracteas* oblong or ovate, the inner ones silky, all more or less glutinous. *Calyx* large, scarcely silky, deeply cut into five, erect, large, foliaceous ovate *lobes*, half an inch long. *Filaments* ten, glabrous. *Anthers* short, and, as well as the nearly straight *style*, included. *Ovary* oblong, clothed with glandular hairs. *Stigma* small, obtuse. *Fruit* setose, rich brown, included in the persistent calyx.

One of the most beautiful of the Himalayan species, and readily distinguished by the bristly petioles and young branches. [Although in cultivation in England, at least in the Upton Nursery, Chester, of Messrs. Dickson, no coloured figure has yet been published. The present one will serve to show what a treasure is in store for our open borders, seeing that it has proved perfectly hardy in the Nursery above mentioned. ED.]

TAB. III. *Rhododendron barbatum*, Wall.; flowering branch. 1. Flower and bract:—*natural size*. 2. Stamen. 3. Pistil. 4. Section of ovary:—*magnified*. 5. Capsule:—*natural size*.

Tab. IV.

J.D.H.del. Fitch.lith.

Reeve, Benham & Reeve, imp.

RHODODENDRON LANCIFOLIUM, Hook.fil.

3.

RHODODENDRON LANCIFOLIUM, <small>Hook. fil.</small>

Lance-leaved Rhododendron.

Tab. IV.

Subarboreum, ramis rugosis tortuosis, foliis oblongo-lanceolatis acutissimis coriaceis basi cordatis margine revolutis glabris, supra indistincte penninerviis viridibus subtus reticulatis luteis, petiolis tuberculoso-rugosis, floribus terminalibus capitatis majusculis puniceis, lobis calycinis late obovatis foliaceis erosis, corollis reticulatis, staminibus 10, ovario dense villoso 5–8-loculari.

Hab. Interior of Sikkim-Himalaya. *Fl.* May.

This constitutes a *shrub*, six to eight feet high, the *bark* reddish, papery, easily separating and falling off. *Branches* spreading, tortuous, wrinkled and knotted. *Leaves* chiefly at the extremities of the branches, three to four inches long, one to one inch and a half wide, coriaceous, oblong-lanceolate, very acute, the margins revolute, the base cordate, above full green, penninerved, the nerves inconspicuous, beneath reticulated and tawny or yellow brown, quite glabrous on both sides, and destitute of dots or furfuraceous scales : *petioles* half an inch long, much wrinkled and tubercled, looking as if diseased, glabrous. *Flowers* of a moderate size, collected into a rather dense *head* at the ends of the branches. *Bracteas* small. *Peduncles* glabrous. *Calyx* large, cut almost to the base into five, obovate, slightly spreading, coloured, erose, foliaceous *lobes*. *Corolla* rich puce-colour, campanulate, distinctly reticulated, five-lobed, lobes rounded, waved. *Stamens* and *pistil* included. *Ovary* elliptical, densely shaggy with hairs, five to eight-celled. *Style* slender, flexuose. *Stigma* capitate.

Allied to the preceding, *R. barbatum*, but forming a stunted shrub, with very differently shaped leaves, tawny beneath when recent, the corollas reticulated, the calyx-lobes erose, and the plant is everywhere destitute of hairs except on the ovary, which is more shaggy than that of *R. barbatum*.

Tab. IV. *Rhododendron lancifolium.* 1. Flower. 2. Pistil :—*natural size.* 3. Section of the ovary. 4. Pollen with tubes :—*magnified.*

Tab. V.

J.D.H. del. Fitch lith.

Reeve, Benham & Reeve, imp.

RHODODENDRON WALLICHII, Hook. fil.

RHODODENDRON WALLICHII, *Hook. fil.*

Dr. Wallich's Rhododendron.

Tab. V.

Frutescens, foliis coriaceis ellipticis acutis basi cordatis supra lævissimis petiolisque glaberrimis marginibus revolutis subtus pallidis costam versus punctis ferrugineis pulverulento-tomentosis, floribus 6–8 capitato-racemosis, calycibus lobis brevissimis coriaceis subacutis, ovarii glaberrimi loculis 5.

Hab. Interior of Sikkim-Himalaya.

A *shrub*, attaining a height of from eight to ten feet, with the *branches* rugged, rather tortuous, clothed with dark brown bark. *Leaves* mostly confined to the apex of the ultimate branches, three or four inches long, of a remarkably neat appearance, almost exactly elliptical, coriaceous, full green, very even, most indistinctly nerved, glabrous above, as is the somewhat wrinkled *petiole*, the base cordate, the margins recurved, the apex suddenly acute, the underside pale green, very obsoletely nerved, and quite glabrous, except towards the costa, where it is dotted as it were with dark, ferruginous, pulverulent tomentum. *Flowers* large, handsome, six to eight in a capitate *raceme*. *Pedicels* less than an inch long, glabrous. *Bracteas* deciduous, exterior ones glabrous, viscid, or sparingly downy. *Calyx* very short and small, the *lobes* triangular, rather obtuse, glabrous. *Corolla* lilac-colour; the *tube* campanulate, the *limb* spreading, of five nearly equal, rounded *lobes*, the upper one however the largest, all two-lobed, sprinkled with deeper rose-coloured dots within. *Stamens* ten, as long as the tube. *Filaments* white. *Anthers* purple-brown. *Style* filiform, longer than the stamens. *Ovary* glabrous, oblong-ovate, five-lobed, five-celled.

A very distinct and handsome species, worthy to bear the name of one who may justly be called " Botanicorum Indicorum facile princeps." Its leaves are quite unlike any Indian species, and the flowers in colour and size resemble those of the much cultivated *R. Ponticum.*

Tab. V. *Rhododendron Wallichii.* Fig. 1. Stamen. 2. Calyx and pistil. 3. Calyx and section of the ovary ;—*magnified.*

Tab. VI.

J.D.H. del. Fitch lith.

Reeve, Benham & Reeve, imp

1.

2.

3.

RHODODENDRON CAMPBELLIÆ, Hook.fil.

RHODODENDRON CAMPBELLIÆ, *Hook. fil.*

Mrs. Campbell's Rhododendron.

TAB. VI.

Arboreum, foliis coriaceis oblongo-lanceolatis acuminatis basi cordatis supra glaberrimis subtus rufo- v.-ferrugineo- tomentosis marginibus recurvis, petiolis pedunculis calyceque furfuraceis, capitulis densifloris, calycis parvi lobis brevissimis, corollæ puniceæ intus maculatæ lobis 4 rotundatis integris unico (superiore) bilobo, staminibus 10, ovario pubescente 7–10 loculari.

HAB. Sikkim-Himalaya, frequent: alt. 9,000–10,000 feet. *Fl.* April and May.

This may be called a *tree*, attaining, as it does not unfrequently, a height of forty feet, detected in various localities, at the elevation just mentioned above the level of the sea. On the summit of Tonglo it is the prevailing plant, and there, when in full flower, it exhibits a truly magnificent spectacle, gorgeous with scarlet heads of blossoms. So far as I could observe, the greater the elevation above the sea at which this species grows, the redder or more deeply ferruginous was the under-side of the leaf. This ferruginous tomentum, together with the obtuse and cordate base of the leaf, are the characters which distinguish it from *R. arboreum*, as the very different outline of the leaves does from *R. Nilagiricum*. *R. cinnamomeum*, Wall. (*R. arboreum*, var. of Lindley and De Candolle) differs in the white (perhaps not the normal) colour of the flowers, and in the two-lobed segments of all the lobes of the corolla. In the present species the peduncles, styles, and base of the filaments are red.

TAB. VI. *Rhododendron Campbelliæ.* Fig. 1. Calyx and pistil. 2. Section of ovary. 3. Stamen :—*magnified.*

6.

RHODODENDRON ARBOREUM, *Sm.*

Scarlet arborescent Rhododendron.

Subarboreum, foliis coriaceis lanceolatis subacuminatis basi in petiolum attenuatis supra glabris subtus argenteis marginibus subrecurvis, capitulis densifloris, bracteis sericeis, calycis parvi lobis brevissimis, corolla punicea fauce supra tuboque intus purpureo-maculatis, staminibus 10, ovario sericeo 8–10-loculari.

RHODODENDRON arboreum. *Smith, Ex. Bot.* p. 9. t. 6. *Lindl. in Bot. Reg.* t. 890. *Hook. Ex. Fl.* t. 168. *Don, Fl. Nep.* p. 154.

RHODODENDRON puniceum. *Roxb. Fl. Ind.* vol. ii. p. 409.

BOORANS. "*Hardw. in Trans. Asiat. Soc.* vol. vi. p. 359."

HAB. Darjeeling, and along the Himalaya, extending east, we believe, according to Mr. Griffith's notes, into Bootan, and west as far as the valley of the Chenaub, in long. 77°. *(T. Thomson.)*

[We need not occupy our space with any description of this species. An excellent drawing of it, sent by Dr. Hooker as a new species from Darjeeling, proves to be the true *R. arboreum*, the first, indeed, of the Indian *Rhododendrons* that was discovered. We can refer with confidence to the synonyms above-quoted, which is more than can be said of many that bear this name. The figure in English Botany, however, does not exhibit the under-side of the leaf; and the purplish spots or dots are omitted by the Indian artist, from whose drawing the plate was copied. Dr. Lindley's figure is very characteristic; but that by Dr. Greville, in the Exotic Flora, is particularly faithful. The distinguishing marks of this species are the almost exactly lanceolate leaves, more or less acuminated, tapering at the base into the footstalk, and clothed beneath with a compact silvery film, neither to be called silvery nor downy. ED.]

Tab VII

J.D.H. del. Fitch lith.

Reeve, Benham & Reeve, imp.

RHODODENDRON ROYLII, Hook.fil.

7.

RHODODENDRON ROYLII, *Hook. fil.*

Dr. Royle's Rhododendron.

Tab. VII.

Arbuscula, foliis coriaceis ellipticis acuminulatis margine revolutis basi obtusis subcordatis supra glaberrimis nitidis subtus ochraceo-fuscis pulverulentis, petiolis transversim rugosis, capitulis 6–8-floris, lobis (pedunculisque resinoso-glandulosis) brevissimis rotundatis, corollæ intus lineatæ segmentis rotundatis acutis, staminibus 10, ovarii puberuli loculis 5.

Hab. Sikkim-Himalaya ; mountains of the interior.   *Fl.* April and May.

This and the following species (*R. cinnabarinum*) belong to a group distinguished by the small size of the plants, the brownish-red colour of the corolla, and its nearly equal and sharp segments.   As species they are all easily recognised. The present is a *shrub*, with almost exactly oval or elliptical leaves, clothed beneath with an ochraceous-brown pulverulent substance.   *Petioles* obscurely winged.   *Flowers* in a lax *head*, from four or five to eight.   *Corolla* subcoriaceous, small, with campanulate tube, striated within, limb not much spreading, the five lobes rounded, but coming to an acute point, the points tipped with bluish-green.   In its unexpanded state, the corolla is tinged with blue.   *Peduncles* slender, short, warted as it were.   *Filaments* slightly ciliated at the base.   *Ovary* short.   *Style* and *stigma* green.

Tab. VII. *Rhododendron Roylii.*   Fig. 1. Stamen.   2. Calyx and pistil.   3. Section of ovary :—*magnified.*

Tab. VIII.

J.D.H. del. Fitch, lith.

Reeve, Benham & Reeve, imp.

RHODODENDRON CINNABARINUM, Hook.fil.

8.

RHODODENDRON CINNABARINUM, *Hook. fil.*

Cinnabar-leaved Rhododendron.

TAB. VIII.

Frutex, ramis gracilibus tortuosis, foliis ovato-lanceolatis acutis marginibus subrevolutis basi in petiolum tuberculosum attenuatis glabris, supra copiose reticulatim venosis subtus pallidis rufisve squamuloso-punctatis, floribus parvis capitatis cinnabarinis, lobis calycinis linearibus inæqualibus pedunculisque grosse glanduloso-squamosis, corollæ infundibuliformis lobis omnibus rotundatis acutis, staminibus 10, filamentis basi pilosis, ovario 5-loculari furfuraceo.

HAB. Sub-Himalaya mountains, interior of Sikkim. *Fl.* April and May.

A small *shrub*. *Leaves* two to three inches long, an inch wide, slightly tapering at both extremities, glabrous, beautifully and closely reticulated above, beneath often reddish, punctato-squamulose : the *costa* terminating in a short produced point. *Petiole* glabrous, wrinkled. *Peduncles* short, clothed, as is the calyx, with large, yellow, glandular scales. *Calyx* cut to the base into five very unequal linear lobes or segments, of which the upper one is much the longest, and almost subulate. *Corolla* small, infundibuliform, cinnabar-coloured, five-lobed, the *lobes* spreading, rounded, acute. *Ovary* oblong-ovate, glanduloso-squamose, five-celled. *Stamens* ten, included : *filaments* stout, hairy at the base. *Style* longer than the stamens, hairy below. *Stigma* capitate, five-lobed.

One of the most distinct of all the Indian Rhododendrons yet known, remarkable for its reticulated leaves and the singular colour and acute lobes of the corolla.

TAB. VIII. *Rhododendron cinnabarinum.* Fig. 1. Corolla. 2. Stamen. 3. Pistil and calyx. 4. Section of ovary, showing the five cells :— *magnified.*

9.

RHODODENDRON ELÆAGNOIDES, *Hook. fil.*

Oleaster-leaved Rhododendron.

Fruticulus ramosissimus, ramis tuberculatis subverticillatis, foliis parvis brevi-petiolatis late obovato-trapezoideis utrinque squamis orbiculatis dense furfuraceis, pedunculis solitariis fructiferis elongatis folia quintuplo superantibus, capsula oblongo-cylindracea 5-loculari 5-valvi basi segmentis calycinis ¼ brevioribus suffulta.

HAB. Mountains of Sikkim-Himalaya, at an elevation of 14–15,000 feet.

Frutex parvus lignosus valde ramosus ; ramis tortis divaricatis 4–8 uncias longis, cortice atro-fusco tuberculato tectis. *Folia* ¼ unciam longa, æquilata, coriacea, plana, obovato-trapezoidea, costa valida percursa, obtusa, basi in petiolum brevem angustata, utrinque squamulis minutis argenteo-furfuraceis ut in *Elæagno*. *Pedunculus* fructiferus uncialis, capsula erecta, 2 lineas longa.

A good many specimens of this plant were brought to me by my collectors from the neighbourhood of the snow in April, growing at about the elevation above stated ; but none in flower. A figure of it is therefore omitted ; and its affinities cannot of course be ascertained.

Tab. IX.

J.H.D. del. Fitch lith.

Reeve, Benham & Reeve, imp.

RHODODENDRON ARGENTEUM, Hook.fil.

RHODODENDRON ARGENTEUM, *Hook. fil.*

Silvery Rhododendron.

TAB. IX.

Arboreum, foliis amplis subcoriaceis obovato-oblongis acutis in petiolum crassum attenuatis planis utrinque glaberrimis subtus argenteis costa nervisque prominulis, bracteis deciduis dense sericeis, pedunculis brevibus crassis puberulis, calyce brevissimo obscure lobato, corolla (inter maximas) alba late campanulata, limbi segmentis breviusculis bilobis, staminibus 10, filamentis glabris, ovarii pubescentis loculis subsedecim, stylo flexuoso crasso, stigmate dilatato.

HAB. Sikkim-Himalaya; summit of Sinchul, Suradah, and Tonglo, elev. 8,000–10,000 feet. *Fl.* April.

A *tree* thirty feet high : *trunks* solitary, or two or three together, spreading, branched above, the *bark* pale, the *branches* leafy at the apex. *Leaves* very beautiful in the leaf-buds, erect and silky, at first enveloped in large scales, so closely imbricated and so large, as to resemble the cones of some species of pine, the outer or lower scales broad and coriaceous, glabrous, coloured (reddish-brown), the innermost ones oblong-spathulate, pubescent. When fully developed the *leaves* are among the largest of the genus, six inches to a foot long, three to five inches broad, coriaceous, nearly plane, glabrous, full green above with parallel rather closely placed nerves, beneath silvery white, with the costa and nerves prominent. *Petioles* short. *Bracteas* deciduous, densely silky. *Flowers* two to three inches long, two to two and a half inches in diameter, always white.

In the silvery underside of the foliage, but in nothing else, this resembles *R. arboreum* ; while in the much divided limb of the corolla, the ten-celled ovary, the stout flexuose style and large stigma, it approaches *R. Falconeri*, but only in those particulars. The blossoms are only second in size to *R. Dalhousiæ*. On Sinchul, the higher parts of the mountain, at from 8,000 to 9,000 feet of elevation, are more or less clothed with it : on Tonglo, as it approaches 10,000, it is suddenly replaced by the following species, *R. Falconeri*. It seems to be shy of flowering, this season at least (1848) ; for it was with difficulty I could procure sufficient specimens to complete my drawing.

TAB. IX. *Rhododendron argenteum.* Fig. 1. Stamen. 2. Pistil. 3. Section of ovary :—*magnified.*

Tab. X.

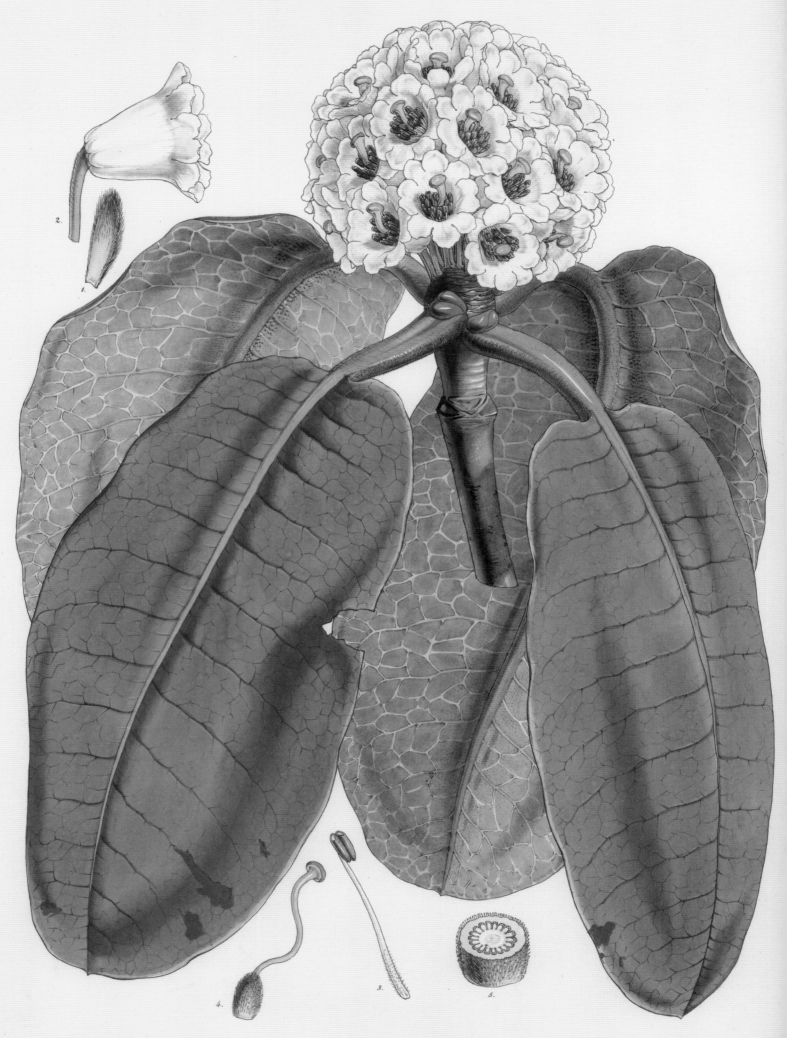

J.D.H. del. Fitch, lith.

Reeve Benham & Reeve, imp.

RHODODENDRON FALCONERI, Hook. fil.

11.

RHODODENDRON FALCONERI, *Hook. fil.*

Dr. Falconer's Rhododendron.

Tab. X.

Arboreum, foliis amplis valde coriaceis obovato-ellipticis obtusis cum mucronulo basi cordatis supra nitidis glabris reticulatim venosis subtus ferrugineis costa petiolisque validis rufo-tomentoso-furfuraceis, capitulis globosis densis multifloris, pedunculis erectis pubescenti-viscosis, floribus parvis (pro planta) albis, calyce minutissimo vix lobato, corollæ lobis 10 rotundatis, staminibus 16, ovario hirsutissimo viscoso 18-loculari, stylo flexuoso incrassato longe exserto, stigmate dilatato.

Hab. Sikkim-Himalaya. Summit of Tonglo, elev. 10,000 feet.

A *tree* thirty feet in height ; two or three *trunks* springing from the same point, and they are often two feet in diameter. The *bark* is pale and smooth : *branches* few, spreading, leafy at the points ; the young leaves clothed with velvety down, and in the state of the bud concealed by downy glutinous scales, of which the outer are subulate, the inner ovate. The perfect *leaves* are very coriaceous, from eight inches to a foot in length, five to seven inches wide, the upper side glossy green, but fading into yellow at the margins, which margins are quite plane (not recurved), beneath, except on the mid-rib and reticulated veins, clothed with a short, dense, pale, ferruginous down. *Petioles* long and very thick, plane and glabrous above, semiterete and clothed with dark rusty down beneath. *Heads* not large, but composed of numerous, rather small, white, densely placed *flowers*. *Stamens* sixteen. *Style* much exserted. *Peduncles* erect, elongated after flowering. *Capsules* erect, eight to ten-valved, hispid, an inch and a half long, with numerous cells.

If not the most showy, this is certainly one of the most striking and distinct of the genus. The noble foliage has some resemblance to that of the variety of *Magnolia grandiflora*, which has the leaves ferruginous beneath. The dense many-flowered head, the multiplication of the lobes of the corolla, and of the stamens and cells of the fruit, and the exserted style, bring it very near *R. grande*, Wight's Ic. Plant., vol. iv. tab. 1202; but the foliage is totally different.

Tab. X. *Rhododendron Falconeri.* Fig. 1. Bracteal scale. 2. Flower. 3. Stamen. 4. Pistil. 5. Section of ovary :—*magnified.*

London : Printed by Reeve, Benham, and Reeve, King William Street, Strand.

THE

RHODODENDRONS

OF

SIKKIM-HIMALAYA;

BEING

AN ACCOUNT, BOTANICAL AND GEOGRAPHICAL, OF THE

RHODODENDRONS RECENTLY DISCOVERED IN THE MOUNTAINS OF EASTERN HIMALAYA,

FROM

DRAWINGS AND DESCRIPTIONS MADE ON THE SPOT,

DURING A GOVERNMENT BOTANICAL MISSION TO THAT COUNTRY;

BY

JOSEPH DALTON HOOKER, R.N., M.D., F.R.S., F.L.S.,

&c., &c., &c.

EDITED BY

SIR W. J. HOOKER, K.H., D.C.L., F.R.S., F.L.S., &c.

Vice-President of the Linnean Society, and Director of the Royal Gardens of Kew.

PART II.

LONDON:

REEVE AND BENHAM, HENRIETTA STREET, COVENT GARDEN.

1851.

PRINTED BY REEVE AND NICHOLS, HEATHCOCK COURT, STRAND.

PREFACE.

IN the few remarks it seemed necessary to offer as introductory to the " Fasciculus of the Rhododendrons of Sikkim-Himalaya," we made the statement that the author of that work, during a limited sojourn in the country and under many difficulties and privations, had been able to detect there no less than eleven different species of *Rhododendron*, of which nine were considered new. A longer sojourn in the country, and more extended travels, and excursions to the more elevated regions of this vast mountain-chain, on the part of Dr. Hooker, have now brought to light no less than forty-three species, natives of Sikkim-Himalaya! many of which even exceed, in the size and beauty of their flowers or their foliage, the handsomest of those which had been previously discovered. Seeds, too, of a large proportion of these, have been sent to the Royal Gardens of Kew, and have arrived in so good a state, that we have been eminently successful in rearing them. Of all, accurate descriptions were drawn up on the spot; a great number of drawings were made, and Messrs. Reeve and Benham have readily acceded to the wish of the author to publish two more Fasciculi each of ten plates ;—the plates executed with the same degree of skill and care, and coloured with the same fidelity to nature, as the preceding ones.

Not content with drawing and describing the species that fell under his own observation in India, Dr. Hooker has occupied himself with a hastily compiled *Conspectus* of all the species known to inhabit *continental India*, and in this we find forty-three species, arranged in eight groupes or divisions. This Conspectus we give in the present portion of the work, and by which it will be seen what species are to appear in the third and last Fasciculus.—ED.

ROYAL GARDENS, KEW,
February 1, 1851.

THE

RHODODENDRONS

OF

SIKKIM-HIMALAYA.

CONSPECTUS SPECIERUM INDIÆ ORIENTALIS.

I. *Calyx obsolete. Corolla broadly campanulate, hemispherical at the base. Stamens 18–20 (rarely 10). Ovary usually glanduloso-pubescent and villous, many (10–20) celled.—Trees. Leaves ample. Flowers white or pale purple, capitate, often crowded.*

1. R. *Falconeri*, Hook. fil. Tab. X.

   Hab. Sikkim-Himalaya; outer and inner ranges. Mountain-tops and valleys. Elev. 10–12,000 feet.

   Note. The natural size of the flowers of this species is often as great as that given for the magnified figure (fig. 2) in the plate quoted, in which case the capitula are fewer-flowered. Leaves often fifteen inches long and eight broad. Capsule densely villoso-tomentose, oblong-cylindrical, obtuse, slightly curved, an inch and a half long, half an inch wide. Seeds pale-brown.

2. R. *argenteum*, Hook. fil. Tab. IX.

   Hab. Sikkim-Himalaya; inner and outer ranges. Elev. 8,000–10,000 feet. It flowered very abundantly in April of 1849.

   Note. Stamens generally eighteen in number. Capsules puberulous, oblong-cylindrical, obtuse at both ends, one and a half to two inches long. Seeds pale.

3. R. *Hodgsoni*, Hook. fil. Tab. XV.

   Hab. Sikkim-Himalaya. Elev. 10–12,000 feet.

4. R. *grande*, Wight, Icon. t. 1202.

   Hab. Bhootan, *Griffith*.

B

II. *Calyx cupular, hemispherical or scutelliform, obsoletely lobed. Corolla campanulate, 5-lobed. Stamens 10–16. Ovary 6–16-celled.—Large flowering shrubs. Leaves very glabrous.*

5. R. *Aucklandii*, Hook. fil. TAB. XI.

HAB. Sikkim-Himalaya. Elev. 7–9,000 feet, rare.

6. R. *Griffithii*, Wight, Icon. t. 1203.

HAB. Bhootan, *Griffith*.

7. R. *Thomsoni*, Hook. fil. TAB. XII.

HAB. Sikkim-Himalaya. Elev. 11–13,000 feet, abundant.

8. R. *Candelabrum*, Hook. fil. TAB. XXIX.

HAB. Sikkim-Himalaya. Elev. 11–13,000 feet.

III. *Calyx subfoliaceous, 5-partite, lobes submembranaceous. Corolla infundibuliform or campanulate, tube elongated. Stamens 10–18. Ovary 5–6-celled.—Shrubs; frequently Epiphytes. Flowers white. Leaves generally lepidote beneath.*

9. R. *Dalhousiæ*, Hook. fil. TAB. I. II.

HAB. Sikkim-Himalaya; outer and inner ranges. Elev. 6,000–9,000 feet. *Fl.* May, June; *fr.* October.

Note. Gemmæ terminal, strobiliform, one and a half to two inches long; scales broad-orbicular, concave, very coriaceous, almost woody, pale-tawny, glabrous, ciliated towards the apex. Leaves glanduloso-punctate and rough with squamules. Petioles sometimes setose. Capsules large, woody, linear-oblong, rufous, slightly curved, muticous, 5-angled, punctato-glandulose, the valves linear, recurved at the apex, obscurely keeled at the back, the axis terminated by the persistent style. Seeds pale yellow.

10. R. *Edgeworthii*, Hook. fil. TAB. XXI.

HAB. Sikkim-Himalaya. Elev. 7–9,000 feet.

11. R. *barbatum*, Wall., Hook. fil. TAB. III.

HAB. Gossaing-Than, Nepal, *Wallich*. Sikkim-Himalaya. On spurs of mountains, and in valleys. Elev. 9,000–11,000 feet.

Note. Branches, peduncles, and calyces glabrous or setose. Leaves beneath quite glabrous or sub-villous. Capsules generally glandulose, rarely quite glabrous, glands stipitate. Very variable in the degree of hairiness, but otherwise a well-marked species.

12. R. *lancifolium*, Hook. fil. TAB. IV.

HAB. Sikkim-Himalaya. Elev. 8–10,000 feet.

Note. Probably only a glabrous small-flowered and small-leaved variety of *R. barbatum.*

13. R. *ciliatum*, Hook. fil. (n. sp.) TAB. XXIV.

HAB. Sikkim-Himalaya. Lachen and Lachoong valleys. Elev. 9–10,000 feet.

14. R. *glaucum*, Hook. fil. TAB. XVII.

HAB. Sikkim-Himalaya. Chola, Lachen, and Lachoong passes. Elev. 10–12,000 feet.

15. R. *vaccinioides*, Hook. fil. (n. sp.); fruticulus laxe vage ramosus, caulibus ramisque gracilibus tuberculatis ultimis petiolis pedunculis foliisque subtus sparse squamulosis, foliis coriaceis obovatis obtusis emarginatisve superne glaberrimis subter pallidioribus, pedicellis subterminalibus solitariis gracilibus, lobis calycinis ovatis obtusis, capsula parva gracili curvata 5-loculari, valvis submembranaceis.

HAB. Sikkim-Himalaya; epiphytal, or growing on moist rocks, in very damp places, on the inner and outer ranges. Alt. 6–8,000 feet. *Fl.* ?

A small, very slender, straggling species, sometimes pendulous from trunks of trees, and then two feet long, of of a bright green colour, and so like a common Sikkim species of *Vaccinium* (*V. obovatum*, Wight, Icon. t. 1193) as not to be distinguishable at first sight.

Stems no thicker than a dove's quill, scabrid with tubercles, indicating the former position of scales, which still clothe the ramuli, petioles, and, more sparingly, the under surface of the foliage. *Leaves* coriaceous, three-fourths to one inch long, obovate or even spathulate, the lamina produced downwards to the very base of the petiole; upper surface a bright green, lower paler. *Peduncles* of the fruit as long as the leaves, slender. *Calyx* small, but manifestly foliaceous. *Capsules* curving, narrow, pale-coloured, and membranous, an inch long, scarce one-eighth of an inch in diameter, valves linear, torulose, a little scaly on the back. *Seeds* pale-coloured.

I have never found the flowers of this singular and very distinct little species.

16. R. *pumilum*, Hook. fil. TAB. XIV.

HAB. Sikkim-Himalaya. Zemu and T'hlonok rivers, rare. Elev. 12–14,000 feet.

IV. *Calyx small or obsolete, rarely 5-toothed, lobes equal. Corolla campanulate, or with the limb contracted below its base, and subinfundibuliform. Stamens 10. Ovary 5–10-celled.—Shrubs, generally glabrous or clothed beneath, sometimes lepidote.*

17. R. *arboreum*, Sm. *Exot. Flora*, t. 6. (supra p. 6), *not Wight, Ic.* t. 1201.

HAB. Himalaya Mountains: from Bhootan to the western extremity. Elev. 5–8,000 feet.

18. R. *Campbelliæ*, Hook. fil. TAB. VI. R. Nilagiricum, *Hook. Bot. Mag.* t. 4381 (*not Zenker*).—*var. β.* flore albo. R. arboreum, album, *Wall. Ic. Rar. Ind. Or.* vol. ii. p. 23. t. 123 ?

HAB. Sikkim-Himalaya; on both the outer and inner ranges, at elevations of from 7–10,—and even 11,000 feet.— β. Mountain of Sheopore in Nepal. *Dr. Wallich.*

Note. It has been already stated that the chief difference between this and *R. arboreum* consisted in the rusty dull (unpolished) tomentum of the underside of the leaf of *R. Campbelliæ*, as compared with the silvery compact filmy clothing of the latter. Dr. T. Thomson assures me that in Western Himalaya, where *R. arboreum* is so common, it is never otherwise than silvery and white beneath. Since I have seen the figure of *R. Nilagiricum* in the Botanical Magazine, Tab. 4381, I am quite disposed to consider the present species identical with that, exactly agreeing with that in the shape of the leaves, as well as in other characters, and since that is acknowledged to have differently-formed leaves from the true *R. Nilagiricum* of Zenker, and also said to be from Nepal, not from the Neelgherries, we can hardly doubt but that it may safely be brought as a synonym to our *R. Campbelliæ*: perhaps, also, Dr. Wallich's *R. nobile* (Wall. Cat. n. 1521, excluding 2) is not different, but this is nowhere accurately described, and possibly *R. cinnamomeum* (which by many is considered a variety of *R. arboreum*) of the same author, from Nepal. I have not seen *R. Campbelliæ* below 7,000 feet, whereas *R. arboreum, verum*, ranges from 5,000 to 8,000 feet.

19. R. *Nilagiricum*, Zenker, *Plant. Nilag. cum Ic.* (*not Hook. Bot. Mag.* t. 4381). R. arboreum, *Wight, Ic.* t. 1201 (*not Sm.*) R. nobile, *Wall. Cat.* n. 1521. 2 (*not* 1).

HAB. Neelgherry hills, abundant. *Wight, Zenker, and others.*

Note. Difficult as it may be to define the characters of this species in words, yet we believe that no one can see our native specimens in the herbarium without feeling assured that it is a distinct species, and truly different from any found in the north of India.   There is a peculiarity in the firm and hard texture of the broad foliage, with its strongly recurved margins, and the deeply impressed venation and opake green colour; and a still stronger distinguishing mark is in the almost globose strobilus, formed by the scales of the united flowers while in young bud, and which is admirably represented in Dr. Wight's plate above quoted.   The nearest approach to this is in the *Rhododendron* from Adam's Peak and other mountains of Ceylon, which, I believe, has never been described, though it has been considered, while there was believed to be only one *tree* Rhododendron in India, as *R. arboreum*, and it is cultivated in nurseries under the name of *R. Zeylanicum*.   This has darker foliage than *R. Nilagiricum*, and is much larger in all its parts.

20. R. *nobile*, Wall. *Cat.* n. 1521 (not 2, which is *R. Nilagiricum*).

HAB. Kamaon.   *Dr. Wallich.*

21. R. *niveum*, Hook. fil.; arbuscula vage ramosa, cortice fusco rugoso, ramulis pubescentibus, foliis obovato-lanceolatis breve petiolatis obtusis v. subacutis super glaberrimis opacis subter petioloque tomento appresso niveo (rarius fuscescente) lanatis, capitulis densissimis, pedicellis brevibus, calyce obsoleto, capsulis oblongo-cylindraceis tomentosis utrinque obtusis 6-locularibus, valvis lignosis, seminibus pallidis.

HAB. Sikkim-Himalaya; rocky valleys and ridges, Lachen, Lachoong, and Chola; elev. 10–12,000 feet, not unfrequent.   *Fl.*? *Fr.* November.

A small rugged-barked tree, having the habit and general appearance of *R. arboreum*, with which and *R. Campbelliæ* it grows frequently intermixed, but may be distinguished, even at a distance, by the snow-white under-surface of the leaf.   On a closer inspection this is seen to be caused by an appressed flocculent tomentum, occupying both surfaces of the very young leaf, and sometimes of a rusty-red hue.   In the two quoted allies the the leaf is narrower and the whitish hue or silvery lustre of the under-surface of the leaf is not removable, and is generally shining.   The upper surface of the leaf of this is opake, but in *R. Campbelliæ*, polished.   *Capsules* of this shorter, more cylindrical, blunt, and straight.   I have never known these species to pass into one another. The present inhabits a much higher elevation than that usually occupied by *R. arboreum*.   The flowers I have never seen.

22. R. *formosum*, Wall., *Pl. Asiat. Rar.* vol. iii. p. 207.   *Hook. Bot. Mag.* t. 4457.   R. Gibsoni, *Hortulan.*
HAB. Mountains bordering on Silhet.   *Dr. Wallich, Mr. Griffith,* and *Mr. Gibson.*

23. R. *campanulatum*, Don, *Wern. Trans.* vol. iii. p. 409.   *Wall. Cat.* n. 756.   *Hook. Bot. Mag.* t. 1944.
HAB. Gossaing-Than in Nepal; and Kamaon.   *Wallich, Hamilton.*

24. R. *Wallichii*, Hook. fil.   TAB. V.
HAB. Sikkim-Himalaya; on spurs and in valleys of the inner and outer ranges; elev. 11–13,000 feet.   *Fl.* June; *fr.* October.

Note. Distinguished from *R. campanulatum* by the conspicuous calyx.   Leaves ferruginous or olivaceous beneath, pubescent or villous.   Capsules linear, slightly curved, nearly erect, woody, glabrous, an inch to an inch and a half long.   Seeds pale.

25. R. *Wightii*, Hook. fil.   TAB. XXVII.
HAB. Sikkim-Himalaya.   Elev. 12–14,000 feet.

26. R. *lanatum*, Hook. fil. TAB. XVI.

HAB. Sikkim-Himalaya, at Jongri and Chola. Elev. 10–12,000 feet.

27. R. *fulgens*, Hook. fil. TAB. XXV.

HAB. Sikkim-Himalaya. Elev. 12–14,000 feet.

28. R. *æruginosum*, Hook. fil. TAB. XXII.

HAB. Sikkim-Himalaya. Elev. 12–14,000 feet.

29. R. *campylocarpum*, Hook. fil. TAB. XXX.

HAB. Sikkim-Himalaya. Elev. 11–14,000 feet.

V. *Calyx short, coriaceous, 5-lobed or 5-dentate, lobes short, one (the upper) generally elongated, sometimes subulate. Corolla funnel-shaped, tube narrowed, lobes rounded or acute. Stamens 10–20. Ovary 5–10-celled.—Shrubs. Leaves lepidote beneath. Flowers closely capitate.*

30. R. *Maddeni*, Hook. fil. TAB. XVIII.

HAB. Sikkim-Himalaya. Lachen and Lachoong valleys, very rare. Elev. 6,000 feet.

31. R. *cinnabarinum*, Hook. fil. TAB. VIII.

HAB. Sikkim-Himalaya; chiefly in valleys and on the skirts of woods, elev. 10–12,000 feet, abundant. *Fl.* June; *fr.* November.

Note. Shrub six feet high, very elegant; branches and branchlets virgate. Corymb spreading. Peduncles half an inch long. Flowers pendent. Capsules small, half an inch long, ovate, obtuse.—One of the most elegant species of the genus, but very inefficiently represented at our Tab. VIII. Its pendulous or drooping flowers, when in perfection, are peculiarly graceful. It is universally considered poisonous to cattle and goats: of the latter I have seen many die, from eating either of this or of a species of *Andromeda*;—which latter is notorious for this property throughout Sikkim, Nepal, and N. W. Himalaya. If employed for fuel, the smoke of *R. cinnabarinum* causes the eyes to inflame and the cheeks to swell.

32. R. *Roylei*, Hook. fil. TAB. VII.

HAB. Sikkim-Himalaya. Elev. 10–11,000 feet.

Note. Very near, it must be confessed, to *R. cinnabarinum.*

VI. *Calyx subfoliaceous, 5-partite, lobes coriaceous or membranaceous. Tube of the corolla short, tinged at the base, the lobes patent, concave. Stamens 8–10. Style subclavate, short, decurved, valid. Stigma thickened, disciform. Ovary 5-celled.—Shrubs, often small, epiphytes or terrestrial. Leaves (except in* R. pendulum) *densely lepidote.*

33. R. *camelliæflorum*, Hook. fil. TAB. XXVIII.

HAB. Sikkim-Himalaya; generally pendent from the trunks of trees, sometimes rocks. Elev. 9–11,000 feet.

34. R. *pendulum*, Hook. fil.   Tab. XIII.

Hab. Sikkim-Himalaya; pendulous from trees, generally, rarely from rocks.   Elev. 9–11,000 feet.

35. R. *obovatum*, Hook. fil.; frutex ramosus, ramis ramulisque gracilibus, ramulis pedunculis calyce corolla extus petiolis foliisque subtus (junioribus utrinque) sparse squamuloso-ferrugineis, foliis petiolatis obovatis basi in petiolum angustatis apice rotundatis apiculatis vix coriaceis marginibus planis superne opacis subtus pallide ochraceo-brunneis, pedunculis brevibus (fructiferis elongatis) terminalibus solitariis, calycis lobis foliaceis obtusis, corolla rubro-purpurea (ut in *R. lepidoto*), staminibus 8, filamentis basi sericeo-villosis, ovario creberrime lepidoto, stylo brevi crasso, capsulis conico-ovatis abrupte truncatis 5-sulcatis 5-locularibus, valvis lignosis lepidotis.

Hab. Sikkim-Himalaya; rocky places. Lachoong valley, 12,000 feet. *Fl.* June, and again partially in September; *fr.* November.

A small shrub, 3–4 feet high, much branched, and very resinous in odour. *Branches* as stout as a duck's quill, not tortuous, but much divided, the upper scabrid where once lepidote. *Leaves* plane, membranous for the genus, of an opake green above and pale yellow-brown below, the *costa* slender, percurrent; lamina an inch and a half long, half to three-quarters of an inch broad. *Buds* nearly globular; scales orbicular, coriaceous, brown, downy on the outer surface, ciliated, the outer ones lepidote. *Pedicels* half to three-quarters of an inch long, one to one and a half inch when in fruit, very lepidote, as is the calyx, base of the corolla, and ovarium, and fruit. *Corolla* altogether like that of *R. lepidotum*. *Capsules* one-fourth to one-third of an inch long, about twice the length of the persistent calyx-lobes.

The form and size of the foliage, and its glabrous upper surface, distinguish this well from *R. lepidotum*.

[There is no original drawing of this species.—*Ed.*]

36. R. *salignum*, Hook. fil.   Tab. XXIII. A.

Hab. Sikkim-Himalaya; above Choongtam.   Elev. 7,000 feet.

37. R. *elæagnoides*, Hook. fil. (supra Fasc. I. p. 8. n. 9).   Tab. XXIII. B.

Hab. Sikkim-Himalaya; open rocky places.   Elev. 12–16,000 feet.

38. R. *lepidotum*, Wall., *Cat.* n. 738.   *Royle, Ill.* p. 260. t. 64. f. 1.

Hab. High mountains, Nepal, *Dr. Wallich, Dr. Royle.*   Sikkim-Himalaya, elev. 12–15,000 feet, *J. D. H.*

Note. A small densely-tufted shrub, a foot or so high, allied to *R. elæagnoides* and *R. obovatum*, with the flowers always on very short petioles. Its common name is " *Tsaluma*," or " *Tsuma*," amongst the Bhoteas, and its resinous odour is very strong, not unpleasant. The description in De Candolle (Prodr. v. 7. p. 724), if, as I do not doubt, it refers to this plant, is very erroneous. The leaves cannot be called " ferruginous below," in the same sense as applied to *R. anthopogon*, &c.; nor are there any setæ or cilia at the bases of the leaves; nor have I observed more than eight stamens, the typical number in this very distinct group, which includes *R. salignum*, *R. obovatum*, and *R. elæagnoides*. The flowers vary from very fine red to a dingy yellow.

VII. *Calyx subfoliaceous, 5-partite or 5-lobed, lobes short, rounded. Tube of the corolla short, funnel-shaped, lobes of the limb elongated, narrow, spreading, entire. Stamens 8, exserted: filaments elongated, slender. Style slender, much exserted. Ovary 5-celled.—Lepidote shrubs.*

39. R. *triflorum*, Hook. fil.   Tab. XIX.

Hab. Sikkim-Himalaya.   Elev. 7–9,000 feet; scarce.

40. R. *virgatum*, Hook. fil. TAB. XXVI. A.

HAB. Sikkim-Himalaya; skirts of Pine-forests. Elev. 8–9,000 feet.

41. R. *nivale*, Hook. fil. TAB. XXVI. B.

HAB. Sikkim-Himalaya; on the loftiest bare slopes on the Thibetan frontier. Elev. 16–18,000 feet.

42. R. *setosum*, Hook. fil. TAB. XX.

HAB. Sikkim-Himalaya; open stony and rocky places. Elev. 13–16,000 feet.

VIII. *Calyx 5-phyllous, lobes membranaceous. Corolla hypocrateriform, tube narrow, cylindrical, limb plane, patent. Stamens 6–8, included. Style short, clavate. Ovary 5-celled.—Small lepidote shrubs.*

43. R. *anthopogon*, Don, *Trans. Wern. Soc.* vol. iii. p. 409. *Hook. Bot. Mag.* t. 3947. R. aromaticum, *Wall. Cat.* n. 1520.

HAB. Gossaing-Than, Nepal, and Kamaon, *Wallich, Hamilton*; Sikkim-Himalaya: rocky, open, especially gravelly places, abundant. Elev. 12–16,000 feet.

Note. A strongly and far more disagreeably and heavily odorous plant than *R. setosum*. This, the *Palu* of the Bhoteas, shares with the *Tsallu* (*R. setosum*) the blame of exciting the headache and nausea attending ascents to the dreaded elevations of the Eastern Himalaya. In the Herbarium its permanent odour is more disagreeable than that of any of the genus. Nothing, however, can exceed the beauty of its flowers, whether we consider the exquisitely tender, membranaceous, translucent texture of the corolla, with its delicate nervation, or the rich blush of the first opening blossoms, which insensibly passes into snowy white, then faintly tinged with sulphur—all colours seen on one and the same plant.

Tab. X

J.D.H. del. Fitch, lith.

Reeve, Benham & Reeve

RHODODENDRON AUCKLANDII, Hook. fil.

RHODODENDRON AUCKLANDII, *Hook. fil.*

Lord Auckland's Rhododendron.

Tab. XI.

Frutex, cortice lævi pallido subpapyraceo, foliis amplis sublonge petiolatis oblongo-ovalibus acutis basi cordatis margine planis subtus vix glaucescentibus coriaceis venis divaricatis, floribus (inter maximos) 3–5 terminalibus albis, pedunculis longiusculis, calyce patelliformi-subrhomboideo inæqualiter obscure lobato, corollæ tubo late campanulato, limbo amplissimo patente, lobis 5 rotundatis emarginato-bifidis, staminibus 12–18, ovario glanduloso 12-loculari, stylo valido curvato, stigmate magno disciformi, capsula oblongo-cylindracea coriacea utrinque obtusa, valvis crassis dorso glaberrimis.

Hab. Sikkim-Himalaya; inner ranges only; elevation 7–9,000 feet, rare. *Fl.* May and June. *Fr.* October.

Seen in scattered *bushes,* four to eight feet high, branching from the base: and there the trunk is six inches in diameter. *Branches* suberect, copiously leafy. *Bark* smooth and papery. *Wood* resembling that of *R. Hodgsoni.* *Leaves* variable in size and breadth, but large for the size of the plant, four to ten inches long, coriaceous, oblong-elliptical, scarcely approaching to lanceolate, acute, cordate at the base, penninerved, the *nerves* patent, the margin plane often tinged with yellow, upper surface light full green, the under paler, slightly glaucescent, everywhere glabrous. *Petioles* two inches long. *Flowers* the largest of the genus, but variable in size, terminal, three to five together, inodorous. *Peduncles* rather slender, longer than the petioles, red or green. The *calyx* represents a shallow, concave, irregular, subrhomboid-shaped platter, an inch and a half in its longest diameter, obscurely lobed, upper lobe most elongated, the back marked with slightly elevated, radiating lines, glossy, as it were varnished. *Corolla* pure white, tinged with pink, veiny, of a firm, rather fleshy, texture: *tube* short for the size of the flower, yellowish and rose-colour towards the base, the mouth very wide, limb exceedingly large and spreading: we have measured some only three inches across, but others five inches and five inches and a half in diameter! *Stamens* twelve to eighteen, small for so large a flower: *filaments* glabrous; *anthers* obovate, ochreous brown. *Ovary* ovate, rather short, glaucous green, granulated. *Style* rather flexuose, curving upwards, terminating in a spreading, concave disc, from which the hemispherical lobed *stigma* rises. *Capsule* an inch and a half long, three-quarters of an inch broad.

It has been my lot to discover but few plants of this superb species, and in these the inflorescence varied much in size. The specimens from which our drawing was made were from a bush which grew in a rather dry sunny exposure, above the village of Choongtam, and the bush was covered with blossoms. The same species also grows on the skirts of the Pine-forests (*Abies Brunoniana*) above Lamteng, and it is there conspicuous for the abundance rather than for the large size of its blossoms.

To this fine plant I have the melancholy satisfaction of affixing the name of the late Right Honourable Lord Auckland, no less in token of my gratitude for the kindness and patronage I received from him, when First Lord of the Admiralty, than in memory of his zealous promotion of every scientific inquiry, and his liberal patronage of the arts and sciences while he filled the exalted station of Governor-General of India.

Tab. XI. *Rhododendron Aucklandii.* Fig. 1. Stamen. 2. Pistil. 3. Section of ovary:—*slightly magnified.* 4. Fruit:—*natural size.*

Tab. XII.

J.D.H. del. Fitch lith.

Reeve, Benham & Reeve, imp.

RHODODENDRON THOMSONI, Hook. fil.

RHODODENDRON THOMSONI, *Hook. fil.*

Dr. Thomson's Rhododendron.

TAB. XII.

Frutex ramosissimus, cortice pallide papyraceo, foliis in ramos terminales coriaceis glaberrimis orbiculari-ovatis obtusissimis apiculatis basi cordatis læte virentibus subtus glaucescentibus margine subrecurvo, petiolo gracili, corymbis plurifloris, pedunculis longitudine petiolorum, floribus radiatim patentibus cernuisve, calyce amplo cylindraceo-cyathiformi basi retuso inæqualiter lobato, lobis erectis obtusissimis, corolla intense sanguinea coriaceo-carnosa nitida, tubo elongato-campanuliformi, limbi lobis 5 patenti-subrecurvis profunde emarginatis superioribus intus maculatis, staminibus 10, ovario conico-cylindraceo glaberrimo 6–10-loculari, stylo gracili, stigmate conico, capsula calyce cylindraceo persistente ⅔ tecta.

HAB. Sikkim-Himalaya; inner and outer ranges; elev. 11–13,000 feet; abundant. *Fl.* June. *Fr.* November.

A *bush* six to ten feet high, or in damp woods fifteen feet, but then spare, and woody. Lower *branches* stout, a foot in diameter; upper slender, leafy at the extremities. *Leaves* two to three inches long, very broad, generally orbicular-ovate, but sometimes almost exactly orbicular, much resembling those of *R. campylocarpum*, Hook. fil., only that in the latter the petioles are often glandular, here never; the texture of the leaves is coriaceous, but not very thick, the apex very blunt, tipped with a short mucro, the base subcordate, the colour pale green, below subglaucous, everywhere quite glabrous. *Flowers* in a corymb of six to eight together from the apices of short branches among the leaves, on peduncles an inch or more long, which radiate, as it were, from a centre, spreading horizontally or curving downwards. *Calyx* large, between cylindrical and hemispherical, or deep cup-shaped, coloured red in the upper half, green below, the base intruse for the reception of the peduncle, three-quarters of an inch long and as much wide, the mouth almost truncate but obscurely lobed. *Corolla* remarkable for the almost unrivalled deep blood-red colour and glossy surface of its flowers, yielding only to *R. fulgens*, Hook. fil.,—deeper coloured than that of *R. arboreum*: the *tube* elongated, often vertically compressed, two inches long; the *limb* large, much spreading, five-lobed, the *lobes* emarginate, upper ones spotted. *Stamens* a little longer than the tube: *filaments* glabrous, white; *anthers* rather large, deep brown. *Ovary* conico-cylindrical, glabrous, furrowed, six- to eight-celled. *Capsule* rather short, straight, glaucous purple, about three-quarters of its length immersed in the persistent calyx.

The whole is perfectly inodorous. Much honey is secreted in the base of the corolla, which has the character of not being poisonous, like what is yielded by *R. Dalhousiæ* and *R. argenteum*. The two latter species are said to render wild honey, collected in spring (their flowering season), deleterious.

To this species I give the name of Dr. Thomas Thomson, surgeon, H. E. I. C. S., late of the Thibetian Mission, son of the learned Professor of Chemistry of Glasgow University, my earliest friend and companion during my College life, and now my valued travelling companion in Eastern Himalaya.

TAB. XII. *Rhododendron Thomsoni.* Fig. 1. Stamen. 2. Pistil. 3. Transverse section of ovary :—*magnified.*

Tab. XIII.

J.D.H. del. Fitch. lith.   Reeve, Benham & Reeve, imp.

RHODODENDRON PENDULUM, Hook.fil.

14.

RHODODENDRON PENDULUM, *Hook. fil.*

Pendulous Rhododendron.

Tab. XIII.

Fruticulus epiphytus pendulus, caulibus gracillimis dichotome ramosis, ramulis pedunculis petiolis brevibus foliisque subter (junioribus utrinque) tomento fulvo laxo dense vestitis, foliis elliptico-oblongis subacutis apiculatis convexis superne nitidis, pedunculis terminalibus subbinis rarius axillaribus parvis, calyce profunde 5-lobo hirsuto, lobis ellipticis submembranaceis æqualibus, corollæ albæ extus lepidotæ tubo brevissimo, limbo patente 5-lobo, lobis æqualibus subundulatis integris, staminibus 10, filamentis (nunc 2–3 basi inter se coalitis) rectis inferne dilatatis supra medium dense barbatis, antheris magnis obovatis, ovario parvo densissime fulvo-villoso, capsula brevi calycem persistentem vix superante villosa basi lepidota.

Hab. Sikkim-Himalaya; pendulous from the limbs of tall Pine-trees (*Abies Webbiana* and *Brunoniana*); elev. 9–11,000 feet, rarely found upon rocks; often covered with *Usnea*.

Stems three to four feet long, sparingly but dichotomously branched, *branches* scarcely stouter than a crow's quill: young shoots very villous. *Leaves* chiefly confined to the apices of the ultimate branches, on short *petioles*, spreading, between elliptical and oblong, acute or nearly so, and further tipped with a short mucro, smooth (never lepidote) and shining above, the margins a little recurved, an inch and a half to two inches long, and about three-quarters of an inch broad, below densely clothed with ferruginous tomentum. *Scales* of the flower-buds coriaceous, the outer lepidote, the inner villous. *Peduncles* two or three from the apex of the young leafy branches, very short, but longer than the petioles, ferruginously villous, bearing one or two linear *bracteas*. *Flowers* small. *Calyx* large in proportion to the size of the flower, deeply cut into five, oval, membranaceous lobes, lepidote below, villous. *Corolla* pure white, about an inch in diameter, externally lepidote, tube very short, gradually expanding into the nearly equally five-lobed *limb*: *lobes* rotundate, waved at the margin, entire. *Stamens* ten: *filaments* straight, sometimes more or less combined at the base, and there dilated; below the middle is a dense mass of white hairs; *anthers* large in proportion to the flower. *Ovary* ovate, densely villous, lepidote towards the base. *Style* very short, curved upwards, and thickened beneath the *stigma*, which is a convex, scarcely lobed *disc*. *Capsule* broadly ovate, acute, hairy, four to five lines long, five-celled, five-valved.

This species is inodorous, very distinct, but clearly allied to *R. camelliæflorum*, Hook. fil., the lepidote character of that species giving place to a denser fulvous or ferruginous tomentum here. In the size and colour and regular lobes of the corolla, and also in the general form of the calyx, the present may be compared with the *R. albiflorum** of the Rocky Mountains of North America, but in little else. Growing, as it does, an epiphyte, upon the trunks of trees in the gloomy and almost impenetrable forests, it is a plant very difficult of detection.

* Hook. Fl. Bor. Am. vol. ii. p. 43. f. 133.

Tab. XIII. *Rhododendron pendulum.* Fig. 1. Flower. 2. Stamens. 3. Pistil. 4. Transverse section of ovary :—*magnified.* 5. Capsule with its persistent calyx :—*natural size.*

Tab. XIV.

J.D.H. del. Fitch. lith.

Frederic Reeve, imp.

RHODODENDRON PUMILUM, Hook. fil.

RHODODENDRON PUMILUM, *Hook. fil.*

Dwarf Rhododendron.

Tab. XIV.

Fruticulus humilis laxe ramosus, ramulis foliis subter petiolis pedunculis calycibus ovariisque lepidotis, foliis parvis brevi-petiolatis lato-ellipticis coriaceis apiculatis superne glaberrimis subter precipue glaucis, pedunculis solitariis 2–3-nis elongatis erectis strictis, flore inclinato, calycis lobis ovatis obtusis, corollæ roseæ campanulatæ extus pubescentis tubo elongato, limbi lobis brevibus rotundatis integris, staminibus 10 inclusis, filamentis rectis basi hispidis, stylo rectiusculo, stigmate capitato, capsula in pedunculum magis elongatum erecta ovata 5-loculari calycem persistentem multoties superante.

Hab. Sikkim-Himalaya; on alpine slopes among ericaceous vegetation, rare; about the Zemu and T'hlonok rivers. *Fl.* June.

The smallest of all the Sikkim Rhododendrons: its slender woody *stem* roots among moss, *Andromeda fastigiata,* &c., ascends obliquely, and bears a few somewhat spreading dichotomous branches, three to four inches in length, rising above the surrounding vegetation. *Leaves* chiefly from the upper ends of the branches, half to three-quarters of an inch long, broadly elliptical, rigid, mucronate, smooth and naked and bright bluish-green above, below lepidote, as is the short petiole, and glaucous. *Bracts* of the flower-buds coriaceous, smooth and downy, and, as is usual in the lepidote species, quite destitute of glands or squamulæ. *Peduncles* moderately slender, erect, one to three from the apex of the branches, and rising an inch and a half above the base of the superior leaves, firm and woody, much elongated, and strict to the very apex in fruit. *Flower* inclined or almost drooping. *Calyx-lobes* rather short, but somewhat leafy in texture, reddish-brown, scaly, particularly towards the base. *Corolla* half to three-quarters of an inch long, rose-colour, campanulate, very delicate, externally all over down, and obscurely glandular: the *tube* rather broad, the *limb* of five, nearly equal, moderately spreading roundish *lobes,* which are quite entire. *Stamens* ten, included: *filaments* nearly straight, hispid at the base. *Ovary* ovate, densely lepidote, five-celled. *Style* rather short, thickened upwards. *Stigma* capitate, obscurely five-lobed. *Capsule* perfectly erect on the elongated strict peduncle, three-quarters of an inch long, large for the size of the plant, ovate, red-brown, five-valved.

Although the smallest among the Sikkim-Himalayan Rhododendrons, it is an extremely elegant species, and apparently of very rare occurrence: for I have never gathered it but twice, and each time in the wild district above indicated, where its elegant flowers are produced soon after the snow has melted: and then its pretty pink bells are seen peeping above the surrounding short heath-like vegetation, reminding the botanist of those of *Linnæa borealis.*

It yields a faint and agreeable odour, like that of *R. glaucum,* to which this has many points of resemblance.

Tab. XIV. *Rhododendron pumilum.* Fig. 1. Upper side of a leaf. 2. Under side. 3. Flower. 4. Stamen. 5. Calyx and pistil. 6. Transverse section of ovary:—*magnified.*

J.D.H. del. Fitch. lith.

Frederic Reeve imp.

RHODODENDRON HODGSONI, Hook. fil.

RHODODENDRON HODGSONI, *Hook. fil.*

Mr. Hodgson's Rhododendron.

Tab. XV.

Arborescens, ramis lævibus, foliis amplis petiolatis (petiolis crassis) obovato-ellipticis obtusis basi subcordatis coriaceis glaberrimis marginibus recurvis læte viridibus subtus tomento appresso subargenteo albido-glaucescentibus, capitulis magnis 15–30-floris, pedunculis brevibus tomentosis, calyce obsoleto, corollæ roseæ tubo (basi intruso) late campanulato, limbo brevi 8-lobo, lobis rotundatis æqualibus emarginatis, staminibus sub-18, filamentis gracilibus glabris, ovario pube viscido dense vestito 16-loculari, stylo elongato, stigmate disciformi radiatim lobato, capsulis anguste cylindraceis elongatis curvatis obtusis tomentosis.

Hab. Sikkim-Himalaya; on rocky spurs, and in the valleys of the outer and inner ranges; elev. 10–12,000 feet, very abundant. *Fl.* May and June; *fr.* December.

A small *tree*, from twelve feet, the average height, to twenty, branching from the base, main branches as thick as the human thigh, spreading horizontally for twenty or thirty feet each way, interwoven with the adjacent plants and shrubs. *Bark* smooth, papery, pale-flesh coloured, flaking off in broad membranous patches. *Wood* white, very close-grained, soft, yet tough, neither warping nor splitting, but, in consequence of the great compression of the larger branches, rarely affording a sample a foot in the square. *Leaf-buds* or *gemmæ* terminal, as large as a hazel-nut; their scales broadly ovate, concave, coriaceous, subtomentose, tapering into a long acuminated point. *Leaves* terminal on the ultimate branches, ample, spreading, twelve to sixteen and often eighteen inches in length, varying in form, oblong-elliptical or obovate or ovate-lanceolate, obtuse, nearly cordate at the base, of a singularly thick coriaceous texture, quite glabrous and bright glossy green above, penninerved (scarcely reticulated), the margins recurved; beneath, all, except the thickened costa, clothed with a pale silvery white, rarely ferruginous, closely appressed *tomentum*, but which is easily abraded by the finger, and is often itself evanescent. *Petioles* one to two inches or more long, very stout. *Capitula* four to six inches in diameter, of several delicate, pale purple or rose-coloured *flowers*. *Peduncles* short, viscid, often downy. *Calyx* obsolete. *Corolla* large, the tube an inch and a half long, broadly campanulate, the base depressed at the insertion upon the peduncle, the margin of the depression lobed, limb spreading, two to two and a half inches across, eight-lobed, the lobes rather short, emarginate, or obtusely bifid, reflexed. *Stamens* sixteen to eighteen, spreading: *filaments* slender, glabrous; *anthers* rather small, dark purple-brown. *Ovary* oblong-ovate, densely covered with a short, white, viscid *tomentum*, many-celled. *Style* rather short, glabrous, thickened upwards. *Stigma* a broad radiately-lobed disc. *Capsules* slightly curved, two inches long, cylindrical, striated, covered with a white loose tomentum. *Seeds* small, winged with a lax aril, jagged at both ends.

This, and the *Abies Webbiana*, I have always regarded as the characteristic tree and shrub (or underwood) at the elevation of 10 to 12,000 feet in all the valleys of Sikkim. *R. Hodgsoni*, in this respect, ranks with the *R. arboreum* and *Campbelliæ*, being typical of a loftier zone of Rhododendrons, succeeded by the arctic one of *R. anthopogon*, *R. setosum*, *R. elæagnoides*, and, finally, far above the ordinary limit of phænogamic vegetation, by *R. nivale*, which is found at an elevation of 18,000 feet above the level of the sea.

Nowhere can the traveller wander, in the limits assigned to the present species, without having his attention arrested by its magnificent foliage, larger than that of *R. Falconeri*, and remarkable for its brilliant deep green hue. In summer the leaves are broad, and spreading all round the plant; in winter rolled up, shrivelled, and pendulous from the tips of the branches. It is alike found at the bottom of the valleys, on the rocky spurs or slopes and ridges of the hills, in open places, or in the gloomy Pine-groves, often forming an impenetrable scrub, through which the explorer in vain seeks to force his way. Nor is this a thicket merely of twigs and foliage, that will fall under the knife or cutlass, but of thickset limbs and stout trunks, only to be severed with difficulty, on account of the toughness and unyielding nature of the wood.

The scentless blossoms expand late in April, and in May and June, but are not very copiously produced in comparison with the majority of its congeners.

Of the wood, cups, spoons, and ladles are made by the Bhoteas, and universally the little "Yak" saddle, by means of which the pack-loads are slung on the back of that animal. Easily worked, and not apt to split, it is admirably adapted for use in the parched and arid climate of Thibet. Nor is the foliage without its allotted use. The leaves are employed as platters, and serve for lining baskets for conveying the mashed pulp of *Arisæma* root (a kind of Colocass); and the accustomed present of butter or curd is always made enclosed in this glossy foliage.

Such are the characteristics of this Rhododendron, which I desire to dedicate to my excellent friend and generous host, B. H. Hodgson, Esq., of Darjeeling, formerly the Hon. East India Company's Resident at the Court of Nepal; a gentleman whose researches in the physical geography, the natural history, especially the zoology, the ethnology, the literature of the people, &c. &c., of Eastern Himalaya, are beyond all praise.

TAB. XV. *Rhododendron Hodgsoni.* Fig. 1. Flower:—*natural size.* 2. Stamen. 3. Pistil. 4. Section of ovary:—*magnified.* 5. Capsule:— *natural size.* 6. Seed with its aril. 7. Seed deprived of its aril. 8. Vertical section of a seed:—*magnified.*

Tab. XVI.

J.D.H. del. Fitch, lith.

Frederic Reeve, imp.

RHODODENDRON LANATUM, Hook. fil.

RHODODENDRON LANATUM, *Hook. fil.*

Woolly Rhododendron.

Tab. XVI.

Arbuscula ramosa, cortice rugoso, ramis tortis, ramulis petiolis pedunculis foliisque subter lana molli subappressa albida vel fulva dense tectis, foliis elliptico-obovatis oblongisve coriaceis brevi-petiolatis apice rotundatis apiculatis basi acutis supra (costa basinque versus lanatis exceptis) glabratis subter lana molli appressa sordide albis v. fulvis, corymbo terminali capitato plurifloro, calyce minuto 5-lobo, corollæ ochroleucæ tubo lato-campanulato intus superne rubro irrorato, limbi lobis 5 rotundatis patentibus integerrimis, staminibus inclusis, filamentis basi lanatis, ovario tomentoso 5-loculari, capsula cylindracea curvata obtusa ferrugineo-floccosa.

Hab. Sikkim-Himalaya ; on the rocky spurs of the humid mountains and gullies ; elev. 10–12,000 feet, most common at Jongri and Chola. *Fl.* June ; *fr.* November.

A large *shrub* or small *tree,* with the *trunk* six inches in diameter in the stoutest part, irregularly and repeatedly branching ; *branches* much gnarled and bare of leaves, covered with a dark-coloured rugged bark, very different from the prevailing beautiful papery clothing of the genus : where it breaks off from the younger branches, however, it exposes a delicate pink liber as shown in our figure, whilst the ultimate ramuli are densely clothed with a soft appressed cottony *tomentum.* The *latter,* generally of a white or tawny colour, is uniformly spread over the petioles, peduncles, ovarium, and the whole under surface of the leaf, also extending to the upper surface of the latter, along the costa, and to the very base in a less degree. These leaves are confined to the apices of the branches, three and a half to five inches long by about two inches broad, obovate or elliptical, obtuse, with a short mucro, the base rather acute, or at most obtuse (not cordate), the colour a full yellowish-green. *Petioles* short, thick, very woolly. *Corymbs* terminal, of several, 6–10, rather large, inclined flowers. *Peduncles* an inch and a half long, thickened. *Calyx* small, reduced to five very minute blunt teeth at the top of the peduncle. *Corolla* ochroleucous or pale sulphur-colour : the *tube* broad-campanulate (like that of *R. Wightii*) within, above, and three of the upper *lobes* in part sprinkled with red dots ; *limb* two inches to two and a half across, of five nearly equal, very spreading, rounded, entire obtuse *lobes. Stamens* ten, included : *filaments* slender, slightly curved, downy at the base ; *anthers* dark brown. *Ovary* oblong-oval, furrowed, thickly woolly, five-celled. *Capsules* more than an inch long, cylindrical, curved, woolly, obtuse.

In the dense tomentum on the underside of the leaves, this species may be compared with *R. fulgens* and *R. æruginosum* among the large shrubby kinds, and with *R. Edgeworthii* and *R. pendulum* among others.

Tab. XVI. *Rhododendron lanatum.* Fig. 1. Stamen. 2. Pistil. 3. Transverse section of ovary :—*magnified.* 4. Capsule :—*natural size.*

Tab. XVII.

J.D.H. del. Fitch lith.   Frederic Reeve imp.

RHODODENDRON GLAUCUM. Hook.fil.

RHODODENDRON GLAUCUM, *Hook. fil.*

Glaucous-leaved Rhododendron.

Tab. XVII.

Fruticulus erectus ramosus, ramulis petiolis pedunculis foliisque subtus lepidotis, foliis ellipticis seu elliptico-lanceolatis mucronatis in petiolum brevem angustatis superne denudatis subtus albo-glaucescentibus, corymbis terminalibus 6–8-floris, floribus suberectis mediocribus, calycis 5-partiti lobis ovatis acutis subfoliaceis, corollæ minute glanduloso-punctatæ roseæ tubo late campanulato intus basi pubescente, limbi lobis patentibus rotundatis emarginatis, staminibus 10, filamentis basi puberulis, ovario dense squamuloso inferne nudo, capsula subglobosa calycem persistentem æquante squamulosa glauca 5-loculari.

Hab. Sikkim-Himalaya; rocky depressed ridges of Chola, Lachen, and Lachoong; elev. 10–12,000. *Fl.* May; *fr.* November.

This constitutes a small *shrub* of the average height of two feet. *Branches* scarcely so thick as a goose-quill, yellowish-brown, often glaucous-white, the younger ones squamulose. *Leaves* rather crowded at the extremities of the branches, 1–3 inches long, usually 1–1½ inch broad, on short petioles, oblong or broadly lanceolate, obtuse, with a mucro, upper side deep green, when old naked above, below remarkably glaucous, almost white, and quite dotted with copious little scales, which in the young state covered the whole leaf, and at all times abound on the bracteas, buds, peduncles, and especially on the calyx-segments. *Peduncles* seven to eight almost in an umbel at the apices of the branches, erect, an inch or more long, rather slender. *Flowers* erect or inclined, pale pinkish-purple. *Calyx* deeply five-partite, the lobes ovate, acute, leafy, almost the length of the tube of the corolla. *Corolla* rather more than an inch long, and about as broad in the widest part: *tube* campanulate; *limb* moderately spreading, of five nearly equal rounded emarginate *lobes*. *Stamens* ten, included: *filaments* downy at the base. *Ovary* ovate, five-furrowed, upper half densely scaly. *Capsule* short, subglobose, acute, five-valved, scaly, included in the large loose persistent calyx, the valves glaucous, lepidote.

The remarkably glaucous colour* of the underside of the leaves, and the great development of the calyx, will readily distinguish this species from every other. In foliage, indeed, it has the closest resemblance to *R. virgatum*: but in that alone,—the inflorescence and calyx are widely different. The whole plant has a powerful resinous smell, due to exceedingly minute globules of a pale yellow colour, which may be seen to exude from beneath the little scales on the underside of the leaves, and which, in this species, too, abound so much on the other parts of the plant.

These scales, themselves, are very curious on the underside of the leaves of this plant: they are of two kinds; the majority are smaller, pale-coloured, exhibiting several concentric circles of minute, nearly uniform cells; the larger ones are setose at the margin, and consist of a centre or disc of small cells, while the circumference forms a limb or margin of radiating elongated cells (see fig. 6, 7).

* This glaucous hue is fully retained in the well-dried specimens, but disappears from those that have been by any accident wetted.

Tab. XVII. *Rhododendron glaucum.* Fig. 1. Stamen. 2. Calyx and pistil. 3. Pistil. 4. Transverse section of the ovary:—*magnified.* 5. Fruit included in the calyx, and with the persistent style:—*natural size.* 6. Portion of a young leaf, showing the scales:—*magnified.* 7. Exhibits the two different scales separated from the leaf:—*more highly magnified.*

Tab. XVIII.

J.H.D. del. Fitch. lith.

Reeve & Nichols, imp.

RHODODENDRON MADDENI, Hook. fil.

RHODODENDRON MADDENI, *Hook. fil.*

Major Madden's Rhododendron.

TAB. XVIII.

Frutex erectus virgatus, ramulis pedunculis petiolis foliisque subter ferrugineo-lepidotis, foliis petiolatis elliptico-lanceolatis utrinque acutis acuminatisve marginibus planis superne nitidis viridibus, pedunculis 2–3 terminalibus brevibus crassis, calycis brevis 5-fidi lobis inæqualibus supremo nunc elongato, corolla extus lepidota ampla, tubo contracto elongato, limbi patentissimi lobis maximis rotundis integris, staminibus 18–20, filamentis glaberrimis, stylo longissimo ovarioque lepidotis, capsula elliptica 10-loculari lignosa.

HAB. Sikkim-Himalaya; inner ranges, very rare: in thickets by the Lachen and Lachoong rivers at Choongtam; elev. 6,000 feet. *Fl.* June to August; *fr.* November.

A *shrub* six to eight feet high, branching from the base. *Branches* erect, supple, covered with pale, papery *bark*. *Leaves* abundant, very bright green, of a coriaceous substance but flaccid, elliptical-lanceolate, acute or acuminate, gradually tapering below into the rather short ferruginous petiole, 4–7 inches long, frequently pendulous; the young ones entirely, the perfect ones beneath only, or sometimes partially above, clothed with dense, white squamules, which become ferruginous in age, the costa below eventually losing them. *Peduncles* about three, short, stout, lepidote. *Calyx* (as in *R. Roylei*) variable in form, always small in proportion to the size of the flower, somewhat membranous at the margin, five-lobed, the lobes obtuse, the upper one generally much prolonged. *Corolla* three and a half to four inches long, and as much across the limb, very handsome, pure white, with a faint blush, chiefly on the upper lobe, rather fleshy, but firm, in substance, the *tube* sparingly lepidote, in shape rather infundibuliform than campanulate, being so much more contracted than is usual with the Himalayan species; the *limb* very large, spreading, of five, nearly equal, rounded, entire *lobes*, slightly crenato-undulate at the margin, delicately but obscurely veined. *Stamens* eighteen to twenty, as long as the tube: *filaments* very slender, glabrous; *anthers* ochreous-yellow. *Ovary* small for the size of the flower, ten-celled, elliptical, whitish with the copious squamules. *Style* very long, exserted much beyond the stamens and the mouth of the corolla, thickened upwards, lepidote. *Stigma* large, often morbidly incrassate and lobulate. *Capsule* oval-oblong, cylindrical, short, straight, obtuse at both ends, about an inch and a quarter long, and half that in breadth.

Of this species the foliage and the flowers are faintly odorous. Very different as this may appear at first sight from *R. cinnabarinum* (Tab. VII. of this work), it clearly belongs to the same natural groupe along with *R. Roylei*. The very large white flowers, the numerous stamens, and ten-celled fruit abundantly distinguish it.

I do myself the pleasure to name this truly superb plant in compliment to Major Madden of the Bengal Civil Service, a good and accomplished botanist, to whose learned memoirs on the plants of the temperate and tropical zones of North-west Himalaya, the reader may be referred for an excellent account of the vegetation of those regions. The same gentleman's paper on the *Coniferæ* of the north of India may be quoted as a model of its kind.

TAB. XVIII. *Rhododendron Maddeni.* Fig. 1. Stamen. 2. Calyx and pistil. 3. Transverse section of ovary:—*magnified.* 4. Capsule:—*natural size.* 5. Portion of the lepidote underside of a leaf:—*magnified.*

Tab. XIX.

J.D.H. del. Fitch. lith.

Reeve & Nichols, imp.

RHODODENDRON TRIFLORUM, Hook. fil.

20.

RHODODENDRON TRIFLORUM, *Hook. fil.*

Three-flowered Rhododendron.

Tab. XIX.

Frutex erectus, ramulis glaucescentibus novellis petiolis pedunculis foliisque subtus creberrime lepidotis, foliis ovato-lanceolatis utrinque acutis v. basi subcordatis superne nitidis subtus glaucis vel subferrugineis, pedunculis sub-3 terminalibus gracilibus, calyce brevi 5-lobato lepidoto ciliato, corollæ flavidæ tubo brevi obconico dorso minute lepidoto lobis oblongis patentibus integris, staminibus 8–10, filamentis elongatis inferne villosis, ovario 5-loculari oblongo lepidoto, stylo elongato, stigmate truncato, capsula oblonga, valvis lignosis.

Hab. Sikkim-Himalaya; inner ranges, on brushy slopes; elev. 7–9,000 feet; scarce. *Fl.* May, June; *fr.* November.

A *shrub* four to six feet high, with erect and rather twiggy *branches* for the genus, the ultimate ones about as thick as a duck's quill: the new shoots lepidote. *Leaves* frequently pendulous, on rather short slender *petioles* (one-third of an inch long), ovato-lanceolate, more or less approaching to oblong or elliptical, two or rarely three inches long, acute at both ends, or cordate at the base and sometimes blunt, with a mucro at the apex, the margin a little recurved, substance rather thin, upper surface smooth and shining, under quite glabrous and glaucous, but so beset with *ferruginous* squamules as to partake of that colour. *Peduncles* generally three together, terminal one-half to three-fourths of an inch long, slender, erect. *Calyx* very short, lepidote, cut into five small rounded teeth or lobes. *Corolla* greenish-yellow, in shape much resembling that of the common garden Azaleas, having a somewhat obconical tube very open at the mouth, and a limb of five spreading oblong entire segments, which are slightly veiny, nearly two inches across the lobes. *Stamens* eight, much exserted: *filaments* slender, hairy near the base. *Ovary* oblong-cylindrical, very lepidote, obtuse. *Style* much longer than the stamens, curved upwards, and terminating in a truncated *stigma*, a little thickened in the disc. *Capsule* half an inch long, straight, cylindrical, often a little swollen at the base, obtuse at the point.

The present *Rhododendron* will form a groupe or section along with *R. virgatum*, Hook. fil., *R. setosum*, Don, and *R. nivale*, Hook. fil.; all of which have peculiarly narrow segments to the corolla. But the present species is well distinguished by its comparatively large yellow flowers, and the larger, usually pointed, leaves.

Tab. XIX. Fig. 1. Stamen. 2. Calyx and pistil. 3. Transverse section of ovary. 4. Small lepidote portion of the underside of the leaf:—*magnified*. 5. Squamules from the leaf:—*more magnified*.

Tab. XX.

J.D.H. del. Fitch, lith.

Reeve & Nichols, imp.

RHODODENDRON SETOSUM, Wall.

RHODODENDRON SETOSUM, *Don.*

Bristly Rhododendron.

Tab. XX.

Fruticulus humilis ramosissimus, ramulis setosis foliis utrinque pedunculis calycibusque creberrime lepidotis, foliis parvis brevissime petiolatis (petiolo setoso) ellipticis subovatisve marginibus subrecurvis ciliatis læte viridibus subtus glaucis v. pallide ferrugineis, pedunculis 3–5 terminalibus brevibus, calycis lobis subfoliaceis ovalibus obtusis coloratis, corollæ purpureo-roseæ tubo brevissimo lobis 5 oblongis obtusis integris patentibus, staminibus 8–10 exsertis, filamentis basim versus barbatis, ovario brevi lepidoto, stylo superne incrassato capsula calycem persistentem æquante brevi crassa lepidota 5-loculari.

Rhododendron setosum, *Don, Wern. Trans.* vol. iii. p. 408. *Prodr. Fl. Nep.* p. 152. *De Cand. Prodr.* vol. vii. p. 784.

Hab. Gossain-Than. *Hamilton, Wallich* in Herb. nostr. Sikkim-Himalaya; open stony and rocky places, abundant; elev. 13–16,000 feet. *Fl.* June, July; *fr.* October.

Stems from a span to a foot high, much and repeatedly branched, *branches* sometimes verticillate, covered with a papery bark, the youngest ones setose and very lepidote, which last character extends to both sides of the leaves, peduncles, calyx, and ovary. *Leaves* small, copious towards the ends of the branches, one-third to half an inch long, elliptical or obovate, coriaceous, very obtuse, dark green above, pale and glaucous beneath, setose on the recurved margin; *petiole* short, setose. *Peduncles* half an inch to one inch long, three to five from the ends of the numerous branches, very lepidote, erect. *Flowers* inclined. *Calyx* coloured, red, large for the size of the corolla, deeply cut into five oval very obtuse foliaceous lobes, very squamulose at the back and edge, nearly naked towards the margin. *Corolla* bright red-rose colour, an inch and a half across, five-partite, the tube very short: the *lobes* spreading, oblong, waved, and sinuated at the margin. *Stamens* eight to ten, much exserted: *filaments* slender, with a dense tuft of hairs above the base; *anthers* oblong. *Ovary* ovate, obtuse, very squamulose, five-celled. *Style* long, ascending, thickened upwards: *stigma* a depressed disc, bearing five prominent *points* or *lobes*. *Capsule* a quarter of an inch long, subglobose, densely lepidote, enclosed by the persistent calyx.

A small and elegant shrub, with a good deal the aspect of *Rhodora*, especially in the flowers, but these are more copious and brighter coloured, and the foliage is Box-like and evergreen. It is the "*Tsallu*" of the Sikkim-Bhoteas and Thibetians, who attribute the oppression and headaches attending the crossing of the loftiest passes of Eastern Himalaya, to the strongly resinous odour of this and of the *Rhododendron anthopogon*, Wall. ("*Palu*" of the natives). The species certainly abounds to within a few miles of the summits of all the passes, and, after hot sunshine, fills the atmosphere with its powerful aroma, too heavy by far to be agreeable; and it is indeed a sad aggravation to the discomforts of toiling in the rarified medium it inhabits. Covering, as it does, extensive moorland tracts and rocky slopes, the brilliant red purple of its flowers renders it a charming and most lovely object. In its late flowering (June and July) and early fruiting (October) it is eminently typical of the briefer and more distinctly circumscribed summer of those elevated regions:—and no less so are its powerfully strong odour and copious resinous secretions of a drier climate than any, except a very few of its congeners, enjoy. The hand, on being passed over the foliage and branches, is imbued with the clammy exudation, and which long retains the scent. An useful volatile oil, of no less marked character than that of the American *Gaultheria* * (now in great demand by the perfumers) would probably be yielded by distillation of the foliage.

* *Gaultheria procumbens*, which yields the "*Oil of Wintergreen*," used by perfumers and by druggists to flavour syrups.

Tab. XX. *Rhododendron setosum.* Fig. 1. Stamen. 2. Calyx and pistil. 3. Transverse section of ovary. 4. Upper, and 5, underside of a leaf, with a portion of the branch. 6. Scales from the leaf:—*all more or less magnified.*

THE

RHODODENDRONS

OF

SIKKIM-HIMALAYA;

BEING

AN ACCOUNT, BOTANICAL AND GEOGRAPHICAL, OF THE

RHODODENDRONS RECENTLY DISCOVERED IN THE MOUNTAINS OF EASTERN HIMALAYA,

FROM

DRAWINGS AND DESCRIPTIONS MADE ON THE SPOT,

DURING A GOVERNMENT BOTANICAL MISSION TO THAT COUNTRY;

BY

JOSEPH DALTON HOOKER, R.N., M.D., F.R.S., F.L.S.,

&c., &c., &c.

EDITED BY

SIR W. J. HOOKER, K.H., D.C.L., F.R.S., F.L.S., &c.

Vice-President of the Linnean Society, and Director of the Royal Gardens of Kew.

PART III.

LONDON:

REEVE AND BENHAM, HENRIETTA STREET, COVENT GARDEN.

1851.

Tab. XXV

J.D.H. del. Fitch, lith.

Reeve & Nichols, imp.

RHODODENDRON EDGEWORTHI, Hook. fil.

RHODODENDRON EDGEWORTHII, *Hook. fil.*

Mr. Edgeworth's Rhododendron.

TAB. XXI.

Frutex sæpe epiphytus, ramulis petiolis pedunculis capsulis foliisque subtus dense ferrugineo-villoso-tomentosis, foliis sublonge petiolatis elliptico-ovatis acutis vel acuminatis subcoriaceis rugoso-reticulatis basi obtusis supra nitidis marginibus recurvis, pedunculis 2–3 terminalibus v. ab innovationibus lateralibus, floribus speciosis albis, calycis ampli 5-partiti lobis foliaceis oblongo-obovatis inæqualibus lanuginosis ciliatis, corollæ tubo breviusculo late campanulato, limbi maximi lobis rotundatis venosis crenato-undulatis, staminibus 10 exsertis, filamentis inferne villosis, antheris elongatis, ovario dense tomentoso 5-loculari, stylo gracili basi lanuginoso, capsula oblongo-cylindracea recta obtusa valvis lignosis.

HAB. Sikkim-Himalaya; in valleys of the inner ranges, usually pendulous from trees, sometimes on rocks; elevation 7,000–9,000 feet. *Fl.* May and June; *fr.* November.

A small *shrub*, with straggling branches, often pendulous upon trees and rocks. *Branches*, the older ones covered with a dark ashy and slightly glaucous bark; young ones and young leaves and bracts, peduncles, petioles, and the underside of the old leaves, densely clothed with a soft ferrugineo-fulvous tomentum, which is easily detached. *Leaves* two to four inches long, ovato-lanceolate, acute or more usually suddenly acuminate, obtuse at the base, the margin recurved, the upper surface fine glossy green, singularly rugose from the deeply impressed reticulated veins; beneath, too, the principal veins are prominent and conspicuous. *Petioles* about three-quarters of an inch long. *Peduncles* terminal or axillary from innovations, usually two or three from the same point, about as long as the petioles. *Flowers* very large, showy, inclined. *Calyx* large, of five deep, membranaceous or foliaceous, obovate, spreading, unequal, coloured lobes, very downy on the back, the edges finely ciliated. *Corolla* white, often tinged with blush and pale yellow: the *tube* rather short, widening much at the mouth, slightly curved, the *limb* unusually large, more than four inches across, spreading, of five nearly equal, rounded, slightly emarginate lobes, crisped at the margin, delicately veined on the surface. *Stamens* ten, a good deal exserted beyond the mouth of the tube: *filaments* slender, a little dilated downwards, villous on the lower half: *anthers* very large, long in proportion to their breadth, linear-oblong, dark purple-brown. *Ovary* ovoid, six-furrowed, six-celled, densely woolly: *style* elongated, red, woolly below: *stigma* five- to six-lobed. *Capsule* more than an inch long, straight, oblong-cylindrical, obtuse, densely covered with ferruginous wool. *Seeds* pale-coloured.

A truly superb species from the size of the flowers and their roseate tinge on a white ground, also on account of the variety of rich colour in the leaves, bracteas, stipules, calyx, &c., while the very wrinkled surface of the leaf adds much to its beauty. In its floccose character and foliaceous calyx it resembles *R. pendulum*; but in the size and shape of the flowers it approaches *R. Dalhousiæ*, next to which I would place it.

The majority of my specimens were obtained from the land-shoots, or -slips, in the rocky ravines, which bring down in their course those Pines on the limbs of which this species delights to grow.

I dedicate this Rhododendron to my accomplished and excellent friend, M. P. Edgeworth, Esq., of the Bengal Civil Service, now Commissioner of Mooltan, who has long and successfully studied the Botany of Western Himalaya, and of North-western India generally.

TAB. XXI. *Rhododendron Edgeworthii.* Fig. 1. Stamen. 2. Calyx and pistil. 3. Transverse section of ovary:—*magnified*. 4. Pistil with its persistent calyx:—*natural size*.

Tab. XXII.

J.D.H. del. Fitch lith.

Reeve & Nichols, imp.

RHODODENDRON ÆRUGINOSUM. Hook.fil.

23.

RHODODENDRON ÆRUGINOSUM, *Hook. fil.*

Æruginose Rhododendron.

Tab. XXII.

Frutex densissime racemosus, ramis cortice papyraceo tectis, ramulis petiolis pedunculis foliisque superne glaberrimis, foliis petiolatis obovatis obovato-oblongisve apice acutis v. muticis basi cordatis subtus dense ferrugineo-tomentosis, capitulo conferto vix densifloro, floribus lilacinis v. roseis, pedicellis subelongatis, calyce breve 5-dentato, corolla campanulata basi intus plaga sanguinea v. lobo superiore tantum maculato, staminibus 10, antheris majusculis, filamentis glabris, ovario glaberrimo 5–8-loculari, capsulis cylindraceis elongatis.

Hab. Sikkim-Himalaya, growing with *Rhododendron fulgens*, and equally abundant, flowering at the same season.

The colour of the flower, the loose capitulum, long pedicels, and campanulate corolla, distinguish this species from *R. fulgens*; in the fruiting season, too, its longer, more slender capsules afford a marked character, as does the more evidently toothed calyx. When dried, however, they are so difficult to discriminate, that I have felt inclined to unite them. The leaves are identical in all respects, except that those of this species have a remarkable verdigris hue. It is still more closely allied to *R. campanulatum*. Of all the Sikkim shrubby Rhododendrons of any size, these two attain the highest level, reaching nearly to 15,000 feet in the remote Lachoong valley, and 14,000 feet in that of the Lachen: 13,000 is their usual level in the ascending zone.

Tab. XXII. *Rhododendron æruginosum.* Fig. 1. Stamen. 2. Peduncle, calyx, and pistil. 3. Transverse section of ovarium :—*all magnified.* 4. Fruit :—*natural size.*

Tab. XX

J.D.H. del. Fitch. lith.

RHODODENDRON SALIGNUM, Hook. fil. | RHODODENDRON ELÆAGNOIDES, Hook.fil.

24.

RHODODENDRON SALIGNUM, *Hook. fil.*

Willow-leaved Rhododendron.

TAB. XXIII. A.

Fruticulus erectus, ramis erectis apice fasciculatim ramulosis, ramulis foliis utrinque pedunculo calyce corollaque extus creberrime squamuloso-lepidotis, foliis breve petiolatis patulis pendulisve elliptico- v. lineari-lanceolatis utrinque acuminatis subtus pallidioribus, pedicellis solitariis v. 2–3 elongatis gracilibus erectis, calycis lobis patulis obtusis subfoliaceis, corolla lutea v. viridi-sulphurea, tubo inflato , brevi, limbi lobis patulis v. recurvis orbicularibus 3 superioribus viridi-maculatis, staminibus 8–10 exsertis, stylo crasso curvo, ovario brevi albo-lepidoto 5-loculari.

HAB. Sikkim-Himalaya ; grassy and rocky hills above Choongtam, elev. 7,000 feet ; common. *Fl.* May, June.

A slender twiggy *shrub*, two to four feet high, branching from a stout tortuous stock ; the *branches* as thick as a crow-quill, rather scattered, bearing fascicled ramuli at the top. *Leaves* often drooping, rather flaccid, of a pale glaucous green, lighter underneath and sometimes ferruginous where the lepidote scales abound, an inch to an inch and a half long, scarcely half an inch broad, acute or mucronate. *Pedicels* always elongated, an inch and a half to two inches long, slender. *Corolla* yellow, an inch across the lobes, lepidote, especially on the outside of the tube ; the upper lobes are spotted with green, the spots occupying the spaces between the very broad anastomosing translucent veins. *Anthers* large, rich red-brown ; *filaments* short, stout, villous below. *Ovarium* covered with white lepidote squamulæ. *Stigma* very stout, curved, gradually thickened towards the truncated stigmatiferous apex. *Capsules* not seen.

The odour of this plant is strongly resinous. As a species it is very closely allied to the *R. lepidotum* ; but the leaves are much longer, and the pedicels always elongated ; characters by no means satisfactory. *R. elæagnoides* may prove another state of the same species.

TAB. XXIII. A. *Rhododendron salignum.* Fig. 1. Plant :—*natural size.* 2. Stamen. 3. Peduncle, calyx, and pistil. 4. Portion of under surface of leaf :—*all magnified.*

25.

RHODODENDRON ELÆAGNOIDES, *Hook. fil.*

Oleaster-leaved Rhododendron.

TAB. XXIII. B.

Fruticulus humilis, nunc depressus, ramôsissimus, more *Ericæ* gregarius, ramulis scabridis ultimis apice foliiferis, foliis pedicellis calyce corolla extus ovarioque dense lepidotis, squamulis ferrugineis argenteisque, foliis verticillatim confertis breviter petiolatis late obovatis obcordatisve retusis obtusisve mucronatis, pedicellis terminalibus solitariis rarius binis elongatis erectis, calycis lobis foliaceis patulis recurvisve rufescentibus, corolla flava pro planta ampla, tubo brevi basi globoso, limbi lobis patulis concavis 3 supremis obscure maculatis, staminibus 8–10, filamentis basi villosis, antheris majusculis, ovario brevi 5-lobo dense lepidoto, stylo crasso decurvo, capsulis parvis.

HAB. Sikkim-Himalaya; open rocky places, elev. 12–16,000 feet; most abundant. *Fl.* June and July.

<hr>

Undoubtedly the smallest species of this section, growing in widely extended clumps, much as heather does, but never so extensively, emitting in sunshine a powerful resinous odour. *Leaves* fasciculated at the apices of the ramuli, generally spreading in a rotate manner, pale yellowish-green, very copiously covered with lepidote squamulæ, a quarter to half an inch long. *Pedicels* an inch to an inch and a half long. *Flowers* large for the size of the plant, of the same form as *R. salignum* and *lepidotum*, but much larger, varying from yellow (the usual colour) to deep red-purple, spotted faintly on the three upper lobes. *Stamens* generally eight. *Capsule* very small, a quarter of an inch in length, twice as long as the calyx, five-valved, five-celled. *Seeds* pale-coloured.

This and the *R. lepidotum* and *salignum* may prove extreme varieties of one species.

<hr>

TAB. XXIII. *Rhododendron elæagnoides.* Figs. 1 and 2. Plants :—*natural size.* 3. Stamen. 4. Peduncle, calyx, and ovarium. 5. Transverse section of ovarium :—*all magnified.* 6. Fruit :—*natural size.*

Tab. X

J.D.H. del. Fitch lith.

Reeve & Nichols imp.

RHODODENDRON CILIATUM, Hook. fil.

26

RHODODENDRON CILIATUM, *Hook. fil.*

Ciliated Rhododendron.

Tab. XXIV.

Fruticulus rigidus, erectus, caulibus plurimis validis, ramulis pedunculis pedicellisque hispido-pilosis, foliis ellipticis acuminatis coriaceis super marginibus ciliato-pilosis senioribus glabratis subtus (costa excepta) glaberrimis pallidis creberrime ferrugineo-punctatis, pedicellis validis subconfertis (2–5), calyce basi hispido, lobis late ovatis obtusis coriaceis, corolla campanulata pallide purpurea, staminibus 10, filamentis basi pilosis, stylo gracili, capsula brevi crassa calyce duplo longiore 5-loculari infra apicem contracta.

Hab. Sikkim-Himalaya, inner ranges only, in wet rocky places, rarely in woods. Lachen and Lachoong valleys; elev. 9–10,000 feet. *Fl.* May; *fr.* October.

A small very rigid *shrub*, growing in clumps two feet high, generally in moist rocky places. Odour faintly resinous and pleasant. Whole plant more or less pilose and setose, the hairs long and fulvous on the young leaves; petioles and pedicels patent. *Leaves* two, rarely three inches long, sometimes obscurely cordate at the base. Upper surface (except in age) pilose, even villous when young, underneath quite glabrous, covered with minute orbicular ferruginous scales. *Bracteas* rather membranous, ciliated. *Capitula* three- to five-flowered, terminal; pedicels very stout, one inch long; flowers inclined. *Sepals* nearly equal, membranous, veined, ciliated. *Corolla* one inch and a half long, nearly as much across at the mouth; *tube* rather contracted below, *limb* five-lobed, colour pale reddish-purple, upper lobe obscurely spotted. *Anthers* large. *Stigma* exserted, capitate. *Capsule* woody, one-third to one-half of an inch long, suddenly contracted below the apex, each of the five valves there recurved or beaked, the back covered with minute scales. *Seeds* pale-coloured.

Allied to *R. barbatum*, but widely different in stature, habit, and the scattered scales on the under surface of the leaves. I have not observed it in other valleys than those flanked by snowy mountains, where it is common, scenting the air in warm weather.

The scales (as in many of its congeners) are orbicular, sessile, and peltately attached, formed of three concentric series of cells, the outer elongated in the direction of the radius. A dark concentric line marks the union of the circumferential series of cells with those next to it. The fragrant oil is secreted chiefly in the discoid cell.

Tab. XXIV. *Rhododendron ciliatum.* Fig. 1. Stamen. 2. Peduncle, calyx, and pistil. 3. Transverse section of ovarium. 4. Fruit. 5. Under surface of portion of leaf. 6. Scales from the same :—*magnified*.

J.D.H. del. Fitch, lith.

Reeve & Nichols imp.

RHODODENDRON FULGENS, Hook. fil.

27

RHODODENDRON FULGENS, *Hook. fil.*

Brilliant Rhododendron.

TAB. XXV.

Frutex densissime ramosus, foliosus, ramis cortice papyraceo tectis, ramulis pedunculis petiolis ovariis foliisque superne glaberrimis, foliis petiolatis late obovato- v. ovato-ellipticis apice rotundatis basi cordatis margine recurvo subtus tomento floccoso ferrugineo dense vestitis, capitulis densifloris, pedicellis brevibus, calyce obsoleto v. brevissimo disciformi lobato, corolla intense sanguinea campanulata, tubo subcompresso, limbi lobis 5 rotundatis breviusculis recurvis, staminibus 10, filamentis glabris, ovario conico basi turgido apice truncato 8-loculari 8-sulcato, capsulis oblongo-cylindraceis obtusis gibbosis glaucis purpureis.

Hab. Sikkim-Himalaya; mountain slopes and spurs, elev. 12–14,000 feet; abundant.   *Fl.* June; *fr.* November and December.

This, the richest ornament of the alpine region in the month of June, forms a very prevalent shrub at the elevations assigned to it, not yielding in abundance to its constant associates, *R. æruginosum* and *R. Maddeni,* and, like the former, pushing forth young leaves of a beautiful verdigris-green in July and August.   The foliage is perennial, and gives a singular hue to the bleak snowy mountain-faces immediately overhung by the perpetual snow, contrasting in August in broad masses or broken clumps with the bright scarlet of the Berberry, the golden yellow of the fading Birch and Mountain Ash, the lurid heavy green of the perennial Juniper, and the bleak raw brown of the withered herbage.   Whether, then, for the glorious effulgence in spring of its deep scarlet blossoms, which appear to glow like fire in the short hour of morning sunlight, or the singular tint it at other seasons wears, this is among the most striking of the plants which lend to these inhospitable regions the varied hues which are denied to the comparatively habitable but gloomy forests of the temperate zone on the same mountains.

Individual shrubs are generally of a rounded outline, about four feet high, and twice as much in diameter, and when growing together they compose an impenetrable thicket, as annoying to the traveller as *R. Hodgsoni* is at lower elevations.   The ramuli are bright green, the thickness of a little finger.   *Leaves* four inches long and three broad, pretty constant in form, and always coriaceous in texture, with a glossy upper surface, and dense woolly clothing underneath, which wholly obliterates the venation.   *Corolla* of a deep, bright blood-red, somewhat fleshy in texture, highly polished and shining.   *Anthers* dark brown; *filaments* pink.   *Style* rather short, curved, ending in a truncate stigma, not materially enlarged.   The *capsules* are one to two inches long, very stout, of a fine plum-purple colour, and covered with a glaucous bloom.

There is no pubescence, glands, or squamæ, on any part of the plant, except on the inner bracteal scales, which are silky, and on the very young foliage, which has often a little villous pubescence: the latter, which is wholly scentless, is not to be distinguished from that of *R. æruginosum.*

Tab. XXV. *Rhododendron fulgens.*   Fig. 1. Flower.   2. Stamen.   3. Peduncle, calyx, and ovarium.   4. Transverse section of ovarium.   5. Fruit:—*all but figures* 1 *and* 5 *magnified.*

Tab. XX

R.VIRGATUM. Hook fil.

J.D.H. del. Fitch. lith.

Reeve & Nichols imp.

RHODODENDRON NIVALE, Hook.fil.

28.

RHODODENDRON VIRGATUM, *Hook. fil.*

Twiggy Rhododendron.

Tab. XXVI. A.

Fruticulus gracilis, erectus, virgatus, ramulis pedicellis foliisque squamulosis, foliis lineari-ellipticis lanceolatisve mucronatis subtus albo-glau-cescentibus vel pallidioribus, pedicellis brevibus axillaribus solitariis rarius binis, bracteis chartaceis concavis suffultis, calyce abbreviato obtuse 5-lobo, corolla campanulata glanduloso-punctata, tubo subcontracto, lobis angustis, staminibus 8–10, filamentis basi lanatis, stigmate exserto capitato, capsula 5-loculari ovata vel breviter cylindracea squamulis ferrugineis tecta, seminibus pallidis.

HAB. Sikkim-Himalaya; skirts of Pine-forests in ravines, elev. 8–9,000 feet. Lachen valley. *Fl.* May; *fr.* October.

Decidedly the most slender twiggy species with which I am acquainted, the stems and branches reaching four feet in height, and scarcely the thickness of a crow-quill. The *leaves* are so like those of *R. glaucum* as to require no detailed description. *Flowers* solitary, rarely in pairs, and axillary: the pedicels two to three lines long, covered with sheathing deciduous coriaceous brown scales, which are longer than the pedicel, very rigid in texture, downy on the back. *Corolla* a pale red-purple, smaller than that of *R. triflorum*, but of the same form: the *tube* short, narrow and obconical, the *segments* narrow and spreading. *Style* long; *stigma* exserted. *Calycine lobes* short, broad and rounded. *Capsules* seldom half an inch long, surrounded at the base by the short appressed calyx.

The axillary flowers and nature of the imbricating bracts are almost peculiar to this species.

TAB. XXVI. A. *Rhododendron virgatum.* Fig. 1. Stamen. 2. Calyx and pistil. 3. Transverse section of ovarium. 4. Fruit. 5. Portion of under surface of leaf:—*all but fig.* 4 *magnified.*

29.

RHODODENDRON NIVALE, *Hook. fil.*

Snow Rhododendron.

Tab. XXVI. B.

Fruticulus depressus, prostratus, ramosissimus, ramis ramulisque tortis cortice fusco tectis, foliis minimis terminalibus confertis patulis ramu-lisque dense ferrugineo-lepidotis, petiolo brevissimo, lamina coriacea elliptico-oblonga obovatave utrinque obtusa, marginibus subrecurvis subtus glaucescentibus, pedicellis solitariis terminalibus brevissimis, calyce laxe lepidoto, lobis submembranaceis ciliatis, corolla parva (rubro-purpurea), tubo brevissimo, lobis oblongis lineari-oblongisve obtusis patulis, staminibus 8–10 exsertis, antheris oblongis majusculis, filamentis gracilibus basi villosis, ovario densissime lepidoto, stylo gracili, stigmate capitato, capsula calyce longiore brevissime obovata 5-valvi.

HAB. Sikkim-Himalaya; on the loftiest bare slopes of the mountains on the Thibetan frontier, elev. 16–18,000 feet. *Fl.* June and July; *fr.* September and October.

The hard woody branches of this curious little species, as thick as a goose-quill, straggle along the ground for a foot or two, presenting brown tufts of vegetation where not half a dozen other plants can exist. The branches are densely interwoven, very harsh and woody, wholly depressed; whence the shrub, spreading horizontally, and barely raised two inches above the soil, becomes eminently typical of the arid stern climate it inhabits. The latest to bloom and earliest to mature its seeds, by far the smallest in foliage, and proportionally largest in flower, most lepidote in vesture, humble in stature, rigid in texture, deformed in habit, yet the most odoriferous, it may be recognized, even in the herbarium, as the production of the loftiest elevation on the surface of the globe,—of the most excessive climate,—of the joint influences of a scorching sun by day, and the keenest frost at night,—of the greatest drought followed in a few hours by a saturated atmosphere,—of the balmiest calm alternating with the whirlwind of the Alps. For eight months of the year it is buried under many feet of snow: for the remaining four it is frequently snowed and sunned in the same hour. During genial weather, when the sun heats the soil to 150°, its perfumed foliage scents the air; whilst to snow-storm and frost it is insensible, blooming through all, expanding its little purple flowers to the day, and only closing them to wither after fertilization has taken place. As the life of a moth may be indefinitely prolonged, whilst its duties are unfulfilled, so the flower of this little mountaineer will remain open through days of fog and sleet, till a mild day facilitates the detachment of the pollen and fecundation of the ovarium. This process is almost wholly the effect of the winds; for though humble-bees, and the " Blues " and " Fritillaries " (*Polyommatus* and *Argynnis*) amongst butterflies, do exist at the same prodigious elevation, they are too few in number to influence the operations of vegetable life.

The odour of the plant much resembles that of " Eau de Cologne." Lepidote *scales* generally rather a bright ferruginous-brown, wholly concealing the ramuli, foliage, &c. *Leaves* one-eighth to one-sixth of an inch long, pale green. *Corolla* one-third of an inch across the lobes. The nearest allies of this species are *R. setosum* and *R. Lapponicum*, from which latter it differs in its smaller stature and solitary sessile flowers.

This singular little plant attains a loftier elevation, I believe, than any other shrub in the world.

TAB. XXVI. B. *Rhododendron nivale.* Fig. 1. Branch and leaves. 2 and 3. Flowers. 4. Corolla laid open. 5. Stamen. 6. Calyx and pistil. 7. Transverse section of ovarium :—*all magnified.* 8. Fruit :—*natural size.*

Tab. XXV.

J.D.H. del. Fitch, lith.

Reeve & Nichols, imp.

RHODODENDRON WIGHTII. Hook fil.

30

RHODODENDRON WIGHTII, *Hook. fil.*

Dr. Wight's Rhododendron.

TAB. XXVII.

Arbuscula ramosa, ramis cortice papyraceo tectis, foliis lanceolatis elliptico-lanceolatisve utrinque acutis superne glaberrimis subtus lana arctissime appressa rufa tectis marginibus planis, petiolo puberulo, capitulis multifloris, bracteis coriaceis glaberrimis viscidis, pedicellis gracilibus puberulis, calyce obsoleto, corolla ampla campanulata pallide straminea sanguineo-notata, tubo turgido, limbo patenti-recurvo 5-lobo, staminibus 10, filamentis glabris, stigmate capitato vix exserto, ovario glanduloso-pubescente albido 10-loculari, capsula glaberrima lineari-cylindracea curva, valvis lignosis, seminibus atro-fuscis.

HAB. Sikkim-Himalaya; wooded valleys and on spurs of all the mountains, elev. 12–14,000 feet; abundant. *Fl.* June; *fr.* November.

A small shrubby *tree*, yielding to none in the beauty of its inflorescence amongst that yellow-flowered groupe of which it is the pride. The *trunks* are as thick as the thigh in the large specimens, and branch very much both upwards and outwards, forming a thickset shrub of ten feet high. *Ramuli* very thick and woody, the ultimate ones puberulous. *Petioles* half an inch long, stout, puberulous. *Leaf* six to eight (rarely ten) inches long, two and a half to three broad, very coriaceous, more plane than is usual in the genus, of a deep bright green above and but hardly glossy, beneath covered with a very closely appressed opaque tomentum of a more or less deep rufous colour, rarely pale and nearly white in the young foliage. *Capitula* much larger than those of *R. arboreum*, twelve- to twenty-flowered, but the flowers are not densely packed. *Bracteal scales* chestnut-brown, very coriaceous and viscid. *Pedicels* one inch to one and a half inch long, slender for the size of the flower. *Corolla* large and very beautiful, truly bell-shaped, being broad at the base and spherical, five-lobed at the insertion of the pedicel. *Capsules* nearly two inches long, ten-furrowed. Flowers have a faint honeyed smell; foliage inodorous.

This exceedingly handsome and abundant species replaces the *R. Hodgsoni* in ascending the mountains, and is the most prevalent species at 12 and 13,000 feet, conspicuous at all seasons for the large foliage, of a rusty cinnamon-colour underneath, and the viscid buds. It bears the name of a distinguished Indian botanist and personal friend, to whose zeal and liberality the botanists of India are no less publicly, than I am personally, indebted for encouragement and the most material aid in our common pursuits. The 'Icones Plantarum Indiæ Orientalis'—an excellent work in all respects, and indispensable to a knowledge of Indian plants—is a remarkable instance of the perfection to which botanical illustrations can be brought by indomitable perseverance under the most discouraging circumstances. The first plates of that work are equal to any produced at the era of their publication in India; the latter will compete with the best outline lithographs of Europe.

TAB. XXVII. *Rhododendron Wightii*. Fig. 1. Flower. 2. Stamen. 3. Peduncle, calyx, and pistil. 4. Transverse section of ovarium :—*magnified*. 5. Fruit :—*natural size*.

Tab. XXVI

J.D.H. del. Fitch, lith.

Reeve & Nichols, imp.

RHODODENDRON CAMELLIÆFLORUM, Hook.fil.

31

RHODODENDRON CAMELLIÆFLORUM, *Hook. fil.*

Camellia-flowered Rhododendron.

Tab. XXVIII.

Frutex plerumque epiphytus, pendulus, laxus, parce ramosus, ramulis pedunculis petiolis foliisque subtus (junioribus utrinque) dense lepidoto-squamulosis ferrugineis, foliis petiolatis ellipticis utrinque acutis acuminatis muticisve, costa valida percursa, pedunculis brevissimis axillaribus solitariis, calycis lobis appressis rotundatis coriaceis, corolla carnosa, tubo brevi basi globoso, lobis patentibus orbicularibus, staminibus 16 radiatis, filamentis crassis, antheris majusculis, stylo crasso decurvo, ovario glabro 10-loculari, capsula brevi oblonga 10-loculari.

HAB. Sikkim-Himalaya; pendulous, generally from trunks of trees, often of Pines, sometimes from rocks, not unfrequent; elev. 9–11,000 feet. *Fl.* July; *fr.* December.

This very abnormal species is more allied, in some respects, to the section including *R. lepidotum*, than to any of the others: in foliage it resembles *R. Maddeni*, though so much smaller a plant, and also *R. cinnabarinum*, from which the dried flowerless specimens are not easily separable. The same very stout percurrent costa of the leaf is common to all these.

Stems two to six feet long, seldom thicker than a goose-quill, branches long, generally pendulous, though when growing on cliffs often obscurely so. *Leaves*, as usual in the genus, at the apices of the branches, differing in little but the size from those of *R. Maddeni*, two and a half to three inches long. *Peduncles* axillary or terminal, very short and stout. *Calyx* half the length of the tube of the corolla, very coriaceous, lepidote, one or more lobes at times lengthened and membranous. *Corolla* sparingly lepidote, an inch and a half across, of a very thick texture, pure white with a faint rosy tinge, all the segments obtuse and entire. *Stamens* very large for the size of the corolla: *filaments* incrassated and hairy at the base, also thickened below the *anther,* which is remarkably adnate and large, orange-red. *Ovarium* short, white with lepidote squamulæ. *Style* very stout, decurved, gradually enlarging to the abrupt disciform stigma. *Capsule* woody, broad, squamulose, obtuse at both ends, three inches and a quarter long; often diseased, and then spherical (fig. 4). The similarity between the flower and that of a single (wild) *Camellia* has suggested the trivial name. Odour, as in all the lepidote species, more or less strongly resinous according to the heat of the day.

TAB. XXVIII. *Rhododendron camelliæflorum.* Fig. 1. Stamen. 2. Peduncle, calyx, and pistil. 3. Transverse section of ovarium. 4. Fruit, diseased. 5. Portion of under side of leaf. 6. Squamulæ from the same:—*all except figure 4 magnified.*

Tab. XXIX.

J.D.H. del. Fitch, lith.

Reeve & Nichols, imp.

RHODODENDRON CANDELABRUM, Hook.fil.

32.

RHODODENDRON CANDELABRUM, *Hook. fil.*

Candelabra Rhododendron.

TAB. XXIX.

Frutex ramosissimus, foliis terminalibus subcoriaceis glaberrimis oblongo-ovatis obtusissimis apiculatis basi cordatis subtus glaucescentibus margine subrecurvo, corymbis plurifloris, pedunculis petiolo æquantibus, floribus radiatim patentibus cernuisve, calyce brevi disciformi obscure inæqualiter lobato ciliato, corolla pallide rosea, tubo elongato campanulato, limbo 5-lobo, staminibus 10, ovario conico-cylindraceo glanduloso-ciliato.

HAB. Sikkim-Himalaya; elev. 10–11,000 feet. *Fl.* June.

The plant from which the accompanying plate and description are taken, was found in thick Pine-woods near Lachen village, before I was well acquainted with the *R. Thomsoni* (Tab. XII.), of which I fear it is only a pale-flowered variety, found growing at a lower elevation than that species usually inhabits, flowering earlier and in a shady protected situation. The much shorter calyx (of the same peculiar character, however), its glandular margin and ovarium, are the only further distinctions I have been able to detect between them, and they are quite unimportant.

TAB. XXIX. *Rhododendron candelabrum.* Fig. 1. Stamen. 2. Peduncle, calyx, and pistil. 3. Transverse section of ovary :—*all magnified.*

Tab. XXX.

J.D.H. del. Fitch, lith.

Reeve & Nichols, imp.

RHODODENDRON CAMPYLOCARPUM. Hook. fil.

33.

RHODODENDRON CAMPYLOCARPUM, *Hook. fil.*

Curve-fruited Rhododendron.

Tab. XXX.

Frutex gracilis, virgatus, ramosus, cortice papyraceo, ramulis ultimis pedunculis pedicellisque glanduloso-pilosis, foliis petiolatis ovato- vel oblongo-cordatis apice rotundatis utrinque glaberrimis superne nitidis subter pallidioribus interdum glaucescentibus, capitulis terminalibus laxis 6–8-floris, pedicellis gracilibus, calyce 5-lobo glanduloso, corolla (elegantissima) campanulata alba v. saturate straminea immaculata, lobis 5 patentibus, staminibus 10, antheris rubris, filamentis glabris, ovario glanduloso, capsulis patentibus valde arcuatis cylindraceis angustis pilis rigidis glanduloso-capitatis aspersis plerisque 6-valvis, seminibus pallidis.

Hab. Sikkim-Himalaya; rocky valleys and open spurs, elev. 11–14,000 feet; abundant. *Fl.* June; *fr.* November.

A small *bush*, averaging six feet in height, rounded in form, of a bright cheerful green hue, and which, when loaded with its inflorescence of surpassing delicacy and grace, claims precedence over its more gaudy congeners, and has always been regarded by me as the most charming of the Sikkim Rhododendrons. The plant exhales a grateful honeyed flavour from its lovely bells and a resinous sweet odour from the stipitate glands of the petioles, pedicels, calyx, and capsules. *Leaves* on slender petioles, three-quarters of an inch long, coriaceous but not thick in texture, two to three and a half inches long, one and three-quarters to two inches broad, cordate at the base, rounded and mucronate at the apex, in all characters, except the evanescent glandular pubescence and spherical buds, undistinguishable from *Rhododendron Thomsoni*. *Flowers* horizontal and nodding. *Corolla* truly campanulate, delicate in texture, tinged of a sulphur hue and always spotless, nearly two inches long, broader across the lobes, which are finely veined. The pedicels of the capsules radiate horizontally from the apices of the ramuli, and the capsules themselves curve upwards with a semicircular arc; they are about an inch long, always loosely covered with stipitate glands.

Tab. XXX. *Rhododendron campylocarpum.* Fig. 1. Stamen. 2. Peduncle, calyx, and pistil. 3. Transverse section of ovarium :—*magnified.* 4. Fruit :—*natural size.*

First published in 2017 by the Royal Botanic Gardens, Kew, Richmond, Surrey, TW9 3AB, UK
www.kew.org

ISBN 978 1 84246 645 2

Distributed on behalf of the Royal Botanic Gardens, Kew in North America by the University of Chicago Press, 1427 East 60th St, Chicago, IL 60637, USA.

British Library Cataloguing in Publication Data
A catalogue record for this book is available from the British Library.

Production Management: Andrew Illes
Design and page layout: Christine Beard

Printed in the UK by Gomer Press Limited

For information or to purchase all Kew titles please visit shop.kew.org/kewbooksonline or email publishing@kew.org

Kew's mission is to be the global resource in plant and fungal knowledge, and the world's leading botanic garden.

Kew receives about half of its running costs from Government through the Department for Environment, Food and Rural Affairs (Defra). All other funding needed to support Kew's vital work comes from members, foundations, donors and commercial activities, including book sales.